HIGHER EDUCATION IN INDIA

Building Robust Institutions

HIGHER EDUCATION IN INDIA

Building Robust Institutions

Dr. Susheel P. Kandalgaonkar

Foreword by

Professor Bhushan Patwardhan

PENTAGON PRESS LLP

First published in 2025 by
PENTAGON PRESS LLP
206, Peacock Lane, Shahpur Jat
New Delhi-110049, India
Contact: 011-26490600

Typeset in AGaramond, 11 Point
Printed by Aegean Offset Printers, Greater Noida

ISBN 978-81-988370-0-4

Disclaimer: The views and opinions expressed in the book are the individual assertions of the Author. The Publisher does not take any responsibility for the same in any manner whatsoever. The same shall be solely the responsibility of the Author.

www.pentagonpress.in

To

Suvarna

my wife, companion, critic

CONTENTS

Professor Bhushan Patwardhan PhD - FNASc - FSAMS
National Research Professor - Ayush - Consultant WHO Geneva
Former Chairman, National Assessment and Accreditation Council Executive Committee (NAAC)
Former Vice Chairman, University Grants Commission (UGC)
Former Chairman i/c, Indian Council of Social Science Research (ICSSR)

FOREWORD

As we mark 75 years of independence during the Azadi ka Amrit Mahotsav, the Indian higher education finds itself at a crucial juncture, confronting a series of challenges and opportunities. The educational systems imposed by the British colonial era are now under scrutiny, prompting a reimagining of the relevance to our heritage, languages, culture and educational roots. Rapid transformations are underway, notably with the National Education Policy (NEP) 2020, aiming to bring about substantive reforms aligning with the ethos and needs of India that is Bharat.

In this context, Professor Susheel P. Kandalgaonkar's book, "Higher Education in India: Building Robust Institutions" emerges as a timely scholarly contribution. The book offers practical insights to assist higher education institutions in India in becoming locally relevant and globally competitive. With its collection of essays, case studies, and learning resources, it serves as a valuable tool for educators, policymakers, and those interested in the future of Indian higher education. NEP 2020 lays down crucial principles like access, equity, quality, affordability, and accountability. The book addresses the evolving landscape by emphasising the need for thoughtful consideration of institutional purpose, values, and methodologies. It challenges the conventional belief that increased funding alone is the solution, highlighting the importance of purposeful institution-building grounded in strategy, methodology, skills, and values. A central focus is placed on the significance of strengthening state universities and affiliated colleges, forming the base of the educational pyramid. The book provides examples of good and bad practices in Indian higher education, incorporating insights on improving institutions through Organisation Development (OD) skills. It underscores that the effectiveness of the new education policy hinges on increased investment in building and developing publicly funded colleges and universities.

"Institution Building for Higher Education in India" is not just an academic endeavor; it is a call to action. Professor Kandalgaonkar, drawing on his extensive experience as a senior teacher and former Director of the Institute of Management

Development and Research (IMDR) in Pune, offers nuanced insights into organisational behavior, human resource development, and qualitative research methodology. The book, comprising eleven essays, nine cases, and four notes on learning resources, serves as a practical guide. It provides a roadmap for leaders and policymakers to comprehend the complexities of institution-building, offering perspectives, strategies, and skills crucial for effective execution. Its contemporary relevance to Indian universities, colleges, and institutions of professional education makes it an essential read for anyone concerned about the quality and access of higher education in India.

I believe that Professor Kandalgaonkar's work will inspire collective efforts towards building institutions that endure challenges and embody values vital for the future of higher education in India.

Professor Bhushan Patwardhan

ACKNOWLEDGEMENTS

I am grateful to *Dr Bhushan Patwardhan*, who holds rich experience in leadership positions in apex institutions of higher education in India, for agreeing to write a foreword for the book. I wish to sincerely thank *Dr Ashutosh Bhupatkar*, former colleague and mentor at *IMDR*, for sparing his time and showing patience while reviewing initial drafts with valuable suggestions. Two of his unpublished notes are included in the section on Cases and Learning Resources. *Prof Rajén Harshe,* former Vice Chancellor of *Allahabad University*, was kind enough to provide specific advice on writing style and to share his vast experiential knowledge of teaching-learning and managing in seven universities. I am grateful to *Mr Rajan Arya*, Partner, *Pentagon Press LLP*, who recognised the contemporary relevance in the theme of the book for publishing. *Mrs Niketa Mulay* has provided excellent inputs on copy-editing.

Similarly, I wish to acknowledge *Dr Vipra Tiwari* for giving me access to reference books from the library. Fellow students of *IMDR* deserve special thanks because, as a faculty in a 'community of learners' on campus for three decades, I gained a lot from the academic climate driven by critical thinking, freedom, and egalitarian values nurtured by students and faculty together. Writing on a serious theme of institution building for higher education in contemporary India tested my stamina and patience, as well as that of my family members. I thank *Suvarna, Tapan,* and *Kanan* for their constant support and encouragement during the prolonged period of writing and rewriting.

List of Abbreviations

ABVP	Akhil Bharatiya Vidyarthi Parishad
AICTE	All India Council for Technical Education
AISA	All India Students Association
API	Academic Performance Indicator
AR	Action Research
AT	Agency Theory
BSC	Balanced Score Card
CBSE	Central Board of Secondary Education
EPSI	Education Promotion Society of India
GST	General Systems Theory
HC	Human Capital
HEIs	Higher Education Institutions
HRD	Human Resource Development
IB	Institution Building
ID	Institution Development
IIM	Indian Institute of Management
IIT	Indian Institute of Technology
IMDR	Institute of Management Development and Research
JMI	Jamia Millia Islamia, University
JNU	Jawaharlal Nehru University
KW	Knowledge Worker
LO	Learning Outcomes

MBA	Master of Business Administration
MCI	Medical Council of India
MoE	Ministry of Education
NAAC	National Assessment and Accreditation Council
NBA	National Board of Accreditation
NEP	National Education Policy
NIRF	National Institutional Ranking Framework
OD	Organisation Development
PAT	Principal-Agent Theory
PBAS	Performance-Based Assessment System
PC	Process Consultation
PGDM	Post Graduate Diploma in Management
PMS	Performance Management System
PR	Phenomenological Research
ROI	Return on Investment
RP	Reflective Practice
SFI	Students' Federation of India
SHRD	Strategic Human Resource Development
SP	Strategic Plan
STEM	Science, Technology, Engineering, Medicine
SWOT	Strengths, Weaknesses, Opportunities, Threats
TE	Technical Efficiency
TEP	Techno-Economic Perspective
TR	Technical or Technological Rationality
UGC	University Grants Commission
UoA	University of Allahabad

A List of Figures/Tables

INTRODUCTION

'To write is to measure the depth of things, as well as to come to a sense of one's own depth.' – ***Max Van Manen*** (1990)

The ideas and experiences presented in this book is a modest attempt of the author to share his understanding of a complex and vast subject, focusing on perspectives and processes of institutional building for higher education in India. It is based mainly on the three decades of teaching-learning experience at postgraduate courses in a management institute in Pune, which is managed by the Deccan Education Society. With a hundred and thirty-five years of existence, the Society has a unique system of teacher-managed educational institutions, schools, and colleges in cities and towns of western Maharashtra. As a consequence, the institutions were managed by committed educationists as faculty and teachers. The purpose and ambience on the campuses remained academic in pursuit of knowledge and learning. Notably, the fee structure remained affordable to many students, and governance reflected a total absence of wealth or profit orientation. Things have changed in the recent past, with covert and overt ideological intrusions in the academic space of educational institutions, and neoliberal economic policy of the state. The author has documented and discussed these experiences in two of the cases in the second section of the book.

Education is primarily an academic engagement between faculty and a collective of students on institutional campuses. The time spent on campus has a significant impact on his or her character because it is not only about what is taught, but, also about how teaching and learning take place, the intellectual ambience, and the culture provided by institutions. The main focus of institution building *(IB)* is to empower those at the centre of higher learning, that is, faculty and students, and strengthen their capability to deliver learning outcomes. Also, institutional building processes strive to combine hard and soft aspects of an institution, that is, structure and systems, with processes, attitudes, and values that impact behaviours to achieve the institutional mission. However, there are forces, internal and external, economic, political, and social, that obstruct or support the process of building educational institutions in contemporary India.

Institutional leadership of higher education is expected to engage with diverse groups of internal and external stakeholders, such as its employees, staff, promoters, governing board, alumni, the state and its regulatory bodies, industry employers, local and professional communities, and society at large. In recent years, one more important stakeholder has emerged: the so-called customer in the market of higher education, who are potential and prospective students who would sustain institutions financially in the years to come. The reputation of the institution is now measured in terms of brand building. Meeting the expectations of such a divergent group of stakeholders is a challenging task of balancing educational and economic dimensions, and therefore, it is crucial to have a sound conceptual foundation that offers an integrated perspective and theory to navigate and govern institutions of higher education.

Higher learning requires institutions to provide pedagogic support, a climate conducive to developing higher-order cognitive, emotional, and action capabilities, and a set of ethical professional values. Hence, the book is about building higher education institutions '*for*' higher learning. An equal and added significance is given to the processes of building and shaping institutions and to '*higher order*' teaching–learning–research processes as mentioned in *Bloom's and Anderson's* taxonomy of education objectives.

The much hallowed University education in India has a long tradition of about two hundred years, and reputed universities and institutes provide higher education in multiple academic and professional disciplines. In the contemporary context, there is a need to review the challenges in *IB* and discuss them in the context of perspectives and methodology of building and developing them to impart a theoretical basis and a value-based approach for solving institutional problems. One finds a significant shift in the conventional role of the state, which provided financial support to universities and affiliated colleges. In the neoliberal regime, the state is actively involved in creating a market for education. It expects public institutions to operate as players in a competitive market, who had to invest in promotional and brand-building activities for their courses. It has made these institutions dependent on market forces to improve efficiency and sustain themselves.

Though the demand for education has increased manifold, and it is difficult to sustain institutions on fees and other sources of government and non-government grants. Exposing universities and colleges to market mechanisms has diverted their attention from the primary purpose and mission. It has made institutional stakeholders like faculty and students insecure about their future. In this situation, it needs to be examined whether the macro level trend in privatisation and marketing of higher education is driven by an economic necessity or is it only an ideological agenda of the state as is seen in developed countries globally. Universities and affiliated colleges, need to search for alternative perspectives and options in the areas of financial support and innovative designs of institution building. Three cases in Section Two illustrate the point.

The perspectives on higher education institutions need to be understood in the larger context of institutional history, social psychology, and work culture. For instance, it is globally observed that colleges, institutes, and universities with better-managed systems can deliver superior quality of education. These institutions are good at managing in areas such as operations management, monitoring, target setting, and people management. Countries like the UK, Sweden, Canada, and the USA are known for better quality education because they have well-managed institutions. Countries like Italy, Brazil, and India have undermanaged educational institutions that lack quality and fail to deliver academic performance. Well-managed educational institutions are governed by professional, academic expertise and values that support excellence in institutional performance.

In the Indian context of higher education, values that support better managed systems would indicate that internal stakeholders of the system tend to take psychological ownership to ensure accountability and monitoring of the academic and administrative processes. State universities and colleges in India have structures and systems, such as quality assurance or research, which are not much different from those in Western countries. However, they are not backed by the professional norms and values that govern them. This is one of the central themes of building robust institutions in terms of setting norms for appropriate behaviours. The process of setting internal norms requires group collaboration and does not work if it is imposed by the top authority or regulators. The perspective of institutional design in traditional universities worldwide is a combination of structural and cultural aspects, a conglomerated systemic collectivity of academic community, with flexible boundaries rather than a rigid hierarchy, functional-subject expertise and roles.

For example, at a more practical level, the bottom line of academic administration covers the key processes of admission, assessment, and declaration of results. The typical complaints of students of universities and affiliated colleges in India reveal a combination of routine and serious problems, such as admissions not based on merit but through influence and donations; denying admission without giving a valid reason; demanding extra fees which are more than as announced formally; late announcement of results; a non-transparent process of assessment; details of fee structure and seats available are not mentioned in the prospectus; not providing adequate facilities for students; discrimination on campus on basis of sex, caste, religion, place of birth; not refunding fees and disbursement of scholarship. (*online grievance Redressal Portal of UGC*)

The list is long, but the message is loud and clear: those people who manage systems or institutional bureaucracy at all levels, in state universities, private institutes, and affiliated colleges, lack accountability and show less concern for the key stakeholders of educational institutions, the faceless student and powerless faculty. Apparently, the problem does not seem to be much about the structure and systems but more about attitudes, mind-sets, institutional culture, values, and perspectives of higher education that govern institutional behaviours. Essentially, it is an issue of both governance and leadership, cutting across all levels of the institutions. If this hypothesis on above diagnosis is valid, then appropriate interventions, methods, and theoretical perspectives are required to influence institutional behaviours. A significant part of the essays and cases address these challenges in quality, governance, campus culture and academic-institutional performance.

The point is that we can bring and implement better technical systems at the operational level, but people who manage systems also need appropriate attitudes, beliefs, and values because they impact institutional behaviours. While borrowing best international practices of management systems and models for *HEIs* in India, it would be beneficial to locate the values, attitudes, and behaviours that sustain these systems at workplaces. Indeed, there cannot be a standardised template for soft aspects like attitudes, behaviours, and values for all institutions. Such a task would require sensing and diagnosing specific institutional behavioural processes at workplaces to capture the reality as experienced by the institutional members. The methodology of Action Research, Qualitative Research, Diagnosis, and Interventions provide appropriate tools for these tasks,

It is necessary to mention that the perspective, theory, and methodology of *IB* mentioned above should not be considered as models of *IB* because there would not be a standardised model applicable at the pan-India level. The systemic model implies an organic evolution based on each institution's specific context, history, and mission. Grafting or importing models would be counter-productive because although copying models of structures and systems is easy, it is impossible to manufacture concurrent attitudes and values that support them. Building robust institutions is about shaping the mind and identity of the institution, nurturing a suitable academic climate and culture, and developing the capability of its people.

In other words, there cannot be one right model and best practices for institutions. However, it is vital to have a grip over the internal and external environment in which the institution exists in order to develop a perspective and methodology for specific institution within a context.

Therefore, socio-economic and cultural reality in which the institution is embedded, also, needs attention in designing the strategy and mission of specific institutions. We have an excellent policy document, like the *National Education Policy (NEP) 2020*, that assumes the right values and behaviours are readily available in institutions. It ignores the development of human resources and climate, which is a much broader subject than faculty development and training programmes in universities and colleges. A comprehensive approach is needed to build the capability of institutions because they are expected to work on implementation of the *NEP* vision.

Unlike the brick and mortar-based physical structures, *IB* in education, constitutes an overt and covert process. The word 'building' in *IB* connotes a sense of shaping and moulding because the core of an educational institution is its people, who are more than a pair of hands but have minds and brains. In other words, technical and task-oriented operations and socio-psychological processes deserve equal attention, because, they are interdependent aspects of a living system called an institution. Institutional leadership has to focus on the primary task or purpose and also pay attention to the human processes that would facilitate or hinder the achievement of its purpose and mission. Well-managed institutions of higher education promote organisation-wide learning based on feedback from the stakeholders to develop robust systems of operations that can sustain innovation and continuity. These institutions distinguish themselves from other organisations by their capacity to learn and remain viable and purposive for a longer time.

While describing the process of *IB*, it is also essential to recognise the external context or the macro environment in which institutions operate, particularly the demographic changes, technological innovations, economic and political climate, and state policy, among other aspects. As living systems, educational institutions are also open systems exposed to the dynamics of the environment. They adapt and adjust to external and internal changes as they evolve and grow.

Institutional leadership and educationists now benefit from a research-based body of knowledge on the theory and methodology of developing organisations and institutions. For the last six decades, it has been available in the discipline of applied behavioural sciences, that is, Organisational Development (*OD*), and in the emerging field of Institutional Development *(ID)*. It offers methods, tools, and techniques for managing change, diagnosing problems in groups and organisations, and designing interventions for institutional change and development. A third section on Learning Resources in this book includes notes on concepts, tools, operational-behavioural skills, and competencies of faculty and VC essential for developing academic organisations.

The second section of the book consists of illustrative cases and case studies that shed light on the ground reality of higher educational institutions in India. Specifically, they focus on problems of social discrimination, governance, leadership, the role of students' unions, political intrusions in academic spaces, and the processes of evolution, growth, and decline of institutions. These cases give a sense of specific challenges in higher education in India and also provide positive examples of self-regulated and visionary leadership in *IB* and negative examples of misuse of power and ideological aggression into educational spaces.

The ground-level reality of the Indian university system of affiliated colleges is that it is governed by an outdated bureaucratic mind-set, structures, and systems that resist change and innovation. The rules and regulations of administration are in place, but the predominant mind-set is to violate the boundaries of systems for vested interests and to beat the regulatory system of admissions, recruitment, evaluation, targets, and academic performance. Those of us who are exposed to the documentary evidence presented in the university series by *Ravish Kumar* on *NDTV* or in his *YouTube* videos, can, easily recognise the chasm between the espoused vision of the Indian university system and the actual practices and reality on campuses. They present sights of depleted infrastructures of state universities and colleges, vacant posts for faculty, resource-starved laboratories and libraries. Above all, the apathy and indifference of the state and central education ministry towards the ground realities of higher education, is too a part of the malaise. It reflects a sad but realistic picture of the Indian higher education system. Even in the grand vision of National Education Policy 2020, there is no mention of and provision for the required financial resources for basic facilities like full-time faculty, classrooms, libraries, and laboratories, among other things. India has produced many visionary documents on education in the past but has consistently failed to implement them.

The core contention of the book is that merely funding or increasing the budget for higher education would not be a long-term solution to the problems. Robust institutions are built on purposefulness and perspective. They also need a strategy, a methodology, relevant skills, and, most importantly, a set of values and convictions to improve the academic and institutional quality of higher education. The weakest link in the higher education system lies in state universities and affiliated colleges, which cover hundreds of *HEIs* in India. Educational reforms of

National Education Policy without strengthening state-level institutions would be a biased strategy in favour of privatisation in higher education institutions. In the long run, it would not be the right approach to ensure access to quality education for future generations. It is a reality that a significant part of state funding is currently used to sustain a few elite public institutions like IITs and IIMs in India.

As an instance, the *NEP 2020* document proposes 'autonomy' to *HEIs,* and a few initial steps to implement the policy proposal are taken. A few reputed universities and colleges in some states are given 'autonomous' status by the UGC. However, the fact is that these institutions would not become self-regulated, autonomous institutions overnight because they have been dependent on the bureaucratic structure and systems and allied attitudes and values. In reality, institutions are only given financial autonomy to decide fee structure and be financially self-reliant, which suits the state's policy of gradually withdrawing funding to higher education. However, what is missing is a genuine attempt to give autonomy to faculty and students. Unless the faculty develops capabilities and is empowered to engage with academic and administrative decisions and the students are involved as co-producers in learning and research, a progressive 'reform' in favour of autonomous institutions would not benefit the key stakeholders; instead, it would only promote corporatisation of higher education and give autonomy to promoters and management of *HEIs* to cut expenditure and raise fee structure. It would affect access to higher education for the lower economic sections of society.

To cover up these deficiencies in institutional processes and values, these autonomous institutions tend to fall prey to the strategy of operating like a commercial setup in the higher education market. In the near future, public universities and their affiliated colleges will regard higher education as an area of private goods rather than that of public goods. They would offer only those courses that have market value and neglect the core areas of academic expertise they have built over the years. Autonomous colleges would thus indulge in wasteful competition with other private colleges when the real need is for inter-institutional collaboration in resource sharing and interdisciplinary teaching and research. This is the area where institutional collaboration or an umbrella-like macro organisation is required—an 'organisation of organisations.' The emerging field of *ID,* discussed in the Essay Six, is meant to address issues created by the market competition that drains the scarce resources of educational institutions and does not benefit the key stakeholders, promoters, students, and faculty. In a competitive climate, the career security of faculty is being left to the market forces, and a contractual, clock-hour basis of employment prevails. In short, a policy push for reform of 'autonomy' without creating robust institutional systems, processes and a change in attitudes, values would be dysfunctional. It would damage the purpose and mission of public universities and colleges.

Value-based Institution

The frequently used constructs in academic discourse are 'institutional values' and 'academic culture', which would need clarification to avoid possible misinterpretation. The essential feature of 'values' is that they are reflected in human behaviours or actions. Hence, there is a difference between 'espoused or stated values presented in the vision-mission document and actual 'values in action' or behaviours at the workplace at a day-to-day level. It implies that those espoused or stated values may remain only a set of beliefs or a wish list that are not actually practised on the ground level. Institutional leadership should regularly review and check whether there is congruence or mismatch between 'espoused values' and 'values in action.'

The desirable values in practice or behaviours must be articulated to understand the concept better. Some of the values much desired on campuses are i) Creating inclusive spaces wherein internal stakeholders like students, staff, and faculty develop a sense of belonging or psychological relatedness, ii) Nurturing institutional commitment to individual growth as a person, iii) Acceptance of students from the deprived classes and castes is consciously built in the culture such as, ability to empathise without discrimination, sense of justice, and iv) Values that teach how to tolerate others' opinions, accept other identities irrespective of gender, religion, geography. In short, when progressive and democratic values are learned and practised in everyday behaviours on campus, it contributes to nation-building processes.

More importantly, values are created by individual and collective efforts, and sometimes, institutional members, have to struggle to sustain them against the dominant values promoted by the prevailing ecosystem. For instance, higher education is now perceived as an area of private goods for individual benefit rather than public or social goods. *HEIs* driven by market forces prioritise efficient use of human resources and individual return on investment for students and promoters. In this context, values that emphasise the equality of opportunities or consider education as public goods are ignored, and its contribution to socially productive work, or search for truth and aesthetics take a back seat.

Nonetheless, it has become increasingly essential to reiterate and reemphasise the normative, institutional values that are more relevant in the contemporary context of higher education in India because they give all citizens of India the same constitutional rights and responsibilities. These values include freedom of expression, equality, equity, brotherhood, concern for others and scientific temperament. They imply that freedom of the individual is as essential conditions of freedom of all. In addition, these values also protect the individual search for truth and beauty and promote active engagement with society with a sense of compassion and justice. "No other organisation and profession match the lofty purpose of educational institutions," as Prof *Pankaj Chandra,* former vice chancellor of Ahmedabad University, in his article on '*Questioning Academic Freedom' (2018),* has rightly stated. These values are more relevant for educational institutions in the contemporary context. A value-based academic culture on campuses implies an inclusive, non-discriminatory climate and a tolerance of diversity of views, customs, human dignity, and a respect for intellectual pursuit that supports a subjective and experiential search for 'truth' beyond ideology. Prof Chandra further adds, 'The purpose and objective of a University is lofty and broad, which is not matched by any other work organisation. A country's progress is measured by the advancement of its universities. They build perspectives on intrinsic values, judgements, and skills for the present and the future. It can also connect with the masses and go beyond the boundaries of the ivory tower. It teaches and practices important democratic values about engagement, compassion, fairness, and justice'.

However, significantly, in the first two decades of the twenty-first century, the role of the state and the market had taken centre stage in the power structure of higher education in India. *HEIs* in both public and private sectors are expected to meet the demands of the regulators who act as agents of the state rather than an autonomous body. This trend has impacted other institutions, such as the banks, police, industry, press and media. It has the potential to weaken institutions that sustain Indian democracy. It only signifies that building and developing robust educational institutions, would require visionary leadership that provides a moral compass, integrity, and good governance to counter such external forces and pressures to focus on the primary purpose and mission.

Universities and national institutions of higher education are expected to provide visionary leadership for higher education and society. They would set an example about what is right and wrong and what is important. '*Courage will be needed from universities and their leaders to stand up for what is right*' as Quentin Thomson emphasised in his article on '*International Reflections on University' (2018).*

In the process of writing, the author was able to understand the complexity and challenges of managing higher education institutions in India; at the same time, he also sensed an urgent need for and the potential to strengthen and shape purposeful institutions with robust systems and vibrant learning communities in hundreds of Indian universities, affiliated colleges and private and public institutes that offer professional courses in engineering, medicine, architecture, and pharmacy. India has exceptional *HEIs* of good academic quality and research. Elite public institutes like IITs, IIMs, and some private universities have excelled in professional programmes in engineering, management, and medicine. Universities like *JNU* have an international reputation in social science teaching and research. However, hundreds of affiliated colleges of state universities are academically and resource-wise under-nourished. They need radical interventions in structure and processes. Moreover, the most serious gap in *IB* in India is the absence of visionary leadership that would resist the corporatisation of higher education and provide a moral anchor to the academic community. Visionary institutional leadership for higher education in India is urgently needed to defend 'what is right' with courage and conviction and protect the inherent sanctity and autonomy of academic institutions that are increasingly facing economic, social, and political pressures.

The contents of the book, the author would like to believe, are appropriate and useful to all those working directly or indirectly in the realm of higher education and have stakes in it: educationists, promoters, vice-chancellors, directors, principals, faculty, students from the field of education and management, policymakers, bureaucrats, and parents concerned about quality and access of higher education in India for their wards. Also, the book is of contemporary relevance to Indian universities, colleges, and institutions of professional education. It can help institutional leaders to comprehend the complexity and challenges of institutional building and develop a perspective and strategy to face them. Writing the book has taken longer time than expected, in order to make the contents more comprehensive; though the language used in Essay section is more academic and less reader friendly, the subsequent sections on Case-studies and Learning Resources use straightforward and descriptive narration.

ENDNOTES

1. **On Building Robust Institutions**
   HEI's in India tend to define themselves as a machine that can be steered, controlled and influenced by setting rules and regulations. They do not have autonomy to build 'robustness' to sustain and grow in the changing environment of 21st century. It is possible to build robust systems to strengthen these institutions if institutional stakeholders are engaged in collective learning from experiences and establish norms of behaviors.
   A systemic perspective, action-research methodology, and process skills are appropriate tools for the purpose. Process sensitivity empowers members to recognise how circumstances of their own making are shaping their attitudes and behaviours. Robust institutions of higher education are longstanding organizations with a capacity to revitalize and remain relevant from generation to generation. It is important to document and learn from their practices and processes.

REFERENCES

1. Chandra, P. (2018). Questioning Academic Freedom, *The idea of a University*, Apporvanand (Ed.) Context.
2. Chattopadhyay, S. (1912). *Education and Economics*, Oxford University Press.
3. Dymoke, S. & Harrison, J. (Ed). (2008). *Reflective teaching and learning.* Sage Publications.
4. Harshe, R. (2023). *Pakshi Unhacha –A first-person narration on work experiences on seven university campuses.* : Sadhana Prakashan, Pune.
5. Padaki, V. & Vaz, M. (2003). *Institutional development in social interventions: Towards inter-organisational effectiveness.* Sage Publications.
6. Padaki, V. & Vaz, M. (2005). *Management development in non-profit organisations.* Sage Publications.
7. Ramnarayan, S. & Rao, T.V. (Ed). (2011). *Organisation development.* Sage Publications.
8. Thompson, Q. (2018). *International Reflections on University Autonomy and Freedoms, The idea of a University*, Context

SECTION ONE

The eleven essays in this section deal with perspectives, practices, and theories related to institutional building and higher educational processes. The key concepts and theories of human and organisational development, institutional building (IB) and leadership are discussed with concrete examples from HEIs in contemporary India. The contribution of the disciplines of Institutional Development and Systems Thinking is highlighted to indicate their significance and application to IB in higher education. The section also covers essays on themes of contemporary relevance, such as the market of higher education, the corporatisation of higher education, and measuring the quality and performance of educational institutions. Two essays specifically focus on techno-economic and humanistic perspectives of higher education. The essay format is used since it is more suitable for describing, explaining, discussing, and debating complex issues of IB processes and challenges of higher education in India. The section concludes with an elaborate note on three qualitative research methods for initiating personal and institutional transformation and change.

Essay One

Challenges in Institution Building for Higher Education in India

The first essay reviews the contemporary challenges faced by higher education institutions (*HEI*) in India. It utilises data based on personal experiences, observations, published literature and press reports to describe the predicament of *HEIs* due to macro-level social, economic, technological and political reasons. The essay tries to chart the road ahead by examining the positive and negative examples of Institution Building (*IB*) in India. The essay also presents a four-dimensional conceptual framework model on the *IB* process that would be helpful in offering a diagnosis of and solutions to the challenges of *IB* in India.

Higher education in India faces challenges in terms of quality and access. The campus climate of *HEIs* fails to provide fair and humane treatment to students. Growing unemployment and under-employment of the educated have also led to a new kind of inequity in society along with traditional socio-economic (caste and class-based) discrimination. The state policy of privatisation of education has led to new business models, such as tutorial and digital classes in higher education that focus on brands and tangible attributes of success in examinations to achieve profit. These trends have negatively impacted the primary purposes of higher education, which are a) generating new knowledge, b) disseminating received knowledge through teaching, learning, and research, and c) developing human capability for lifelong learning. The processes of building *HEI*s are affected by the policy focus on a rapid expansion of access to *HEI*s at the state level as a response to the growing demand from the aspiring middle class in India.

Education policies of successive governments have influenced the operations and climate of institutions. Dilemmas of quality vs. quantity, issues emerging from reservation policy for admission, and decrease in state funding remain unresolved.

Moreover, institutions in higher education lack both academic culture and capacity for organisational learning and innovation for development. Building this kind of culture and orientation is the main role of leadership in institutions of higher learning. Fortunately, there are models and cases available in India to guide the *IB* process. In this essay, some of the positive and negative instances from the Indian context are analysed to draw conclusions on the best practices and pitfalls in building sustainable institutions of higher learning. The essay also highlights the role of leadership and governance in *HEIs*.

Context: After the liberalisation of the Indian economy, education has been officially a part of the service industry, and the consequences of this policy decision are now visible. For instance, in Pune city, students are offered courses by fourteen universities, some funded by the state government, while others belong to deemed or private universities. Many affiliated colleges and institutes offer conventional courses in the humanities, science and commerce, as well as professional courses in engineering, management, medicine, and law. Higher education in India is a quasi-market, wherein *HEIs* compete for their space in the national market and try to attract their student customers through aggressive coverage in print and digital media. The advertisement and promotional budget of some private universities are in the millions, which is evidence of over-emphasis on the marketing function of promoting the brand to remain competitive. This is at the cost of substantive academic goals of curriculum design, research, teaching, and quality of learning resources in order to produce and disseminate theoretical and applied knowledge.

A few questions emerge in the context of *HEIs* – How does higher education in India address the needs of Indian industry and society? What is the meaning of the terms 'quality', 'performance', 'merit' in our educational institutions? What are the appropriate structures, processes, attitudes, and behaviours that help build *HEIs?* How are issues of quality, access and equity in higher education addressed?

It is evident that many of the management concepts, techniques and practices of business organisations are also very pertinent to different kinds of educational institutions. Though management concepts and techniques, as such, are value-free and, therefore, relevant to all domains of organisations, the fact is that the larger developmental role of education in India is to sustain economic growth and nourish democratic values in society. It has now become more critical in the 21st century in India due to the recent changes in economic, social and political context.

However, it is essential to recognise that the domain of education is not similar to other sectors of the economy, such as industry, business and commerce, because the context and values are different. For instance, in medical education and practice, one cannot relate to a patient like a customer of consumer goods and services. If a patient is suffering from tuberculosis or cancer, he/she has no choice but to seek medical treatment. In contrast, one can choose from consumer goods companies for products A, B or C and even decide not to buy. This option is not available in medical and educational domains. Every citizen should have good medical facilities and better education since they are connected with the fundamental right to live and work. In the Indian context, it is essential to focus on the purpose and mission of *HEIs* and examine the underlying assumptions of higher education policy of the state and its regulatory institutions.

It is commonly observed that the primary goal of knowledge generation and developmental orientation of higher education is side-lined in the rush to expand higher education access. It was is carried out by private initiatives in educational entrepreneurship with the backing of the state education policy. However,, the responsibility of institutional leadership is to give academic direction to sustain a vibrant intellectual climate on campus. The experience of the young generation concerning the intellectual climate and teaching and learning processes on the campus has a long-term impact on their careers. A young person with clarity on ethical values and a concern for others and society, is, a national asset compared to those focused on personal gains and who treat higher education as a private good. This would require a foundation of a robust theory of institutional building *(IB)* and a perspective on educational leadership that goes beyond making higher education function like a market.

Foundation of Institution Building

A closer and incisive look at the theory and application of *IB* processes in higher education, deserves special attention. More clarity on the concept and definition of the institution is relevant at this point of time in the discussion. Some of the definitions and concepts of 'institution' are mentioned below.

> *"An institution is an organisation that has acquired greater value and wider impact on people's lives" (McGill, 1996).*
>
> *"Organisations... become institutions (when they assume) larger roles and wider responsibilities ... it is an innovative organisation that brings about and protects change." (Esman et al., 1974)*

Broadly speaking, an institution is a longstanding organisation steeped in tradition and culture to claim an institutional status. Some writers distinguish organisations from institutions to imply that the latter have a greater degree of ownership and inner drive as well as the internalisation of values, which is unlike organisations "wherein functions are imposed from outside and not self-run, self-managed and self-assessed." (Fernandez, 1999)

Institutions are also seen as governmental organisations "that create policies, mobilise and manage resources" (McGill,1996), for example, the Ministry of Education (ex MHRD) and apex regulatory organisations like UGC and AICTE, AIMA. In the realm of higher education, these institutions are created as an agency of the state for regulation and coordination. They also function as "... a central authority that has control over the actions of its members... so as to maximise the benefit to the whole society." (Sundrum, R.M, 1983)

There are macro institutions, overarching, umbrella-like organisations, that, are, conceived as 'inter-sectorial institutional linkages' to overcome weaknesses of one sector; for example, public and private universities in India do not have a common institutional platform in India (Padaki et al., 1984). A few years ago, an organisation called the Education Promotion Society of India (EPSI) was formed with an agenda of resource sharing, joint action and lobbying to influence national policy and business corporations favourably on behalf of private universities and institutes of higher education.

Institution Building (*IB)* is used at the micro level in *HEIs,* while Institutional Development (*ID)* is used at the macro level, referring to the institutions as 'overseeing bodies', 'umbrella organisations' and 'an organisation of organisations.' In the case of *ID*, institutions are held together by a set of values to which the constituent members or organisations adhere without giving up their individual pursuits or interests. (Padaki & Vaz, 2003). The theory and practice of *ID* in India is at a nascent stage.

Micro institutions like *HEIs* include affiliated or autonomous colleges and institutes of higher learning that hold their community or collectivity of stakeholders together by a set of values and processes that help maintain their independent identity and values while being a part of regulatory or macro institutions like the state university, *UGC, and AICTE.*

One of the important dimensions of the *IB* process, is, 'to build a capacity of organisations to revitalise and remain relevant from generation to generation'. In essence, investment in *IB* leads to longevity, sustainability, and the ability of the institution, which distinguishes itself from other workplaces called 'organisations' to regenerate or renew itself and focus on capacity building for long-term sustenance. The perspective of *IB* is based on identity and values of collectivity. In this sense, institutions go beyond building task-related structures, systems and human capital. Hence, the concept and processes of *IB* are relevant for all stakeholders and, more so, for those in leadership positions in HEIs.

Institutional Processes

Due to larger time frames in consideration and growth prospects, institutions are rightly conceptualised as 'organisations of organisations'. The boundary of an institution as an open system connects it with other parts or subsystems of the organisations. A university as a macro institution is an umbrella structure that holds affiliated colleges together, and it also holds a micro institution on its campus that runs post-graduate departments in various disciplines. It is like a federal structure and, therefore, is more complex and challenging to manage. Conventional rigid structures of bureaucracy are not adequate to deal with its complexity.

An institutional model proposed by *Prof Pulin Garg* is a community model wherein boundaries of tasks, systems, values of individual and collective identities are permeable and flexible so that rational and emotional dimensions of the living system-like institution are better channelised towards the purpose and the attendant objectives. The critical competence of well-managed institutions is their 'self-managing or self-regulating capability' based on the group or collectivity/ community's ability of 'learning to learn' from experience and collaboration within and with other organisations or its parts. Unlike organisations, where the boundary separates itself from the environment, in the institutional context, the boundary is expected to be more inclusive, allowing the process of give and take more freely. It is a relatively more open system, so that interface with the complexity of the environment is maintained with adequate variety and creativity within the system. In the contemporary context of globalisation and the expansion of knowledge-based industry, only open systems based on values have a better chance to sustain longer and remain purposeful. In the Indian context, the structure of a 'Cluster university' that holds affiliated colleges and institutes at one location is designed to mobilise all resources towards a specific mission of interdisciplinary studies or specialised courses. However, only structures do not ensure a collaborative culture and shared values. This would require systemic perspective wherein the whole system avoids the sub- optimisation of the subsystems. Here comes the role of building robust *IB* processes.

The reality is that in the contemporary, competitive market of higher education, at institutional level, competing universities, colleges and their distinct stakeholders would not engage in a collaborative way or share resources with others. The point is relevant in the context of higher education where colleges within domains of professional education such as engineering, management, and medicine are in an intense competitive mode with inevitable wastage of limited resources and loss of synergy. Even in business and industry, companies have learned the lesson the hard way and taken the initiative to collaborate strategically with competitors for synergy. Similar attempts are also made to create umbrella institutions for sharing resources and other collaborative activities to influence the government and the education market, as done by *EPSI* (2005), an initiative in higher education. (Essay Six)

Educational Institutions as Learning Organisations

The institutional capacity to learn and self-renew as an open system is essential to adapt and resist the inevitable process of 'organisational entropy,' a universal process in all man-made living systems. All living systems tend to move towards disorganisation, chaos and decline. Since institutions are man-made designs, entropy remains a major threat to their survival and growth in institutional evolution. Building institutional capability to get and act on the negative and positive feedback received by the open system is one of the ways to arrest entropy so that institutions can remain viable for a longer time frame. It ensures that institutional intelligence is spread across all levels and its parts. All members have the potential to learn and sense the conditions of organisational health and decay. Learning organisations arrest decay effectively. Robust institutions are able to coordinate and balance external changes in the environment with internal capabilities. The gaps in structures, systems, knowledge, skills, attitudes, and behaviours are filed to help institution survive and grow in turbulent times.

The key feature of an institution is its purposefulness, which is shaped by how people hold the purpose consciously in terms of its mission and behaviours and covertly in terms of beliefs and values. Institutional performance is influenced by the structures, systems, and processes, which are its body or physical aspect and, more importantly, by the orientation and values of those who work for it, which is at the core of the institutional mind and its identity. This way, institutions sustain and grow from the synergy and balance between body and mind, purpose and values, systems and identity, conformity and innovation.

Contemporary Context of Higher Education in India and Challenges in IB

Institutions as living systems are embedded in a context at micro and macro levels. It is important to comprehend how institutions are organically connected with the larger socio-political and economic environment. *HEIs* are a part of higher education market in India. The structure of the market is hierarchical, and it operates at three layers or tiers, that is; the top layer is of reputed, elite institutes like IITs, IIMs and reputed universities like Jamia Millia University, Jawaharlal Nehru University (JNU), and other central-regional institutes. The second tier consists of private universities that tend to invest in building a 'brand' through media hype, and the third layer consists of public and state universities and their affiliated colleges.

The concepts of 'market' and 'brand' are actually used for describing corporate business of goods and services; they also, reflect a toxic effect on the educational institutions due to the neoliberal economic policy of the State. *HEIs* tend to offer expensive courses and invest resources in brand building. In this market competition, the conventional courses of affiliated colleges and public universities tend to lose because the so-called competition and quality are more of market-driven ideas based on media surveys, ranking systems and market perceptions rather than actual experiences of those who study or work in these institutions. The point is that it is very challenging to build a mission-driven identity of a higher education institution based on egalitarian values in the contemporary context. There is no solution to it in the prevalent framework of the higher education market, that, is effectively monitored and supported by the state, which in turn is increasingly influenced by a neoliberal ideology to privatise higher education and support the market system. This policy approach is based more on a political ideology rather than economic and educational rationale.

As an attendant consequence, educational institutions in India are compelled to imitate the model of brand building used by business organisations without considering the long-term impact and mismatch of such a myopic view of institutions. For instance, industry employers who recruit students of business schools observe that the media hype about MBAs and their institutions on placement salaries causes students to develop unrealistic aspirations. They believe that these expectations need to be moderated and educational institutes should conduct an aspiration check of students periodically. (Vikapa, 2014).

Those institutions that offer professional courses in medicine, business management, engineering, and law are primarily managed by trusts, political leaders and industrialists, and their fees range from two to thirty lakhs per year, even for students admitted on merit. Needless to say, after completing education, their employers and clients pithily observe that these professionals operate under anxiety to cash in on their investments in professional education. Moreover, access to higher education in India is limited to those who can afford such fees. Though education loans are available, bankers give last priority to these loans since there is a risk of non-performance in payment. The most recent example is of thousands of medical students in Russia and Ukraine who migrated due to a huge gap in education fees, which is almost four times more in India. The point is that access to higher education in professional courses is limited to only those families with above higher middle-class income. Issues of *quality, access* and *equity* in higher education have remained unresolved for decades. (*RUSA report, MHRD, 2013*)

The role of higher education in nation-building for a democratic country with a strong constitutional framework of India, takes, a beating when brand building and marketing overtake content and purpose of education. If the essence of *HEIs* is serious academic pursuits of knowledge and truth, then brand building would be a divergence of resources and direction. However, the problem can only be solved at the next highest level of higher education, and that is the policy and, most notably, the funding strategy of the state, centre and region. The vision of *NEP 2020* is conspicuously silent on the point of funding. It implies that higher education in India shall rely mainly on private investment.

Some of the questions confronting *HEIs* are: What is the present state of higher education institutions in India? How do stakeholders like students, parents, faculty, employers, regulatory bodies of the government, and society at large see the role and issues in higher education?

The weakest link in the higher education system in India is the affiliated colleges of the state universities. Some anecdotal observations are presented below. These are subjective observations of the author, based on experiences on educational campuses in Pune, considered the hub of higher education in India, and from published secondary sources presented below. These statements indicate only first-cut sensing of problems and issues but do not indicate the solutions to them because it is not a systematic diagnosis to find the root causes of problems. However, they deserve attention because they are based on the personal experiences of the major stakeholders of the higher education system in India: students, faculty, parents, promoters of *HEIs*, employers, and society at large. At this stage, one can only say that a deeper analysis is required to understand the issues of higher education so that alternative solutions and models are offered. However, the author has identified a potential area for further exploration, wherein specific perspectives and models to address the challenges in higher education seem to exist; this is an area of building and strengthening existing and new institutions, broadly recognised as *IB*.

It is necessary to focus our undivided attention on the ground-level reality of *HEIs* in India. Some random observations based on personal experiences, secondary data and informal conversations at institutional spaces of *HEIs* are given below:

1. Students and parents are concerned about the timely declaration of results and quality of teaching in classrooms and administration
2. Faculty are anxious about their tenure on contract and employment security, and it affects teaching-learning processes on campus.

3. While selecting a college for admission, parents and students depend on hearsay and first impressions about the infrastructure rather than the quality of academic delivery due to the absence of reliable information and experience in the college.
4. Industry and employers expect competencies relevant to their sectors but are not greatly interested in investing in industry-academia collaboration or mentoring for internship projects.
5. Regulatory bodies like *UGC*, *AICTE*, and *AIMC* emphasise compliance with the norms and control over institutions. However, malpractices in the admission process, fees, faculty appointments, and assessment continue covertly, and criminal cases for corruption charges in areas of *NAAC* certification and appointment of VCs in public universities are often published in the media.
6. Private universities and institutes promoted by education entrepreneurs see higher education as a business opportunity and bring a new kind of inequity due to higher fees and resources spent on branding than state universities.
7. Successive governments have shown inconsistency in educational policies and introduced procedural changes without addressing the fundamental problems of quality, funding and *IB*.
8. Institutional leaders and faculty fail to focus on the mission and values due to the marketisation of higher education.
9. A former Chairman of a regulatory body, AICTE (Interview in India Today, 15 Sep 2021), had justified mass closures of engineering colleges as a 'market adjustment to excessive growth,' and he believes that it would benefit in improving the quality of technical education. The contradiction between the AICTE policy of increasing engineering colleges and permitting closure is apparent and exposes the myopic and opportunistic approach of state regulators.

These observations are divergent views on various aspects that only indicate the complexity and contradictions in the higher education system in India. Take, for instance, the response of the AICTE Chairman to the problem of large-scale closures of engineering colleges. He does not perceive it as a problem but as a solution to poor quality of education due to a greater number of colleges than required. It is an oversimplification of the issue of the quality of higher education. It is strange logic to connect closure with better quality of education for the future. It is instead an insensitive comment since it is the AICTE that grants permissions to open engineering colleges, and no responsibility is taken for wrong decisions to grant permission without checking the merit of the proposal.

Interestingly, the previous chairman of the same regulatory body explained that many engineering graduates remain unemployed because of a lack of data on the projected employment generation by the government. In the absence of data, how can regulators plan the target growth of technical education in India? Moreover, how can the balance between the growth, access and quality of education be maintained? There are more questions than answers on *HEIs* in India.

This is a picture of the predicament of higher education in India, based on the author's experience in postgraduate teaching, administration, and information from published literature. Indeed, it is not an encouraging scenario for the higher education system in India, but if we are concerned about it as a community of educators, we can work on it by using the positive aspects of the Indian institutions of higher education. One can be optimistic because, in some corners, the work of *IB* is being done and has positively impacted its stakeholders. The reader would find the case study on institutional leadership at IIM-A and a case incident of institutional entropy in a reputed college managed by a 135-year-old education society in this Essay.

The Role of Leadership in IB

Prof Udai Pareek (1981), then faculty in Organisational Behaviour, interviewed Mr *Ravi J Mathai* to learn about his ideas and experiences on *IB* as the first Director of IIM-A, an autonomous management institute, during his tenure from 1965 to 1972. Though the social, economic, and political context of India has changed drastically, *Mathai's* thoughts on the purpose and values of institutional processes and the role of leadership in building *HEIs* remain relevant even now for the following reasons: i) emphasis on institutional leadership and his personal values and preference for innovation over bureaucratic mindset, ii) a professional commitment from the depth of being rather than for vested interests, iii) emphasis on critical thinking, self-regulation, and creativity, and iv) his focus on developmental orientation at individual, group and community levels are equally crucial in contemporary context of higher education in India.

Ironically, *HEIs* in India in the twenty-first century have opted for autonomy, but they want to use it to benefit the promoters rather than the faculty and students. Also, they neglect the non-financial or academic parameters to measure the success of educational institutions. *Mathai's* experiences and ideas would provide valuable input for *IB* in public and private universities and affiliated colleges in India.

In India, university education is largely funded and regulated by governmental bureaucracy. However, post-liberalisation, many deemed and private universities with academic and financial autonomy were established. They are regulated by national-level bodies like *UGC* and *AICTE* to address issues related to governance and academic management. The Indian experience is that autonomy in higher education is used for funding rather than academic purposes. In fact, *HEIs* in India do not have a shared understánding of the standards of quality and governance in higher education. Also, there is a lack of adequate coaching, mentoring, training, and orientation for faculty and staff development. Therefore, there are lapses in governance and mediocre outcomes from academic teaching and learning. Since higher education is seen as a profit-making enterprise, very often, promoters' credibility in establishing education institutions raises questions on the intent. More than half of the *HEIs* operate without an accreditation from *NAAC* and *NBA*, agencies that accredits universities and institutions of technical education.

Behavioural Impact on Key Stakeholders: Faculty and Students

The above discussion points out that the challenges of *IB* in the contemporary context have resulted in the following consequences on the motivation of faculty, students and academic practices in *HEIs*:

(a) Prevalence of uniform or standardised courses of state universities that are controlled and regulated by regional governments,

(b) Private universities are competing to occupy a space in the education market since it is encouraged by neoliberal policies of the state,

(c) Students rate the quality of *HEIs* based on their potential to give a higher return for investment *(ROI).*

(d) In this context, it is interesting to note the impact on the upcoming generation of faculty members employed in *HEIs,* which reveals a distinct mindset very similar to those of neo-professionals in the IT industry.

For young faculty, the organisation is an employment and career arena, rather, than a membership arena which the authorities fail to understand. An deft and attendant, Engagement with the organisation is an assignment specific to building a resume and remaining viable in their career's progress. They seek economic, social and professional mobility – upward and sideways. Commitment is to professional fraternity rather than the organisation or the institution. Since any commitment is always unilateral, it is risky for them to commit to an educational institute or university that is privately funded and micro-managed by promoters with a commercial focus. In such an environment, seeking a sense of belonging or membership is not a welcome idea. It is seen with cynicism from both ends by individual faculty and institutional management.

A Positive Case of Institution Leadership

In the backdrop of market-driven higher education in contemporary India, it is appropriate to revisit and reiterate an exceptional example of leadership in *IB* for deeper insights into institutional processes. It concerns the first full-time director of IIM-A, *Mr Ravi J Mathai*. The description is based on excerpts from an interview by *Prof Udai Pareek* when *Mathai* was the director (1965-72).

Mathai's approach was to build a faculty culture that was responsive to the expectations of the external stakeholders. In his words,

> *"Influencing external expectations was important because it reinforced integrity within the institute (IIM-A). Also, it reduced the pressure for procedures and rules and centralisation of authority that is commonly seen in government-funded organisations. Also, it would have resulted in externally imposed regulations rather than self-regulation. This approach of building a responsive culture freed the institution of IIM-A from the bureaucratisation of professional education. Moreover, building the reputation of the institute was based mainly on behaviours of faculty and students through academic processes of teaching, learning, consulting and research."*

Some of the features of *IB* at IIM-A initiated by *Ravi Mathai* are summarised below:

(a) Primacy of faculty development and management by self-regulation.
(b) Emphasis on the Open Systems Theory perspective with a focus on the openness of the institute to the environment and organisation-wide learning by responding to feedback from external stakeholders.
(c) Emphasis on authority of the self and individual responsibility without the use of formal authority
(d) Minimising power orientation and maximising collective autonomy and development of competence of individual faculty through self-managing committees

A significant part of the interview of *Mr Ravi J Mathai* is devoted to the role of leadership in a new educational institution. Some of the key leadership features are listed below as lessons on leadership for *IB*:

(a) Emphasis on engaging with faculty, staff, industry, and students in order to influence their relationships, attitudes and behavioural norms
(b) Developing conditions in the institute conducive to the development of the individual and the group in terms of reinforcing self-esteem, autonomy, and creativity, which could later become a characteristic of the institution itself.

The director is expected to take a long-term view of his role that goes beyond personal interests so that it would not be seen only as a career for personal gains but for building and developing the institution. The most important qualification of a leadership role is that the person should not need the job. Metaphorically, he should be able to carry his resignation in his pocket and not be vulnerable by being dependent on the job.

In the words of *Prof. Mathai,*

> *"The leader should see himself as a part of the continuum of a very long process; then, he would be less vulnerable to the fear that something may go wrong. If his need is to be regarded as a builder of the institution, it would be self-defeating. Then, his priority would be to achieve personal success, and he would not be able to face the risk of failure.*
>
> *"The leader is expected to spend more time on institutional aspects that go beyond short-term five-year plans, budgeting, research projects, faculty and courses. Instead, he should spend more time on reflecting and thinking about his own perceptions of the task he had accepted, the philosophy of developing the institution. He has to be honest with himself in terms of his needs and the extent to which he can adjust his needs to the task of the situation. Intellectual dishonesty and rationalisation can be avoided if there is less ambiguity about the director's self-assessment of personal needs and the task of the* IB."

A Conceptual Model

From the specific case example mentioned above and the experiences of those in leadership roles in business and non-business organisations, one can conceptualise and operationalise a model of Institution Building. This would provide guidance on designing appropriate structures, systems, attitudes and behaviours for educational institutions in the Indian context. One of the models is a '2 by 2' model of institutional processes.

This aforesaid model of four institutional dimensions is conceptualised by *Mr Sushant Banerjee* (2003), a senior management consultant and process facilitator in OD. It constitutes four main institutional processes captured in the diagram below. They represent human capabilities and faculties with rational and emotional emphasis. It also includes two institutional orientations to focus on instrumental or task-related activities and expressive activities or activities meant to release human articulation. Together, these four dimensions balance individual and collective capabilities and orientations so that institutional behaviours remain channelised and purposeful towards vision and mission.

Explanation of the Model

Four dimensions of institutional behaviours as a collectivity are *Rational, Instrumental, Emotional, and Expressive.* It is expected that the main focus of work organisations, both in industrial and educational domains, is on the rational and instrumental aspects of work. As depicted in Table 1, the first quadrant addresses the question of 'What do we do' as a collectivity? However, not so evident in the organisational space are 'emotional' and expressive dimensions, as quadrant two on professionalism focuses on 'How do we do the work?' and Quadrant four is about 'Why we do it?' referring to the articulation purpose of the institution. Quadrant three is about 'Who are we?' as a collectivity and its institutional identity. The main strength of educational institutions lies in quadrants three and four, as they give clarity and legitimacy to their existence. Organisations in both business and educational sectors over-focus on rational/instrumental aspects of Quadrant 1 and 2 of the workplace and repress and undervalue emotional and expressive dimensions. However, *IB* processes draw primary inspiration and nourishment from the emotional and expressive potential of people in order to balance institutional bias towards rational and instrumental dimensions.

The foundation of *IB* is based on the belief that emotional and expressive faculties of human collectives could be converted into purposive behaviour of organisation through convergence with their counterpoints of rational and instrumental orientations. In other words, leaders of institutions are expected to give equal emphasis to all four dimensions of the model: rational, emotional, instrumental and expressive. These dimensions operate at individual and institutional or collectivity levels, as depicted in Table 1.

	Instrumental	Expressive
Rational	Work Q1	Articulation Q4
Emotional	Professionalism Q2	Identity Q3

Table 1: 2×2 Matrix of Institutional Processes

In other words, the core aspects of *IB* processes are about engagement with work and professional values and the articulation of individual and collective identities for meaningful contributions to the institution. In this way, institutions need a foundation of individual and collective values and identity.

The work of *IB* is to bring the four quadrants mentioned above into synergy, syncretisation and coherence so that the four dimensions of human abilities of doing, thinking, feeling, and expressing are deployed constructively. Specifically, for the health of institutions, quadrant four is the most precious asset from a humanistic point of view. Ironically, it is a missing part in both kinds of organisations, business and education. Educational institutions do not invest in this dimension for a variety of reasons; for example, developing students and faculty through creating a space for self-expression cannot be the right thing to consider in the context of temporary and contractual employment at the workplace of *HEIs*. Also, it is not a safe thing for those in authority positions to allow faculty, staff and students to speak their minds on campus.

The crucial insight into the *IB* process mentioned above is that the primary source of human convictions and commitment spawns from the emotional-expressive domain of the human mind deployed in a collectivity space. However, in reality, only the rational-instrumental dimension of the human mind is used to fulfil the instrumental purpose and related tasks of organisations. Thus, the focus moves to 'skills development' for outcomes. The worrying fact is that only instrumental knowledge and related skills for employability are delivered in formal education systems, which fail to touch the students emotionally and ethically. The 'being' part of the identity of institutional members gets neglected and even suppressed as impractical and irrelevant. This is the impact of the dominance of Technical Rationality (TR) perspective on all types of organisations. It has a more damaging influence on educational institutions whose mandate is to provide sensitive and ethical leadership to society at large.

In institutes of professional education, it is common to find that considerable emphasis is placed on resume writing, business etiquette, and interview skills to remain competitive in the entry-level job market. Paradoxically, those who employ the young consider 'conscientiousness' or responsible behaviours and attitude towards work as the most desirable quality of employees. Needless to say, those who have taken coveted education in elite institutions like *IITs* and *IIMs* are very functional and territorial, committed to their functional expertise, careers and narrow-minded or one- dimensional in their thinking. At workplaces, they cannot influence non-reporting relationships, which is an important leadership quality. They are unable to take a multi-functional, holistic perspective that can integrate functions, structure and geographical locations. The reality is that such a holistic perspective and skill set are usually learned on the job by those who wish to be upwardly mobile and are ambitious individuals in terms of professional careers to take leadership roles.

In other words, at the level of collectivity in institutions, questions on identity like '*Who are we and how do we feel?*' are as important as those about tasks and systems such as '*what do we do and how do we do it?*' It is a state of involved essentiality where institutional identity emerges from the articulation of experiences and reflections, which in turn are possible at the workplace in a climate of openness, trust, and interpersonal and group competencies. It requires a high level of interpersonal trust and shared purpose and values. They are core processes that integrate individual self and identity with the purpose of individual and collectivity to make the institution realise its purpose, vision and mission. It is observed that in the education sector, there is a dominant trend of the corporatisation of institutions, and it raises a question for further exploration as to whether this trend has strengthened or hampered the process of *IB* around the four dimensions.

An institutional model that proposes and visualises an integrated view of the four dimensions of *IB* and makes them effective is an ideal state or model for those engaged with *IB* processes in *HEIs*. However, the reality does not always match the ideal state since institutions are open systems exposed to internal and external changes in a dynamic environment. Hence, thinkers and practitioners of *IB* have to use the methodology of sensing, diagnosis and intervention to rectify the dysfunctionality in the evolution and development of institutions and address the inevitable challenges and situations of crisis in *IB* processes.

Process of Entropy: A Negative Example of Disorientation of an Educational Institution

One of the inevitable processes commonly found in the evolution of established educational institutions, happens to be a state of entropy or disintegration of the core identity and values of the institutions. It is recognised as a state of institutional entropy. Below is an example of such a disorder in a century-old, reputed college and its damaging consequences on institutional development. It would be an eye-opener for other institutions to consider the possibility of similar crises on educational campuses. However, it is important to note that organisational entropy is a process that happens or keeps happening gradually, covertly, for some years, though the visible outcome may look like a sudden crisis. Institutional builders should read the symptoms of entropy from feedback and check the damaging process as a part of performance review and audit to diagnose the state of organisational health and robustness of the systems.

Organisations with robust systems, processes, behaviours and values in place possess a capacity to resist and overcome the inevitable process of entropy. Institutions become viable living systems because of their capacity to detect the processes of entropy within and, therefore, can initiate the process of self-renewal.

Hence, they can avoid or postpone the inevitable process of decay and death in all living systems, whether nature-made or man-made. As mentioned before, such a case of institutional entropy is presented below to highlight the importance of maintaining the process of *IB* alive, even for well-established, century-old institutions.

An Illustrative Case of Institutional Entropy

This illustrative case study describes and illustrates the evolution and current state of a reputed institution in Maharashtra to highlight the issues and problems in the evolution of the *IB* process in higher education.

Pune City is considered the hub of educational institutions in India. It has several trusts and educational societies with a hundred and more years of experience of running schools, colleges and technical institutes. The case below describes such a society with a legacy of managing reputed colleges and schools in western Maharashtra. It was founded by leaders and intellectuals who participated in the freedom struggle and who believed that local and Indian initiatives in education were much needed to strengthen the nationalist movement during the British era. Notably, the society is unique as it is primarily managed by faculty and teachers of colleges and schools. It is considered and rightly called a 'teacher-managed society', which is rarely practised in other societies and trusts in India.

The established practice and structure of this society is that faculty who had committed themselves for twenty or more years as 'Life Members' are on the board of the Trust and Governing bodies. The quality of faculty and students remained exceptional since the pre-independence era, when higher education was limited in access and teaching was a noble profession taken up by only those with scholarship and academic interests. The legacy of life membership continues but is vulnerable to covert and overt disruptions in the recent past.

After the 1970s, things started changing due to the growing dependence of higher education entirely on the state government to get grants for sustenance. Also, the teaching profession became another job with security rather than a vocation or passion. The main purpose of many a schools and colleges has been to prepare students for board or university examinations. Merit is rated in terms of marks and percentages. Passing percentages and college results are the criteria to measure the quality of college education. The academic and intellectual competence of faculty is limited to acquiring a Ph.D. degree, which is mandatory for promotion as per university rules and relevant for careers in teaching.

A more significant transformation in the case of the above institution is the change in composition and influence of governing boards that make policy and operational decisions. From the initiation of Life Members who were faculty of colleges managed by the Society had control over decision-making, and those elected non-faculty members were mainly in the role of advisors and trustees. Slowly, elected members of the Society have taken over the control in terms of financial management and the collection of donations for admission from management quota, the recruitment of faculty, and administrative staff. Now, schools and colleges have principals monitored by board members who have no direct experience or involvement in academic processes of teaching, learning and research. They are mostly practising professionals in finance and engineering, builders or entrepreneurs. More worrisome fact is that important decisions that determine the values and behavioural norms of campus climate are now taken on a political, ideological basis rather than for academic reasons. The dominance of the right-wing ideology on educational campuses in Pune, post-emergency of 1975, is significant. Selection criteria for faculty and lower-level staff jobs are biased towards those from a specific ideological grooming and affiliation. When political leaders are invited to address the students, which is relatively common, college campuses witness students' protests from time to time, which are to be controlled by police interventions, as the task is often beyond the control of college administrators.

It would be appropriate to describe and evaluate, one of the incidents of students' protest and the subsequent chaos on the college campus in this highly reputed college in Pune. The narration is mainly based on a press release written by a senior journalist and former editor of Times of India, *Dilip Padgaonkar*, an alumnus of the said college. He had written a piece in the Times of India rather passionately about his Alma mater, and two of the excerpts are given below to highlight the decline in institutional climate and culture. The article is titled '*A Taste of Ash*' (*TOI, 2016*) and reflects the sadness and loss felt by a past student of this prestigious college.

> *"Conservatives and reformers have locked horns since college was established in 1885 in Pune...; the difference between what happened then and what has been happening of late is this ... in the past the rivals were thinkers and exchanged ideas and not blows. The incident (of the present) speaks not only about poor administrative qualities but, more distressingly, it is the college Principal's supine acceptance of the dictate of those who call the shots in the governance of the college.*
>
> *"Several members of various governing bodies of the Society which effectively run the college are said to belong to or close to Sangh Parivar. The Principal can ill afford to rub them in the wrong way, especially after the change in power at the center and in Maharashtra... Until my time, the college principals, each one a scholar of repute, refused to trim the sails to the prevailing wind. Those who succeeded them possessed*

the spine of an eel... I weep for my Alma mater that was a font of liberal thought."

The alumnus of a century-old college remarks and comments on the difference between ideological battles fought with means of ideas and thoughts in the past rather than with blows and physical violence now, now, highlights the prevalent the prevalent institutional climate on the campus. Moreover, in the name of ideology, a power-seeking game is played on educational campuses that have damaged the academic authority of the principal and faculty. It points to the decline of the integrity of the teaching profession and those responsible for protecting the autonomy of education institutions in contemporary India. The case is a reflection of institutional entropy caused by drifting away from the purpose and mission of the institution known for excellence and liberal values in higher education in the past. Also, it is a sad comment on the political ideological invasion on educational campuses covertly and overtly, and many such cases occurred in other universities and colleges campuses at pan-India since 2016.

Paradoxically, the college mentioned in the case is the most preferred for higher education and the cut-off of admission remains at the top in the city. *NAAC* accreditation to the college is above A, and recently affiliated colleges and this Society are granted autonomous university status by the Ministry of Education (MoE). The decline of institutional values and governance has not affected the rush for admissions in institutions, but invisible damage has already been done in terms of low morale of faculty and deteriorating quality of academic processes. Institutional entropy or decay is gradual and not directly visible unless one goes deeper into the organisational diagnosis based on primary data of internal and external stakeholders.

The case may appear as an astute and poignant anti-climax to the discussion on the *IB* process at the end of this essay wherein the conventional parameters of *IB* are standing on its head. Concepts of institutional autonomy, governance and quality are concepts that not only need urgent attention in the contemporary context but also require a critical reflection based on the individual and collective experiences of students, faculty, educationists, and institutional builders. The *IB* process needs experience-based reflective learning at the level of individuals and collectivity as well.

It is important to note that the reputation and the present context of the political and ideological patronage to the college may help hide the reality of entropy in institutional processes, as in the above case. However, it raises a deeper question: 'What makes an educational institution different from other work organisations?' It highlights the unique mandate of educational institutions to resist the corrupting impact on the primary purpose of higher education. Ironically, slogans of nation-building and patriotism are invoked to cover up the entropic state of the systems and to maintain the power equations of vested interests. The challenges in *IB* have taken a critical shift in the recent past due to the intervention of the state in *HEIs* on ideological grounds. In this context, the theory and practice of *IB* in India need an urgent attention so that universities and colleges would renew and build robust systems, processes, values to achieve the primary goal, mission and institutional autonomy of higher education.

REFERENCES

1. Agarwal, P. (2009). *Indian Higher Education: Envisioning the future.* Sage India.
2. Datar, S., Garvin, D.A., & Cullen, P.G. (2010). *Rethinking MBA: Business Education at Crossroads.* Harvard Business Press.
3. Dymoke, S., & Harrison, J. (Eds.). (2009). *Reflective Teaching and Learning.* Sage.
4. Esman, M., & Uphoff, N. (1974). *Local Organisations for Rural Development: Analysis of Asian Experience.* Springfield: NTIS.
5. *Economic Times* (16 January 2019), The Times Higher Education World University Rankings.
6. Banerjee, Sushant, IMDR (2003), Proceedings of the Second Pulin Garg Memorial Symposium on 'Institutional Building'.
7. Padaki, V., et al. (1984). *The Challenges in Indian Textiles.* Ahmedabad: AITIRA.
8. Pareek, U. (1981). *Beyond Management.* Oxford & IBH.
9. Padgaonkar, D. (2016, April 2). *A Taste of Ash.* Times of India.
10. Vaz, M., & Padaki, V. (2003). *Institutional Development in Social Intervention.* Sage.
11. Vikapa, IIM-A, *Journal,* (vol.39, 2014), *Responding to industry needs: Reorienting management*

ESSAY TWO

TECHNICAL-ECONOMIC PERSPECTIVE OF HIGHER EDUCATION: A CRITIQUE

This essay discusses key concepts utilising a techno-economic perspective (TEP) that has impacted the discourse on higher education in recent times. The Techno-Economic perspective, which is used in the production process of manufacturing companies, is applied to the domain of educational processes. It deploys the logic of technical rationality (TR) with an emphasis on the efficiency of input-process-output and economic returns on investment in evaluating higher education systems.

Some of the key concepts and terms discussed in this essay are human capital, input-process-output of production process, private and public goods, experienced goods, return on investment, market of higher education, quality parameters, performance indicators, evaluation of faculty and institutional performance, and accountability.

The essay critiques and questions the use of *TR* method of analysis and furnishes instances to enumerate that processes of teaching-learning-researching and improving the quality of *HEIs* need an organic and humanist perspective. Since *TEP* is primarily driven by the logic of technical rationality, the essay first explains the logic of *TR* and its impact on policies, management systems and values of *HEIs*. The key concepts used in applying *TR* in education are explained with examples to critique the assumptions of the *TEP*. *TR* is a type of analytical reasoning, while *TEP* is a view that focuses on technical and economic dimensions of productive functions.

The essay is primarily premised upon the analysis of *Prof Saumen Chattopadhyay* in his book on *Education and Economics (2012)*, which focuses on the key elements in producing goods in factories for the free market economy. These elements directly affect the contemporary discourse and debates on issues of quality and academic performance in higher education. A closer look at these concepts is essential to appreciate the main argument of the essay that higher education and industry are two different domains of human activity: a) production and dissemination of knowledge to students and b) manufacturing/providing goods and giving services to customers. Therefore, it is vital to recognise the distinguishing features so that the autonomy and essence of the two domains are not violated by mixing two distinct metaphors: mechanistic and organismic. In other words, combining the mechanical metaphor of industry and the organic metaphor of education would be unfair and harmful to the theory and practice of teaching, learning, research and management processes of institution building *(IB)*.

In the backdrop of classical economic theory, the production functions in a factory are analysed and explained with the help of concepts like efficiency, productivity, costs, and revenue. However, their straightforward application in the educational domain is not possible because each function has an objective, and it operates in a specific context or the domain it belongs to. For example, educational institutions like the universities in India do not have a profit-maximisation objective or function as is the case with business organisations. Also, the teaching-learning activity or delivery of educational services constitutes processes that are different from those in a factory system. Historically, *HEIs* are not considered as service providers, and students are not expected to behave as passive consumers of that service. *HEIs* are created as spaces where the development of the untapped potential of students is emphasised. The faculty and students play an active role as co-producers in imparting and generating knowledge and skills in classroom learning, research and co-curricular activities.

In the contemporary context, it is paradoxical to find that the core features of higher education, as articulated in the 'humanistic-developmental' perspective of *Amartya Sen*, *Rabindranath Tagore* and other intellectuals (Essay Nine on Human Development: Humanistic Perspective), are better understood when analytical concepts and tools of technical rationality are applied in the domain of higher education. One can appreciate the distinguishing features of two distinct domains, education and industry, when juxtaposed to underline the contrast sharply.

The commonly utilised concept to enumerate the process of a technical system is 'input-process-output', which explains the production process used in a factory system. However, when it is applied to understand concepts like 'learning outcomes' and 'value addition' in higher education, it reveals the fundamental difference in the assumptions of two perspectives: The Mechanical systems perspective and the

Humanistic developmental perspective. This happens because it is a comparison between the two separate domains, which can be identified as distinct metaphors to describe designs of organisations: Machine metaphor and Organismic metaphor. It is necessary to highlight the differences between the two to avoid mixing them, which is often evident in contemporary thinking on higher education. Modern thought on higher education innocuously mixes the two metaphors overtly or covertly due to ignorance of the different premises and values that govern them. The essay questions the common misconceptions that have led to serious problems in policy-making and *IB*.

To better comprehend this problem, let us extend the logic of 'efficiency' used in *TR* in the Machine metaphor to the so-called 'inputs' used in the Organismic metaphor of the education system. The main inputs of the higher education system are faculty, students and other knowledge resources. In the language of conventional economics, they constitute 'human capital', which is distinct from physical capital, such as land, machinery, money and hard assets. Unlike physical assets, human capital does not depreciate. On the contrary, it can be developed further and can even appreciate in terms of human abilities, adding to a higher order of motives, needs, desires and other capabilities of individuals.

In a manner, human capital (*HC*) is deftly encased or embodied in an educated person through knowledge, capabilities and skills. Therefore, it remains active and appreciates as long as the person engages herself in continuous learning. In fact, with lifelong learning, human capital appreciates its value in terms of wisdom and judgement over time and with subsequent accumulation of more experience and reflections added to knowledge acquired in formal education.

In other words, the educational investment of an individual adds value to her *HC*, more so when the person is provided learning resources like books, journals, computers, and study groups. However, as a student, she needs to spend adequate time and give attention to her studies to develop her capabilities. This kind of involvement of students in the learning process is implied or assumed in the concept of *HC*, which is an essential input in personal and professional growth. Thus, individual investment in terms of 'time and personal attention' during the process of education by a student adds value to her *HC* in the process of education. Hence, one cannot deny that *HC*, as an input in educational processes, contributes to enhancing the productive ability of a person. However, it must be recognised that the most important and distinguishing feature of the 'conversion process' in education is that both the input and output of *HC* in education are the same: the student. This is not so in the case of input and output of a production/conversion process of a factory. The inputs of raw materials and labour are transformed into a product in a manufacturing company. In the education system, *HC* or student is both an input and output. In this sense, an educated student with capabilities rather than her degree certificate is an output of the education process. Learning in education is a 'process' rather than a 'product' to be consumed. It operates as a verb or action, not a noun or object!

For instance, in the service industry, such as hospitality, the output of service is a satisfied customer but the person who provides the service (input) may be stressed while delivering the service. (*Bolton S.C.*, 2005). In an educational institution, the student is an input and also a product or outcome of her engagement with the learning process. More importantly, in the process of learning in education, the faculty and students are co-producers; together, they develop capabilities by engaging in learning simultaneously.

In the contemporary discourse of higher education, which is influenced by *TEP*, education is seen as a quasi-market rather than a production process. Hence, in the 'market' of education, the 'value' of a person, as a part of *HC*, is ultimately measured not only in terms of her contribution to the output of the production process in the form of her capabilities but also on its market-determined, monetised value, such as the salary she receives after education.

This kind of obvious market orientation of higher education would inevitably take us back to examining the logic of *TR* about how we have defined *HC* as an input and output in the educational process. In other words, the question is, 'How do we define and measure the input value of a student? Can it be, or should it be standardised? The answer is that when the education process is significantly determined by personal involvement and engagement of input, that is, the student, who is also an integral part of that output, it is not possible to get a standardised output like factory goods. Each student is unique and deserves to be treated as such.

Therefore, a student is neither an input nor a product of the education process because she is an active participant who determines what personal resources and attention she would bring to the process. Therefore, the value of both input and output can be monetised only superficially, as in the case of fees paid and the first salary received on the job after education, which is considered a 'return on investment', similar to a return on investment or *ROI* in business parlance. In a way, it is a trivialisation of the learning and development process of higher education due to the quasi-market treatment of the education process to achieve better efficiency through the *TR* perspective. As pointed out by *Herbert Marcuse,* a reputed German-American thinker and philosopher, the logic of *TR* is, in real terms, an irrational view based on false or pseudo-consciousness. It emphasises the manifest or overt features of reality by ignoring the latent or covert reality. Human learning and development are both overt and covert processes. This is more so in the case that involve *IB* processes.

Although the contribution of higher education to economic growth at the macro or national level is well recognised, the intrinsic value of education in terms of finer aspects and values of human life, such as human dignity, ability to make choices, and sense of freedom, are equally important. They are described by liberal humanist thinkers like *Dr A. Sen, J.H. Newman,* and *Rabindranath Tagore*. These finer aspects are also the outcomes of higher-order learning, and they are as important as a person's capacity to earn a decent living through employment.

Another distinguishing feature of higher education processes is the inability (though it is not to be considered a weakness, but only as one of its features) to specify its value-added function in quantitative or so-called objective terms of measurement. One cannot directly measure values and behaviours like dignity, choice-making, freedom, concern for others, and search for truth in numbers, but one can recognise them only as experiential data. These behaviours and values can be identified through field surveys only in terms of perceptions or opinions.

The challenge of measurement occurs because, unlike business, education institutions do not hold an objective function like profit-making to measure their performance. Traditionally, education is not considered a commercial or business enterprise for profit in India. However, it is possible to accumulate surplus revenue so that it can be used to acquire more learning facilities. However, generating a surplus as profit is not expected to be a mission of an educational institution. in fact, the surplus revenue is expected to be invested further in developmental tasks to achieve its institutional mission. The more pertinent questions are about the meaning of institutional performance in education, who benefits from it and how.

Ironically, educational institutions can contribute astutely to their mission or primary task of 'generating and disseminating knowledge and wisdom' only when they hold reserve funds accumulated as surplus in the past. However, in many *HEIs*, particularly colleges and universities that are privately managed, the accumulated surplus is often used for investment in real estate or stocks rather than for investing in and upgrading learning resources like libraries, laboratories and institutional development. On the other hand, government-aided *HEIs* suffer from a lack of resources and funding due to a significant reduction of grants in line with the neoliberal perspective and policy of withdrawal of the state from its responsibility to fund higher education. Higher education in India is now considered as part of private goods for personal use rather than public goods meant for social benefit.

However, the diversion of funds to non-academic goals in privately managed institutions occurs primarily because almost all education institutions, public and private, have come under the influence and pressure of neoliberal policies of the state that regulates *HEIs*. They are directly exposed to and compelled by the quasi-market dynamics of generating revenues to recover costs. Thus, they are forced to spend funds on promotional activities to attract potential students and help institutions survive and grow. Therefore, this competition driven higher education market leads to institutional practices that dilute its focus on primary educational task and mission. Unfortunately, self-generated resources from fees and donations are spent on promoting institutional brands and advertisements to attract students in the emerging, competitive education market.

On the other side, state-funded universities and 35,000 affiliated colleges face market competition from private universities in cities and towns while grappling with diminishing government grants for higher education. Therefore, cost-cutting measures like not filling up faculty and staff positions or temporary recruitment of low-paid faculty staff on a contract basis are the short-term measures taken to maintain efficacy. There is an absence of a long-term state policy on funding higher education. The *NEP 2020* is also conspicuously silent on the issue of funding. The message is certainly in favour of the privatisation of higher education. It fits well within the conceptual framework of *TEP* and neoliberal premises.

This predicament of universities and colleges in India is an outcome of the *TR* perspective and focus on technical efficiency, which is assumed but not articulated openly in the education policy decisions of the MoE. It aims at efficient use of state resources in terms of input-output equations and thus influences investment decisions on higher education at macro and institutional levels. The question is whether the logic of technical efficiency helps to achieve the larger purpose of higher education, which needs closer examination. More importantly, the question is, 'What are the consequences of low-quality education of resource-starved institutions on the development of human capital at the national level, specifically in the case of young minds, society and nation?' Neither the logic of technical rationality prompting efficiency nor the education policy of the state have adequate answers to these questions.

The promotion of the neoliberal perspective to support privatisation and use state regulation to achieve it appears to be more for ideological rather than for economic reasons in the context of higher education in India. The same trend is evident at a global level as well. Then, the questions arise: 'Who is at the receiving end of poorly managed higher education in public institutions, and what is the social cost of expensive private universities? Needless to say, the students, parents and society at large would have to pay the price for it.

In summation of the above discussion and deliberation, we can safely contend that that the problems and contradictions that arise from the application of *TR* of factory system to educational processes, are, evident from the mixing and merging of metaphors wherein one-directional, linear process of input, process and output of a mechanical system, (I-P-O) is grafted on an essentially organic process of learning and development in education. One can separate the 'input' material in a factory from the 'output' of the finished product since the features of input-output are visible and distinguishable. However, in the domain of education, the output of the educational process is the student, who is its input as well. Therefore, an exact or arithmetic valuation of output in the domain of education is problematic for three reasons mentioned below:

1. Depending on the efforts and involvement of the student in the learning process, the output of the learning process varies.
2. Students' output is measured in terms of grades or marks, and for professional courses, it is placements in the job market. Standardising the grade/ marks output across colleges or universities is difficult.
3. Valuation in the job market in terms of pay packages does not refer to quality of work done in educational institutions. The brand and reputation of an institution impact the selection for students' placements in the employment market. Also, campus placements do not directly signify student quality as they are also influenced by the availability of jobs in the employment market, which is determined by time and place.

Other issues related to the measurement of faculty and institutional performance in the context of the *TE* perspective are discussed below.

The logic and rationale of 'Return on Investment' *(ROI)* in education and the measurement of academic performance in *HEIs* are governed by some common assumptions which are given below:

1. *TR* evaluates the viability of a production system in terms of feasibility and efficient use of resources and is measured primarily on economic criteria such as the *ROI*. This emphasis on output measurement creates a need to design various methods to track and evaluate the efficiency and productivity of education conceptualised as a production function. One of the methods is the performance evaluation of faculty and institutions.
2. Academic Performance Indicators *(API)* used by regulatory institutions like *UGC* and *AICTE* for faculty and Institutional Accreditation conducted by regulators of *MoE* are two methods developed to measure the efficiency and productivity of faculty and institutions. A careful examination of these methods would reveal a mismatch of *TR* in the educational context.

The unintended consequences of this objective and data-based methods to assess the performance of faculty and institutions need careful consideration.

3. In the case of institutional performance, the output is identified in terms of grades or placement, which is the *ROI* for the individual students. However, grades and *ROI* for students do not provide any means for the institution, faculty and the government to recover the costs of education directly. It is the *ROI* for the students and not for the institution, even though it is used as a brand-building and a promotional tool by the latter. This needs to be compared with the case of factory products that can be priced higher in the market based on input costs and output benefits. The *ROI* benefits the student after education with better earnings on the job but does not benefit or offer more income to the faculty and more surplus to the colleges to which the student belongs. The irony can only be explained by two types of goods, 'public goods' and 'private goods', which are concepts used in discourse on the economics of education.

Higher Education in India: Is it a Part of Private or Public Goods?

It needs to be understood that higher education is not merely a part of private or individual goods, but, also of public or collective goods because it benefits society at large and has a long-term societal impact. Therefore, the issue of its funding by the government is pertinent. The Human capital (*HC*) theory is an essential part of the conceptualisation of *TR* used in the context of the neoliberal economic perspective. It tends to consider 'manpower' only as a resource and education as an area of private goods. Hence, the benefits of higher education are primarily for the individual because it is an *ROI* of a student or his/her family for investing in higher education. Such a concept of *HC* used in neoliberal economics promotes a view that higher education is for the benefit of individuals rather than a part of commonly shared goods with society. The perspective on *HC* fits well with the ideology of neoliberalism in terms of its overemphasis on individual benefits and less concern for social equity. It helps us to analyse and comprehend better the opposition of the upper castes to the reservation policy of the state for admissions and employment.

An artificial artifice of the separation of individual benefit from societal benefit is the root cause of the above problems that emerge from applying *TEP* backed by neoliberal economic policies. Consequently, in policy decisions to expand the higher education market, the state assigns a larger role to private educational institutions and reduces the role of public universities at the macro level planning through reduced funding. In this way, directly and indirectly, the control of the state, both at central and federal levels, over the education market increases to promote private universities at the cost of public/state universities. This is a serious obstacle in building and strengthening educational institutions in India, particularly state-funded universities and affiliated colleges, which show signs of sub-optimisation or deprivation of resources in the higher education system.

The logic of Technical Rationality (*TR)* in the measurement of faculty performance using Academic Performance Indicators (*API*) and National Institutional Ranking Framework (*NRIF*) have unintended consequences for *IB,* are discussed below.

In measuring the academic performance using *API* for faculty and institutional performance for accreditation by *UGC* and *NAAC,* the evaluation of students' output is considered in terms of cognitive and problem-solving capacity. It is captured through Learning Outcomes *(LO),* where it is technically possible to measure *LO*. However, the allocated grades to students may not reflect learning performance accurately. Also, the assessment may not be rigorous and transparent in a market-driven higher education system where institutions compete for space to survive and grow in terms of course enrolment. As an instance, in allocating internal marks in schools and colleges in India, a tendency to be liberal in rating is widespread. As a result, a school or college faculty benefits from institutional rating, which helps their brand rating in the higher education market.

Research Output of Faculty and its Evaluation: Defining and Measuring the Performance of Faculty and Institutions

One of the aims of higher education is to contribute to knowledge generation, which is achieved by faculty engagement with two closely related academic activities: teaching-learning and research. In professional education, providing consulting services to industry clients or conducting field or action research is also expected of faculty since it enriches their teaching and research competence.

There are a few issues in the evaluation of research output as well. When the quality of research output is equated with the number of papers produced by a faculty in a university system, the output may not correctly refer to value addition or spread of knowledge. It is a documented fact that the gap between the spread of scientific and applied knowledge through university education and its conversion into innovative products and processes in industry takes not less than twenty years (*Forbes N., 2019*). It implies that the major role of undergraduate colleges and universities in India remains to disseminate knowledge of various disciplines at undergraduate and postgraduate levels so that its recipients, the students, can work on advanced research later in central research institutions, universities or industries.

The prevalent method of measuring and calibrating the academic performance of faculty and institutions has been such that individual-institutional performance on various parameters is finally 'aggregated'. It neglects the contextual factors responsible for performance in education institutions. As an instance, differences in performance among institutions arise not from people themselves but from 'sub-system' factors such as resources of library, laboratory, industry-academia collaboration, academic climate in peer groups, quality of students, information technological support, physical-geographical location of institutions, and stable employment provided to faculty. In other words, these factors are controlled by the promoters, board members and the state or central government; they are not under the control of faculty, staff or even institutions. The focus on measuring individual and institutional performance in isolation from other related subsystems also discourages teamwork and the development of group norms to improve the quality of performance. Not surprisingly, the Quality Management guru *Edward Deeming* (1986) was a strong opponent of measuring and rewarding individual performance and believed in total systems improvement for better quality.

Some of the practical difficulties related to doing research in the university system need consideration here. The quality of academic research output in universities suffers from less allocation of funds by the state and an over-emphasis on classroom teaching-learning. It results in a neglect of research or consultancy in institutions that offer professional courses. It would limit serious academic pursuits of institutions in the long run, which is apparent from low research activity in state universities and affiliated professional course institutes. On the other hand, prioritising research publication and consulting in the context of a less number of full-time faculty impacts the classroom learning output of students as faculty engagement is reduced on the campus. Balancing the two, research-consultancy and teaching-learning, is a matter of institutional culture, and it depends on the academic mission and financial strength of each institution.

Appointing the designate faculty on a contract basis as a cost-saving method in private and public institutions of higher education is another offshoot of *TR's* focus on the efficient use of resources. However, it impacts teacher-student interactions as less time is given by faculty for interactions with students outside the classroom since they are not available on campus for the purpose. Moreover, counselling time is not counted in the workload of faculty in the *UGC* norms.

Synthesis: The analysis of the impact of applying the input-output framework of *TR* to educational processes exposes many loopholes due to the fundamental difference in the domains of factory systems and educational processes. It shows that a clear and precise demarcation of input-processes-output and in teaching-learning-research of educational processes is an unrealistic and misplaced idea because its assumptions are borrowed from a linear production system of a factory. It is applied to a more complex and interrelated organic process of teaching, learning, researching, and consulting in *HEIs*. Moreover, limitations and adverse effects of measuring the individual performance of faculty and institution in isolation from its contextual factors of material resources, academic climate and culture, staff, location, mission and other macro systems of the institution make the performance management exercise ineffective in improving the academic performance of individual faculty and institutions.

Accountability for Academic and Institutional Performance

Performance measurement criteria *(API)* also aim to identify and squarely ensure accountability of individual faculty. Also the institutional ranking (*NIRF)* is designed to promote internal competition among institutions for improvement in the quality of higher education and ranking in the higher education market. The aim of the performance measurement of faculty is to establish a system of accountability, which is a desirable objective, considering the historical legacy of dependence on the government-funded public university system since independence. It is observed that academics in post-independence India saw the university system as another space for stable jobs with limited responsibility rather than as an opportunity for academic pursuits and excellence through teaching, research and scholarship in a subject or discipline.

However, it is necessary to note that specification of accountability should not be confused with and limited to the principle of accounting and audit function of regulators. Accountability is not an accounting of data since the outcome of the education system is not like a product or goods manufactured in a factory. It is intrinsically connected with human intentionality, care and values. Intrinsic accountability is an integral part of professional values, which are expected to be nurtured by collective norms as is evident in IITs, IIMs, IIS and some of the reputed universities. Faculty is expected to be an important stakeholder in institutional and academic performance.

Emergence of Higher Education Market in the 1990s and Need for Regulation of Academic Practices

It is pertinent to note how regulatory organs of the *NAAC, NAB,* and *NIRF* regulate faculty behaviours and institutional performance to achieve efficiency and productivity. The *API* is a set of criteria used to evaluate faculty performance in teaching and research. It is designed to encourage productivity in terms of the number of papers written and teaching hours in an academic year. However, a careful examination of its impact reveals that it impacts the quality of education negatively and induces malpractices in institutions where academic traditions of excellence and governance are not strong enough to control it internally.

For example, in API, quantification of performance is based on the number of hours put in i) teaching-learning, ii) assessment, and iii) activities for professional development and extension activities engaged by faculty. When the input-to-output ratio is calculated in terms of the number of hours put into these activities, the 'qualitative aspects' of work, such as depth of teaching and learning and learning outcomes for students, are not considered.

It also influences faculty behaviours, as, they tend to conduct teaching as a mechanical ritual to be finished in the assigned hours that the administration stipulates as workload, particularly in public Universities. Unlike the production function in a factory system, the nature of academic work varies according to localised factors, such as the faculty strength of a department, the nature of subjects taught, the level of difficulty in courses and the geographical location of a university. For instance, quantifying research activity in terms of journal articles and projects ignores the basic difference between pure and social sciences regarding theoretical/ empirical orientations. Since faculty has no role in the formulation of performance parameters to determine its relevance to the local context or mission of the institution, they tend to focus on the acquisition of points to improve ratings that determine the promotional benefits. The real issue is the impact of centralised decision-making on academic processes in a top-down bureaucratic structure, where those expected to implement the system, that is, the faculty, are not involved in critical academic matters that concern their work. It leads to an absence of internal commitment to the primary task of teaching-learning-researching.

Higher Education Market and Institutional Ranking

At the national keel, the ranking of *HEIs* is a policy meant to promote competition and improve the quality of education. It fits well with the assumption of neoliberal and *TR* perspectives that competition in the market of higher education would improve quality and efficiency. This assumption invites a review of its impact on the ground reality in the Indian context.

The ranking of *HEIs* is meant to indicate and reflect the relative performance of institutions. The *API* make faculty individually accountable for their work, and a system of audit is designed to help the monitoring and control by regulatory bodies of*MoE*. The system is designed to deter the faculty from taking advantage of loopholes in the system and, at the same time, presupposes dishonest practices in academics. Joint research is discouraged as the first author gets 70 per cent of the total score, which may negatively impact collaboration in team research. The purpose of research, which is to create new knowledge and expand the frontiers of thinking through interdisciplinary research, is ignored. API system is not designed to build trust in academicians and academic professionalism, which is essential for collaborative interdisciplinary teaching and research, as stated in *NEP 2020.*

Paradox in Measuring Institutional Performance

Akin to the assessment and monitoring of faculty performance, the output of the overall educational process of an institution is evaluated at the national level by *NAAC*, with a system of grades based on criteria such as i) the quality of teaching and research, ii) curriculum flexibility, iii) institutional values, and iv) leadership.

Treating the above qualitative criterion as rating points and then adding them up ignores and hides an important synergetic development of institutional processes. The principle of 'living systems' informs that its components show an organic and not a mechanical synergy; thus, any change in one part of a sub-system impacts the properties of a combination of other parts of the total system. For example, the combination of oxygen and hydrogen results in water, though the properties of each substance are different. Organic systems resemble chemical synergy rather than an arithmetic summation of parts. In short, a more integrated system of evaluation of institutions is needed to serve the purpose of assessment of institutions. More importantly, the assessment methods should hold the potential for guidance on improving and strengthening academic and institutional processes, which is the core of *IB*. In short, the mechanical assessment model needs to be replaced by an 'integrated model' and a developmental perspective for assessment of institutions.

Purpose and Process of Performance Review

Therefore, it is pertinent to suggest and add that that quantitative methods used for evaluating qualitative processes of teaching-learning and research need to be replaced with qualitative methods of behavioural observations, group interviews, self and peer review to arrive at ratings for a Performance Management System *(PMS)*. The main issue is defining the meaning of 'performance' in the context of higher education. Pertinent questions that need to be addressed for improving the process of performance review are: i) Is academic performance of faculty an addition and delivery of output? ii) Is it also for improving the group processes and developing behavioural norms? iii) And importantly, is *PMS* primarily meant for controlling or for improving academic performance and faculty behaviours?

The engagement with these issues indicate that such a task of creating relevant parameters for identifying performance cannot be accomplished by a bureaucratic system where experts and consultants from the apex bodies like *NAAC* or *NBS* visit the campus for a couple of days and evaluate institutional performance by marking ticks in the rating scale boxes. A genuine and participative internal system of quality assurance and review process is necessary in higher education. Above all, it requires clarity on the meaning of performance in the context of the specific mission of the institution. An inflexible, standardised system of institutional performance evaluation needs a radical change in approach and methodology. The fact is that the outcome of the top ten to fifteen institutions selected by the national ranking system has almost remained unchanged for the last five to ten years. It only shows that institutions with better resources provided by the central government and backed by past reputation could do better in the ranking system, while hundreds of other institutions would never be able to upgrade their standards because there is no long-term plan and perspective for their upgrading. This is an example of the rigid, hierarchical, status-oriented, even though merit-based, institutional ranking system in India. The *SPAB* model of institutional levels mentioned in Essay Five on Understanding Behavioural Processes in *HEIs* indicates that performance assessment systems have the potential to influence downwards the processes, attitudes and behaviours of institutional collectivity.

Defining Education as an 'experienced good and service'

At this stage of discussion, it is essential to revisit and reiterate the definition and main features of higher education as an open and living system in order to conceptualise a better evaluation model of the performance of *HEIs*. As mentioned earlier, the products of a factory can be checked on objective quality parameters because their input and output features and characteristics, can be defined precisely concerning the objective function of business, that is, 'to earn profit.' This kind of objective reference point does not exist in the case of education for various valid reasons explained in Essay One. Therefore, there is no single reference point to evaluate both the input and output of education. The valuation of quality of output in higher education would not be in monetary terms, but it can be considered with reference to the 'development of capabilities' of students. Moreover, development is not merely in terms of addition to knowledge and 'doing' or action skills of students but also as an addition to their personal needs, desires, attitudes, and values, which are anchored in the 'being' of learners.

However, a student is neither a customer nor is the faculty a bland supplier. Both indicate unilateral, passive roles as indicated in a production system of a factory where the producer and the consumer have distinct roles. In buyer-seller relations, there is no mutuality and interdependence, as in the case of faculty-student relatedness in the education system. In business, it is a *transactional* relationship; in education, it has a potential for *transformational* relations. It is so because academic learning emerges from an exchange of views, perspectives, dialogue, and debates. Moreover, it is collaborative and involves teamwork. The faculty-student relationship is not one-sided and dependent or a passive relationship but an interactive dynamic relatedness based on human values of trust, mutual respect, care and concern for others.

A suitable example of the above-mentioned point is that of a lady student from Mumbai who got admission at *IIT Guwahati* but dropped out of a *PG* course in social sciences after a yearlong experience on campus. It illustrates the point that higher education belongs to the category of '*experienced goods*' rather than of '*consumer goods*'. The student found the campus climate and attitude of faculty and staff insensitive on gender issues. Even though it was an *IIT*, the teaching-learning was bookish. The course structure was badly implemented by the humanities department. She was depressed because others thought her decision to join another university after a year was an immature thought. However, her parents supported her and helped her do so because the experience of the student was more relevant for the decision than the brand image of the *IIT* degree. The episode highlights that a higher education degree/diploma is not a product or commodity but an experienced good. (*Indian Express, 20/12/2021*)

To consider a student as a customer is relevant only in a narrow sense at the institutional level, that is, of 'having a sense of care and concern for the welfare of students'. However, it has less to do with the academic processes of teaching and learning. The assumption of 'supplier-customer' relations would make the learner dependent and faculty manipulative in the process. Hence, the analogy of production process in a factory and marketing goods for business profit is misplaced in the educational context.

The process of education, at the core, is an '*experienced*' good or service, which can be described and evaluated experientially and not by aggregate rating points of ranking of institutions at the national level or the so-called external/objective performance evaluation. One who has undergone 'experience' on campus can describe it at individual and collective levels. In this context, it is relevant and revealing to compare *APBS* and *NACC* criteria with the *Baldrige* scheme of quality-excellence in education, which is used in American colleges and schools. The latter offers an integrated, overall rating to highlight the point that it is not a scheme of rating but an approach to view, evaluate and improve the performance of an organic, interconnected system.

It is relevant to compare the design *of NAAC* criteria with the *Baldrige* quality parameters used for measuring institutional performance in the American education system. The frameworks of *NAAC* and *Baldrige* represent two approaches to the performance management system, as well as the definition of 'performance' in this context. It would be interesting to compare the two frameworks of *NACC, NAB* in India and Baldrige excellence framework in the USA, in measuring the quality of education in *HEIs*.

Baldrige framework is designed on the following premises. (*Refer to the graphical representation of the framework in Essay Ten on 'Quality of Higher Education'*)

(a) Though the individual components of the quality framework are essential for evaluation, the overall effectiveness of educational institutions and management systems depends on how these components 'relate to one another'.

(b) The framework is conceived as three concentric circles of '*systemic*' perspective; that is, it views organisations as living and social systems which combines technical operations with people processes. It includes institutional quality and excellence, such as a) the innermost circle of core values, b) the outer circle of processes and systems, and c) the circle on the periphery of performance and results.

(c) It recognises the linkages between foundational values and concepts; the intermediate processes and management systems that facilitate achieving results in areas like leadership, governance, workforce, student learning, academic processes, budget, market, and strategy.

(d) However, unlike the Indian framework of *NACC* and *NAB*, it emphasises the critical role of shared values and understanding the core concepts mentioned as values such as Ethics and Transparency; valuing people and societal contribution in delivering values and results. It also mentions core concepts like organisational learning and flexibility, as well as visionary leadership that is strategic and long-term. It also includes 'student-centred excellence', 'management by facts', and 'management for innovation'.

The message and the attendant implications embedded in the design of the *Baldrige* quality framework is that without a foundation of core professional values and beliefs such as accountability and integrity, institutions of education would not be able to move to the next level of management process in areas like leadership, strategic planning, student learning, measurement, analysis and management of workforce and operations. These two levels contribute to results and reach high-quality performance. The framework acknowledges that institutional values and systems govern and contribute to institutional behaviours, which are necessary for managing academic performance.

In contrast, the perspective behind the Indian framework used by *NAAC* and *NAB* regarding the process of measuring the quality of institutions is rather mechanistic and bureaucratic in the sense that it takes the components of quality as independent, isolated entities to be tick-marked and summed up to arrive at the total of marks of the stakeholders and external experts. It uses an arithmetic logic that misses the organic linkages between different functions and ignores the systemic principle that the total of a system could be more or less than the parts due to the systems' ability or inability to integrate parts and functions. The mechanical perspective ignores the possibility of sub-optimisation of some functions wherein some functions get more resources, which is a serious barrier in building robust institutions. It is important to recognise that when it occurs, it is always at the cost of other functions, which are considered less important. Hence, some functions may be rated higher, yet the overall system may be impacted negatively. For example, research and consultancy functions in professional institutes may be rated better. However, its impact on teaching and learning processes may not be good because the faculty may not be available on campus, which would negatively impact students' learning.

For building robust institutions, unless foundational concepts, professional values, and systemic perspective on institutional processes are in place, a unilateral focus on management control through rating and ranking systems would remain an exercise on tick-marked rating sheets and fail to rate the institutional performance authentically. As reported in the media and NDTV Prime Time slot, on the university series, the official rating by *NAAC* and actual institutional reality documented by the reporter found severe discrepancies. For example, an affiliated college in the state of Bihar got an A+ *NAAC* rating, and a video recording by the reporter on the campus showed students complaining about the faculty shortage in subjects, fewer classrooms and laboratory facilities. It raises serious questions about the credibility of the performance evaluation system of *NAA*C and *NAB*. More importantly, it is also an outcome of the absence of governance and institutional leadership of state universities and affiliated colleges.

The above mentioned analysis and debate may also explain why there are fewer institutional takers for accreditation schemes in India because the whole exercise is conceptualised in a mechanistic-bureaucratic mind-set to give credibility and recognition *of HEIs* in the higher education market without offering guidance on how to improve the level of quality and achieve academic performance. More importantly, *NAAC* accreditation provides no guidance or help in improving academic and institutional performance. Even when offered, *HEIs* are not convinced about the proposal that accreditation would ensure better institutional performance and better ranking in the higher education market. It does not recognise the serious efforts needed for *IB* to improve and strengthen academic and institutional processes. Simply put, affiliated colleges in Indian universities remain uneducated on the concepts and processes of *IB* that facilitate quality academic performance. Perhaps, there appears to be a larger issue and attendant theme of an absence of a suitable ecosystem to nurture an academic culture of quality and performance at national level.

However, it needs to be acknowledged that there is a limited relevance of accreditation of a state regulatory body because it assures parents and students of some quality benchmarks; it is a recognition and an assurance of quality standards for the grades assigned by an accredited university or college. However, unlike the production process in a factory, the teaching-learning process is determined by the quality of peers and interactions in the classroom and related institutional factors.

Therefore, it is not surprising and startling to find that almost similar *NAAC* grades are assigned to *Amity* University, a relatively new private university, and *JNU*, an old, internationally-reputed public university. The grades are similar and do not distinguish the climate and values of governance of these two different campuses and how it impacts the development of students. The ratings of institutional features are averaged, and thus, they become meaningless for an accurate understanding of the distinguishing features of two micro institutions with distinct missions, strategies, perspectives and performance.

The Missing Link of 'Institutional Mission' in Performance Evaluation of HEIs

Notably, the ranking and rating systems fail to consider and perhaps completely neglect the "mission" of specific institutions and evaluate the performance without reference to the mission and indirectly downplay the unique, local and distinguishing features of the institutions in terms of the content and process of curriculum, delivery, research, institutional purpose, strategy, culture and values. Non-inclusion of mission helps legitimise the 'one model fits all' policy of *HEIs* in India. The mission reflects the 'identity' of the institution when it is consistently followed. In fact, institutional performance is not evaluated with reference to its mission.

The intent, and approach of the regulators betray the bureaucratic values that do not intend to recognise or appreciate the differences or identity of institutions that add substantive value to the institutional outcomes but are more inclined to standardise the processes and make them similar to factory goods so that efficient production of services is possible. It promotes uniformity in universities that denies them an institutional identity and mind as a living system. It fails to recognise that an institution is made up of a collective conglomerate of people, which is the essence of systemic, humanistic perceptive of institution building and development. This was envisioned by *Rabindranath Tagore* in his concept of the universal principle of a university. He was the first Indian to argue for a humane educational system that was in touch with the environment and aimed at the overall development of the personality. Tagore said, "Our university must not only instruct but live; not only think but produce."

It would not be surprising to find that about 50% of universities and affiliated colleges have not applied for NAAC accreditation in 2019. It does not help them either in improving quality or in getting a direction on how to plan strategically for survival and growth and even to solve their problems of surviving in a competitive market environment. The macro institutional system for regulation also needs review and reflection for double loop learning, which questions and reviews goals to reconsider their relevance and generate better solutions to strengthen universities and colleges in India. The local problems in university systems can be effectively solved only when they are addressed at the national policy level.

Synthesis: Key concepts from the field of Economics and Management are used in this essay to understand the impact of the Technical Rationality perspective on the mainstream thinking of higher education systems in India. However, the mechanistic perspective that considers education a factory system needs to be balanced by adding an organismic or systemic perspective that combines procedures and systems with people, culture, and values, as *HEIs* differ from factory systems. Hence, discourse on the higher education system needs concepts and systems specifically relevant to the education domain. The essay ends with a review of two models of evaluation performance of faculty and institutions to highlight differences in assumptions of the two models. It recommends using a more holistic framework for measuring the performance of academic institutions.

REFERENCES

1. Bolton, Sharon C. (2005). *Emotion Management in the Workplace*. Palgrave Macmillan.
2. Chattopadhyay, S. (2018). Neoliberalism and Freedom: The Emerging Scenario. *The Idea of a University*. Context. Apoorvanand (Ed.)
3. Chattopadhyay, S. (2011). *Education and Economics*. Oxford.
4. Baldrige Excellence Program. (2019). Retrieved from https://www.nist.gov/baldrige
5. *Indian Express*, 20 January 2021, IIT Dropout Series.
6. Tagore, R. (n.d.). *Rabindranath Tagore on Education*. Retrieved from https://www.academia.edu/4659110/
7. Forbes, N. (2019). *Sampada*. MCCIA, Pune.

ESSAY THREE

THE QUASI-MARKET OF HIGHER EDUCATION IN INDIA

This essay presents the context of HEIs in India with reference to the neoliberal economic policy, which has led to complex dynamics of two centres of power: the market and the state. An analysis of the emerging trend in the marketisation of higher education is presented, so that institutions can address the contradictions in the so-called business of education in a quasi-market.

Neoliberal ideology first impacted economic policies in the last decade of the twentieth th century, and consequently, the approach of successive governments towards higher education has changed drastically. Neoliberalism shares some features and assumptions about individual and social behaviours with the earlier school of classical liberalism in economics, such as a) the individual is an economic animal in pursuit of self-interest, b) the institution of market can distribute resources with efficiency, c) market competition can bring both quality and efficiency in the production of goods and services, and d) individual and social interests can coexist in harmony.

However, neoliberalism is different from classical liberalism on one count: in a neoliberal framework, the state is expected to perform a positive and active role in the creation of a market and also in regulating the market indirectly through its regulatory organs. In the sphere of economy, the state protects individual freedom and choice and also allows competition through processes of regulation, auditing and management from a distance. In this way, neoliberalism indirectly, if not overtly, rejects the idea of a welfare state.

It is important to note that, from a neoliberal perspective, higher education focusing on new knowledge generation and research in sciences and technology is considered an important instrument of the national economy (National Education

Policy-2020). Therefore, it is logical that the role of the state in higher education is considered crucial by the policymakers for the growth and development of the national economy. As a consequence, the state is actively interested in creating and supporting a higher education market through competition among public and private players. Moreover, the state also monitors institutional performance through its regulatory bodies and central and state ministries.

In the last three decades, it has been observed in the Indian context that the state has allowed entry for private universities and colleges, and the number would soon surpass government-aided universities. The Ministry of Education (MoE) controls institutional activities through regulators like *UGC, AICTE, IMC* and similar bodies. More importantly, the role of the state has changed from funding and expanding public universities to creating a market that actively encourages investment, expansion and sustenance of public and, more importantly, private institutions of higher education. Hence, the access to higher education is substantially increased. However, the entry of foreign universities in India is restricted in order to maintain a level playing field, and perhaps reputed universities abroad are also not very keen to come to India for various reasons, including the quality of higher education in India.

At the global level, the neoliberal approach has pervaded higher education in many European countries and is most prominent in the USA. It would be worthwhile to examine the impact of this policy based on the critical dimensions of access, quality and equity in higher education so that one can draw relevant conclusions about *IB* processes in higher education in India.

Access: The enrolment in HEIs has increased dramatically in the first two decades of the 21st century. However, over 70% of enrolment is in 345 self-funded private universities. The government of India spends slightly more than one per cent of its GDP on higher education. A large part of government expenditure is spent on operating expenditure at central and state universities, and a significant chunk, about 50 %, is taken by elite institutions like *IITs and IIMs.*

Steps have been taken to hold public institutions accountable for managing their operating expenditure independently without government support. Reputed colleges are given autonomous status, though they remain affiliated with state-owned universities, which gives them legitimacy in the education market. Importantly, they are free to decide the fee structure to adjust to rising costs and survive without government grants. This is a clear sign of the withdrawal of the state from the responsibility to consider education as a public good and its role to support it financially. This is the primary difference between the ideas of a welfare state of the past and the neoliberal approach towards higher education.

There are around 1,000 Universities in India, of which 345 are private Universities. Infrastructure facilities are somewhat uneven in 395 universities located in rural areas (*Maharashtra Times, 19 August, 2021*). There are 35,000 affiliated colleges of state universities under the *UGC*, 2,000 management institutes and 5,000 engineering colleges under *AICTE*. However, the gross enrolment ratio is only 19.4%, which means that 80% of the young population in India in the age group of 18 to 23 years does not have access to higher education.

Quality: Regulatory bodies like *UGC, AICTE, Medical Council of India*, and centres of excellence like *IIT*, *IIM*, *NID*, and *ISI* have been created to improve the quality and regulation of higher education. For a growing, innovation-led, knowledge-based economy, investment in research is important, but research in Indian universities and affiliated colleges is limited.

The immediate impact of the neoliberal approach of recent governments, post the year 2000, is reflected in the market dynamics and management of higher education. Some of the features and consequences of the higher education market at the macro level and on the management practices of *HEIs* at the micro level are explained below:

1. Students and parents are considered consumers, and educational institutions are considered providers of educational goods or services in the market.
2. The higher education market in India has remained hierarchical, ranging from a few elite IIT and IIM-like institutions of repute and some central universities that offer professional courses, to hundreds of public and private universities with affiliated colleges that offer conventional courses in Science, Commerce and liberal Arts.
3. The product of the higher education market is not homogeneous and differs widely in terms of access, equity and quality.
4. Consumer students in the higher education market are not well informed. Since education is an 'experience good' and not a consumption good, the students would know the actual quality of the product only when they take admission and have a first-hand experience of teaching-learning on campus. However, it is too late to correct it and to change the decision later.
5. As a consumer, a student is free to choose the provider, that is, the institution of her choice. However, seats in the elite or reputed institutions are very much limited compared to the population of aspiring students. The recent inorganic growth in the number of *IITs and IIMs* has impacted their quality negatively because the quality of institutions depends on

processes and the evolution of institution building, and they cannot be built or managed by government orders overnight. The central theme of this book elaborates on the process of building robust academic climate and culture in *HEIs* in other essays.

6. Freedom to choose educational products or courses from private universities depends mainly on the financial and other resources that the students/parents possess. This unequal spread of purchasing power in India has triggered a climate of social inequity, which can potentially build social and political tensions in developing countries like India. A demand for a share in reservation seats in *HEIs* by other communities indicates this trend. Failure to get admissions to professional courses in medical and engineering colleges to students of lower economic class and who study in regional state board schools is a serious challenge in the higher education system in India. It has in recent years, caused tragic suicides of young students in some states mainly due to inequitable distribution of higher education.
7. When education policy considers higher education as a private good, students tend to prefer a particular product with the calculation of return on investment, or *ROI*, that is, a return on the first salary, immediately after education. As a consequence, at the individual or micro level, there is a possibility that too many students may have made the same choice in the selection of courses, and hence, the job market fails to provide the expected return on investment as it happens in engineering courses with too many graduates and limited jobs opportunities in a specific year.
8. Though the espoused purpose of the state-driven education market, is, to build excellence in institutions of higher education, the ground reality in practice is that admissions in *HEIs* are not always available based on merit but on the purchasing power of the parents. It leads to corruption and commercialisation of education as if it is available for sale or auction through donation seats. In other words, the education market tends to protect the privileges of a particular section of society and denies other students easy access to it. India's gross enrolment ratio is very low compared to that of China. The recent policy attempt to increase the enrolment ratio without adequate investment for improvement in quality, governance and human resources in *HEIs* would fail to yield the desired results. In fact, it would be harmful to future generations of young men and women in India, who would hold a paper qualification without developing the necessary knowledge, skills and capabilities.
9. In the case of professional education in Medicine, admissions are based

on money power or also on the economic position of parents to pay for coaching classes to prepare for competition in entrance tests like *NEET*. It diminishes the trust level of *HEIs* in society and questions the credibility of ethical practices, as well as the competence of the practising doctors. Though capitation fees are banned on paper, they are not applied in practice as several providers and promoters of *HEIs* are politicians who have made heavy investments in the infrastructure and expect a return on it. The state has abdicated the responsibility to invest in human development through quality education for all. Similarly, doctors who have paid hefty fees indulge in malpractices later in the profession to recover the cost. When merit is not valued, consumers and parents of higher education in India have initiated a movement called "*Save Merit*", but, the covert and unintended agenda seems to be a demand for elimination of reservation for socially and economically disadvantaged groups and covert resistance to increase reservation quota. Moreover, it is difficult to determine 'merit' in absolute terms in the prevalent system of higher education in India because examination marks do not signify the potential of the students but depends on the resources to prepare for board and competitive examinations.

10. An inadequate information and review mechanism to determine the quality of programmes offered in the higher education market, has, been unfair to the students since they are taken for a ride by lesser-known privately owned and run colleges. The *NAAC* accreditation is not a mandatory condition for undergraduate colleges, and the credibility of its assessment process is also questionable. In addition, there is no effective regulatory body that can alert the students in advance and act on it to safeguard their interests. The data shows that two-thirds of undergraduate colleges are not accredited for their programmes by the state regulators since accreditation is not mandatory but only a recommended qualification to operate in the education market. It is rather obvious that accreditation is optional and has become the norm. *HEIs* are not convinced of its necessity when opportunity and access to higher education are limited, and students have no option but to take admission to available state colleges, though with poor quality and inadequate faculty and staff. In short, the higher education market is not uniform and does not promote real competition or support academic merit. As a consumer in the market, the student does not have reliable information about the quality of institutions to make a choice. Bluntly stated, it is a failure of the higher education market controlled by the state and the Ministry of Education.
11. From the perspective of the providers or promoters of higher education

services and goods, freedom of entry in the market is available to all. Since there is less restriction on market entry, promoters who have no expertise in the education field take advantage on the basis of their capacity to fund and reap the benefits due to the commercialisation of higher education via malpractices in admissions, etc. The absence of quality standards and inadequate and ineffective monitoring by regulatory bodies like *UGC, MCI*, and *AICTE* benefit the promoters or providers, and the consumer students and parents suffer at the receiving end.

12. The price of the higher education products or fees is left to the discretion of the providers. However, this kind of freedom available in the commodity market is not of much consequence in the education market in India because the seats are limited in reputed institutions. The discretion over fees is given to private players in the market, where it is difficult to measure and compare prices with the quality of education. Moreover, reliable data is not available to consumers on the actual costs of the education processes of *HEIs*.
13. Choice of products in the market: When educational programmes are self-funded by higher education providers and remain market-driven in terms of student preferences, only those programmes that have a potential for immediate return on investment are offered by private players or universities and colleges. Furthermore, this is usually at the cost of traditional disciplines like philosophy, history, literature, Indian languages and other subjects in social sciences that shape the intellectual and cultural foundation and values of the society. This has negatively impacted the social capital and demographic advantage of India because well-educated professionals from (*STEM*) Science, Technology, Engineering and Management often lack grounding and perspective on history, culture and social-political issues. As a consequence, they succumb to the propaganda on social media and join regressive, right-wing ideologies that are not conducive to a healthy and secure democracy and equitable society, which is founded on a visionary constitution of India.

Marketisation of Higher Education and the Issue of Equity in the Context of National Education Policy, 2020

The abovementioned discussion and analysis makes it pertinently clear that the role of the state is very crucial in terms of policy decisions on marketisation because they have profound implications for not only bringing excellence to *HEI* and improving the overall quality of education at all levels but also for maintaining inclusiveness and equity in society at large.

From this perspective, it is ironic that the state and *MoE* have created a space in the higher education market for private players but have not simultaneously changed the bureaucratic structure and controls of public universities and affiliate colleges. The basic structure of the University system has remained centralised, bureaucratic and undifferentiated, as, it was in the colonial period.

The weakest link in the overall higher education system is the regulation of quality and delivery of education at state universities and colleges. Periodically, academicians and people at large participate in the national debates on the *NEP 2020*. However, radical changes in the structure and policy rarely occur because they require a bottom-up rather than the prevalent top-down approach. The involvement of micro institutions in design and implementation is essential to work on behaviours, attitudes, mind-sets and processes to design appropriate structures for universities and colleges. Therefore, it appears that the outcome and implementation of *NEP 2020* would be half-hearted and confusing. There is a lack of coherent vision for higher education, particularly in the last two decades after liberalisation. The *NEP* has succumbed to the global trend of marketisation of higher education that does not squarely address the core problems of low credibility and uneven quality of undergraduate programmes of state universities in India. They also face imminent problems of underfunding, political interference, corruption in academic appointments, admissions and examinations, inadequate and ill-maintained infrastructure, and overburdened systems due to a large number of affiliated colleges. Instead of reforming the structure and processes of these universities, the state and *MoE* have taken policy decisions for free access to private players and investment in elite institutions of excellence at the cost of state university education. This has led to a serious systemic imbalance in higher education in India.

Conclusion

The Higher Education market and the attendant context, in India is not ethically and structurally mature and differentiated enough to safeguard the interests of students and large sections of society. In the absence of a robust system of quality assurance and governance at the institutional level, that is, at universities and colleges, it is necessary to strengthen and build the quality of *HEIs*. Institutional interventions and reforms are imminent, in order to attain the desired goals of *NEP 2020* can be a reality in the near future.

The neoliberal concept and ground reality of the 'market' of higher education is a mismatch due to deeper contradictions in the Indian context. The higher education market is not based on the principle of free and equitable competition with access to information for all stakeholders. In fact, such a 'market' would be a utopian expectation that is possible only in financial stock markets. Therefore, educationists and decision-makers should take the concept and processes of building robust institutions for higher education seriously to save the problem-ridden higher education system and make it purposeful and vibrant. The challenge is both at the level of policymaking at the top and in managing at the micro-institutional level.

India has a very wide array of socio-economic disparities, and the role of higher education is crucial to promote social mobility, the productivity of young men and women for a vibrant economy, excellence for innovation, and social harmony to maintain democratic institutions. They would define the purpose of higher education in the twenty-first century in India.

Most significantly, policy-makers and institution builders of higher education need to examine critically and deeply the limitations of applying market principles mechanically or mindlessly to the higher education sector and accordingly modify the approach and model of higher education in order to make it a robust organ of Indian economy and society as well.

REFERENCES

1. Chattopadhyay, S. (2012). *Education and Economics*. Oxford University Press.
2. *Maharashtra Times*, 19 August, 2021.
3. Nigvekar, Arun. (2011). *Higher Education: Issues and Trends*. Uttakarsha Prakashan, Pune.

Essay Four

Corporatisation of Higher Education: A Critique

'Education without values, as useful as it is, seems rather to make man a more clever devil.' – ***C.S Lewis***

'In the world of entrepreneurs, you don't need college education. You need proper education.' – ***Robert Keppel***

This essay is an extension of the previous essay on the market of higher education. It focuses on the dominant model of HEIs that prevails in private universities in India. They resemble corporates or big businesses in terms of values, systems and behaviours. The essay analyses the model with examples to highlight the long-term consequences on higher education regarding equity, access, quality and governance.

The first above mentioned quote of *C.S. Lewis* refers to values in education, which gives primacy to human freedom and the search for truth rather than using knowledge for instrumental and personal gains. Thinkers like *Newman, Tagore* and *Amartya Sen* proposed similar values for higher education. The second quote is somewhat critical of contemporary higher education with its standardised courses of state universities and expects a 'proper' utilitarian orientation to the curriculum. The two quotes may seem contrary, but they are relevant views for the discussion and debate on the theme of this essay on corporatisation and the commercialisation of higher education in India.

Present Context of Higher Education

With the growing privatisation of higher education that began in the last decade of the twentieth century in India, education is considered as private goods or services.

Hence, the student is seen as a consumer and higher education as a commodity or product offered to the consumer. Colleges and universities are considered suppliers and service providers. Inevitably, the concepts from economics and management, such as efficiency, productivity, and markets used in the production and marketing of things, are transplanted into the domain of higher education. Earlier, education at school and college levels was considered a part of public goods, and a primary responsibility of the welfare state.

Corporates and large-size companies that operate and assiduously function in the area of business and commerce at national and global levels are a post-industrialisation phenomenon. Higher education, now considered one of the sectors of the economy, is a recent entrant in the service sector market. The immediate impact of this trend is that privately funded universities in India have ambitious plans for rapid expansion of campuses at the pan-India level. For the private sector, higher education is a business proposal with good potential for growth and expansion. India has seen a rapid increase in the number of campuses, students, courses, and colleges in the last two decades of the 21st century. They compete for a share in the higher education market, with concurrent spending on promotional activity and brand building. Therefore, the conventional academic focus on the intrinsic value of higher education to contribute to the overall development of individuals and society has been a thing of the past. The social, intellectual and academic purpose of university education is side-tracked in the race for market expansion and image or brand building.

In the larger and broader context of institution building for *HEIs,* financial and marketing strategy gets the upper hand over developmental strategy for institutional reputation, which involves enhancing the quality of teaching-learning and fair practices in the governance of people management, that is, the faculty, students and staff. These changes in the orientation of higher education are an outcome of the centralisation of power in the hands of the promoters of private universities and also of neoliberal ideas of the state. These ideas and views are very similar to those of corporate management in industry and business, even though profit-making is not yet legalised for educational institutions in India as it is in business and industry.

In the same manner and tenor, there is a significant shift in the objective of higher education in the 21st century at global and national levels; it is now directly linked with the economic development of nations worldwide. Away from the initial focus on the '*universal humanistic perspective*' of institutions like the university, as articulated by *Henry Newman* and *Rabindranath Tagore*, higher education is now reduced to a narrow focus as a primary supplier of human capital for production and innovation in business and industry. The logic and rationale of factory and business systems fit well with the new objective and functioning of institutions of higher learning as a supplier of human resources.

When one reviews the process of the corporatisation of higher education in India, the key point that emerges is the mixing of two metaphors, that is, of the production system of a factory on the one hand and the purpose of university education as envisaged in Newman's idea of '*search of truth and knowledge*' on the other. Here, it is necessary to recognise the process of how the concepts of corporate management, such as efficiency, productivity, return on investment, accountability, quality assurance, and excellence, are being smoothly transferred to a traditional centuries-old university system. This change has occurred due to the benign environment of the university system in India through regulatory bodies like *UGC* and *AICTE* controlled by the Ministry of Education (MoE). This benign transfer of metaphors is readily accepted as inevitable, without questioning the fundamental premises by the academics and authority of universities. It has led to contradictions, emerging from the two opposite metaphors from two different domains of human activity: producing goods or services in a factory system and generating knowledge through a higher cognitive order of learning in sciences, humanities and other academic disciplines in universities.

Historically and traditionally, the university was considered a distinct, autonomous space, often criticised as an ivory tower due to its separation from the mainstream practices in business and commerce, where students learnt to question, critique, think, explore and develop perspectives rather than simply acquiring tools, techniques, and skills for the employment market. Such a space is possible when there is recognition of the autonomy of those engaged with knowledge creation. In the present context of higher education in India, the credibility and independence of faculty in *HEIs* as professionals have eroded drastically due to rapid changes in socio-cultural, economic and political fields at national and global levels.

Similarly, faculty and students, have, become a part of a new hierarchy where the state, *MoE* and the promoters of the university have complete power over them. The rationale of the market logic of corporates is used in HEIs to disempower faculty as professionals and experts in their field of knowledge, as well as students as active learners whose role is beyond exam-givers or competitors in the job market. In professional education institutions, they are asked to follow practices of so called good governance modelled on corporate practices in terms of regimented behaviours. Uniformity is an acceptable norm, and individuality is considered a deviation.

Professor *Saumen Chattopadhyay* (2018) has deconstructed the logic of the neoliberal approach to higher education and analysed in depth the national higher education policy that envisages a new socio-economic order. The revised education policy requires competitive and entrepreneurial individuals who need a market to participate in business transactions. The critical assumption is that the students and faculty are considered or assumed to be '*self-interested*' individuals who can be easily manipulated by those in power rather than a part of a community of learners with shared educational values.

In the new policy regime, *HEIs*, both public and private, are granted autonomy primarily because they are expected to build a climate of competition. Consequently, institutional authorities of public and private universities have accepted many corporate-style practices and ethos that curtail the academic freedom of faculty and compel them to actively create and contribute to the market of education. Inevitably, the faculty of higher education institutions is trapped between management pressures for more efficiency and productivity and students' demands for better quality education or sometimes the opposite, easy qualification and shortcuts, depending on the culture and context of each institution.

Competition for more enrolments among colleges and universities for their courses is a direct outcome of the policy of granting autonomy because the market is strictly homogenised by the regulators with standard courses, nomenclature, norms of size, etc. For instance, in the city of Pune, about 15 public and private universities offer almost similar courses, competing in the same market of 5 lakh students. (https://seamedu.com>blog)

It is observed that increasingly, many *HEI*s in India tend to initiate collaboration with foreign universities as a part of their brand-building and promotional activity, aiming to attract more students that they consider as potential customers for enrolment in the future. The motive and the core objective is often to enhance the brand value of the courses rather than any genuine institutional interest in upgrading quality and research. This is evident from the conspicuous absence of inter-university, inter-institute collaboration with similar elite institutes in India to build centres of excellence. Considering the scarcity of resources available for higher education, it is a much-needed requirement. It explains the reason behind the lack of synergy and wastage of available resources in *HEIs*, which is a barrier in institutional development and collaboration. It is also true that academics and researchers in universities abroad are not very keen to invest in collaboration with Indian counterparts as the state-level university research in India is less developed. It is primarily done by the national research institutions funded by the central government, which is yet another example of a serious structural defect in higher education in India, resulting in an uneven quality of university research output.

Private Universities indulge in competition that requires efficient use of resources. However, this efficiency is achieved through the use of faculty on contract and the use of surveillance technology to monitor faculty operations and output. The use of *CCTV* cameras, biometrics, and *SAAP* technology are common practices to improve faculty efficiency. It shows that institutional authority would trust information technology more than its human resources, which is another mark of corporate value in practice in *HEIs*.

One can only imagine the impact on the quality of the institutional climate where faculty is distrusted and closely monitored, which is not much different from the close supervision in factories as depicted in the classic film by Chaplin, '*Modern Times*'. What is missed in the neoliberal logic of market efficiency is its inability to understand the process of creation of knowledge and research. This has more to do with the absence of a campus ambience conducive to free thinking, openness in sharing ideas, the playfulness of experimentation, courage, and conviction of character.

There is no standardised format to generate original knowledge and ideas to deliver quality education. Also, it is inappropriate to set fixed criteria and methodology to conduct teaching and research and to measure the quality of an institution. The process of creation and dissemination of knowledge is unique to specific subjects, the quality of faculty, history and the academic climate of the institution. These institutional factors tend to evolve, develop, or degenerate and decline due to changes in the internal and external environment.

Similarly, one cannot expect students to learn when they are treated as consumers, as if they can buy education services with their capacity to pay and where teachers are considered service providers with no self-respect as academicians or professionals. In fact, the corporatisation of higher education de-professionalises academics and expects them to respond to the command of institutional authority and/or market forces. It breeds a sheep mentality to conform in faculty and students.

In other words, market-driven educational policy and procedures do not recognise those organic linkages and interdependence of the academic freedom of faculty, the academic climate based on independent thinking, the professional identity of academics and their impact on the quality of teaching-learning-research in higher education. These links can be better understood if one examines the performance indicators used for measuring faculty output by *NAAC*.

Measuring Faculty Performance in PBAS-API or Performance Based Appraisal System

Let us examine and analyse the process of faculty performance evaluation to recognise the values that govern it. The measurement of faculty performance with a rating scale is similar to the institutional rating scheme used by *NAAC*. The espoused purpose is to improve the capability of individuals and institutions for a competitive environment and market. Inevitably, the idea comes from the corporate sector, where a performance appraisal system is used to weed out non-performers so that only the fit can survive. It is presumed that competition among institutions, colleges, and faculty would bring better quality to higher education.

There is a grave conceptual mistake in this kind of logic because education institutions are essentially 'learning organisations' built on the foundations of mutuality and collaboration rather than isolated individuals competing for personal benefits. The logical consequence of performance management systems like Performance Based Appraisal Systems *(PBAS)* is that they lead to performance appraisal and not performance enhancement. The system is expected to improve faculty performance, but in reality, it remains highly competitive and exclusive at the core.

At the institutional level, the focus of performance needs to go beyond individual or departmental levels and reach the frontiers of interdisciplinary knowledge. Such a shift in focus is possible by nurturing a collaborative culture among faculty, particularly when the distribution of resources is unequal. Specifically, *PBAS* measures faculty performance in six areas: *1. Teaching, 2. Learning, 3. Evaluation, 4. Professional developments, 5. Extension, and 6. Research.*

However, the fact is that measurement is only possible when the output is quantified. The output of the first five activities is quantified based on the number of hours put in by individual faculty. Research output is measured in terms of journal articles, book chapters, book review reports, research projects, research guidance, and participation in seminars.

Teaching, learning and developmental or extension activities, are, measured in terms of time where input is equal to output. Here, quality is not considered in the equation since the core focus is on time spent on the activity. A classroom session, allotted in the timetable, is taken as the output and is mentioned as '*workload*' by the administration and faculty on the college campus. Consequently, it indicates a '*load*' rather than a joy of the teaching-learning process from the institutional or managerial perspective. Students' involvement and engagement with the learning process are not considered since attendance is taken as input of classroom learning and marks or grades as output. In other words, quantification or number crunching overrides qualitative or process aspects of teaching-learning.

This system of equating learning output with input hours makes the process of education a ritual to be carried out mechanically without much concern for the mutual involvement of faculty and students as adults engaged with higher-order learning, emphasising critical thinking and creativity.

It must be recognised that teaching-learning is always context-dependent in terms of the size of the class, maturity of students, and campus climate in terms of student-teacher relationships. Similarly, when the research quality is measured in terms of the number of papers, it fails to give a critical direction on the qualitative aspects of research like originality, grounded data and contribution to knowledge.

It is important to emphasise that the dysfunctional impact of corporate systems and values on the education sector can be minimised only by examining the assumptions and purpose of the appraisal system. More importantly, it is necessary to question the perspective and values of corporate management imposed on academic performance. In other words, without suitable changes in the systems and processes of managing institutions, appropriate behaviours and attitudes cannot be developed for collaborative cultures and academic values in *HEIs*.

For instance, the prevalent work designs of *HEIs* are unilateral, that expect individual accountability and ignore mutual accountability. The decisions are taken at a single point of HODs and institutional leadership and not at multiple points among other members of the academic community. Such a decision-making process does not develop facilitative leadership essential for educational institutions. The performance output of the group in this system is taken as a sum of individual work contributions. In contrast, facilitative leadership expects synergistic output emerging from interactivity and additivity across individual roles. It encourages interdependence among members of the group or team in a positive sense because it requires a high level of mutual trust and individual initiative. Moreover, *facilitative leadership* relies on the complementarity of skills rather than on individual skills only so that the expert power of one individual is not overemphasised, causing neglect of team building.

The *PBAS* promotes a unitary and centralised leadership. However, improving the academic and institutional performance of *HEIs* would require multilateral structures and facilitative leadership. (*Refer to the Case Study Two on Leadership and Institution Building*)

Recently, *UGC* had to publish a list of authorised journals for publications to restrict the commercialisation of research activity. The implicit assumption of this otherwise well-intentioned initiative is that more surveillance and control over the outputs of academic activities would ensure better quality. In fact, external controls lead to a decrease in faculty autonomy and loss of self-esteem of the faculty. What is certainly needed is the development of internal norms of behaviours in the institution so that mutual controls and individual conscientiousness are maintained.

On campus, when students attend classes for attendance and learn only to get certification and placements, it becomes a ritualistic and demoralising exercise for the teaching community as students are not motivated to acquire knowledge and learn its application.

Stakeholders vs Consumers of Higher Education

The *'corporatisation'* of higher education is an outcome of a conscious education policy to create a market for higher education. It promotes the 'individualisation' of students and their families in a market economy sense so that they remain consumers of education rather than active stakeholders involved in education as part of the community of learners on the campus and as socially responsible citizens. Unlike stakeholders, consumers tend to focus on the immediate need for satisfaction and benefits in the short term. However, higher education remains a long-term investment in time frame. Personal resources and the collective experiences deployed in longer-duration courses have a profound impact on the future lives and careers of students. It is an orientation for a lifelong learning process, essential to cope with the complexity and challenges of the 21st century.

Neoliberal Economics and Corporatisation

In the neoliberal perspective, persons are seen as individuals isolated and decontextualised from the community. In reality's tandem, though each person is unique or special, their personality is also shaped by the context in which they subsist. Therefore, the term individual is not an abstraction or only a number, as mentioned in *W.H. Auden's* poem on a nameless and faceless '*Unknown citizen*'. The true meaning of the word 'individual' is someone who is indivisible because the individual cannot be isolated from her unique self or the community she lives in.

In the neoliberal view, the individual is not a citizen of a welfare state but a consumer who fulfils her needs in a state-driven market. In this way, the process of identity formation of individuals as consumers and identity of *HEIs* as suppliers are subsumed under a larger macro-system of the higher education market. However, the painful reality in the Indian context is that individuals, as consumers, have no protection or help if they do not have the purchasing power to buy goods and services available in the market. In a country like India, with deep pockets of economic and social inequality, market logic brings more inequality. It deprives many young men and women of opportunities to access higher education to progress their careers. The contradictions of the neoliberal view have come out sharply during the pandemic crisis in India and other developing countries. Parents could not pay fees then, and schools and colleges demanded it, threatening to deprive education for young boys and girls. Also, it exposed the myth that privatisation of schools and universities would bring more efficiency in the use of resources. The neoliberal economic perspective appears to be more of a pro-privatisation ideology than an economic perspective oriented towards resource mobilisation and distribution. Certainly, it fails to create an equitable and just society by providing education for all sections of society, which is relevant in contemporary India with a large young population.

The concept and the criteria of faculty performance and institutional ranking designed by the higher education regulatory bodies of the state, like *UGC, AICTE, and MCI,* are meant to facilitate the creation of a single uniform market for higher education so that it can be promoted and controlled covertly by the state as expected in the neoliberal policies world over.

When tangible and quantifiable criteria are preferred over qualitative and subjective ones, researchers opt for the easier option with a short-term focus on career benefits rather than long-term involvement or in risky research area of study. Hence, faculty and researchers tend to select empirical rather than conceptual research proposals/studies because the former are more conducive and less time-consuming for approval of measurement criteria.

Research faculty tend to put forth deliberate efforts into winning points in academic appraisal and focus on output rather than learning processes, creativity and originality. Focus on output is an orientation of industries but does not essentially suit the higher education domain. Corporate ethos of speed and efficiency overtakes academic orientation towards reflection, contemplation and perspective building. Pressure to earn points in the rating system forces the faculty to use her discretion to allocate time for teaching, administration and research in order to move up the career ladder. When this choice is driven by a rating scheme, it is likely to bring imbalance in their domains of teaching, research and academic administration.

It is essential to recognise that the corporate model primarily uses higher education to promote an individual or institutional brand for prestige maximisation and success. Hence, winning in the competition and acquiring a larger market share for expansion and empire-building are more important than long-term benefits to the students and the institution as a collectivity. It is no surprise that the growth of private universities and colleges has increased significantly in the first ten years of the 21st century.

Impact of Neoliberal Ideology of Institutional Behaviour

The corporate model of higher education in India relies on the state policy of promoting private universities, where institutional promoters create a market for their benefits. They are oblivious to the social impact in terms of access, equity and quality of education because the model assumes that an individual is an economic agent interested in self-benefit and would maximise self-gains. It ignores the social-political-moral dimensions of the perspective. These assumptions about self-interested individuals are self-fulfilling prophesies driven by the *neoliberal ideology,* which is more of a political than an economic perspective. It is an ideology that empowers the state to influence the higher education market to achieve political objectives. Consequently, it has led to frequent fee hikes and has not improved the quality, equity and access to higher education in India. Moreover, neoliberal ideology supports the view that higher education is an area of private rather than public goods and has resulted in disastrous consequences for medical education and public health systems, as evident during *COVID* pandemic 2020-21 in India.

Privatisation of education often coincides with the withdrawal of grants to higher education and the beginning of self-financed courses. Inevitably, it led to exorbitant fee hikes and admitting those students who could pay higher fees. Hence, the idea of merit or quality loses relevance and meaning because only those who have the capacity to pay high fees would have access to professional education. Even admission based on the merit list is a questionable exercise because only those families that can afford to provide additional fees for private coaching classes would succeed in the competition for the merit list. Merit is turning out to be more about financial ability or purchasing power to access higher education rather than better academic quality and excellence.

Emerging Campus Culture and the Role of Faculty in *IB*

When students are treated as consumers, the faculty is expected to tolerate their misbehaviour and appease them on campus. *Sharu Rangnekar,* management educationist vividly described his experience as a guest faculty member in a class of misbehaving students who had been admitted through management quotas with higher fees. (*Refer to "Menace of management quota students in Essay Ten on 'Quality of Higher Education in India)*

It is vital at this point to locate the causes of these distortions and malpractices while applying the economic logic of the market to education, which is generally described as a 'Corporate Model' of higher education. It is understood or assumed that, unlike the commodity markets, education providers, that is, the HEIs, are supposed to be 'not-for-profit' organisations (*NPO*). However, private universities and colleges have autonomy in managing their own sources of funding without government grants.

'Autonomy' of colleges and universities is a misleading term in the Indian context because questions like 'autonomy for what purpose and for whom'? are not squarely addressed by private, autonomous institutions. Most of them do not have financial autonomy in the real sense of self-financing since there is no significant means of self-funding to pursue institutional missions. Inevitably, they are directly exposed to market mechanisms to survive and compete with other universities and colleges. Only elite institutions like *IITs, IIMs, IIS, TISS* and a few public and private universities can maximise their reputation and prestige because they are either funded by the State or sponsored or supported by business houses. Also, they can compete for academic reputation and ranking to attract the best students, faculty, and advisors to achieve higher status in the hierarchical structure of the Indian education system. They try to maximise institutional prestige to remain economically viable without specifically pursuing goals of profit-making or surpluses.

For other players too, that is, state and private universities and affiliated colleges, survival in the market is a major challenge that diverts their attention from the purpose, mission, and institutional values that they have officially stated. Every year, AICTE announces a list of institutes of professional courses like Engineering and Management that have applied for closure of their courses since they have become unviable for the promoters due to reduced enrolment. This is symptomatic of the short-sightedness of higher education policy driven by market logic.

The national ranking system proclaims the rating scores of *HEIs* in the merit list that indicates the relative status and quality of institutions. However, the ranking has failed to motivate the lower-ranked institutions to improve their performance. Thus, inevitably, the top ten names of *HEI*s in the ranking list have remained unchanged for a decade.

Ironically, the ranking system reinforces the inequity because competition in the higher education market is not perfect since several *HEIs* are not on a level playing field due to disparity in the economic and social development of states in India. Also, the so-called consumers in the higher education market, that is, students and parents, do not have access to complete or reliable information about the quality of the product and the institution. Unlike consumer products like ice cream or chocolates, education is an 'experienced good' or service, and one can know its real quality only when she experiences it. This requires a facility to experiment or test by attending initial sessions, as it happens in developed countries. However, it is not available in Indian universities for obvious reasons like shortage of faculty and other resources. It is a fact that once a student takes admission, she is unable to shift her college easily later. Therefore, though tall claims are made by private universities and institutes about quality and placements, they remain misleading because once admission is taken, the student has fewer choices but to continue with it. The costly option is to pay fees again for admission to another college.

In short, the picture of the 'Corporate Model' of education is certainly not an encouraging one. It needs more than procedural reforms made by regulatory bodies of *MoE* and envisioned in the *NEP 2020*. It requires serious questioning of the neoliberal approach along with a review of the primary purpose of higher education.

Relevance of Agency Theory (PAT) in Understanding Corporatisation of Higher Education

Corporatisation in industry and education is marked by a hierarchical structure of authority and responsibility, which may appear similar to a bureaucratic structure, but it is different. Formal authority and power are at the top of the pyramid and are delegated downwards. This is theoretically described as a Principal-Agent relationship (*PAT*). The power and authority of the Principal emerge from ownership, which makes it different from the authority of the bureaucracy given to the office. In the Agency framework, it is a contractual relation wherein the agents are those who manage institutions like HoD, Dean or the Director. They are expected to identify with the goals of the principal (read owner), as it happens in the case of managers or CEOs of business houses. Agents or managers identify with the goals of the owners and work on their behalf. They are also expected to protect the owners' interests. This happens because the final and core objective in business, is, clearly stated as '*maximisation of profits*'. The Principal-Agent relation is an easier and efficient way to operate and achieve the objective. In contrast, the purpose of education has economic, social and ethical dimensions, and the nature of the psychological contract between institution, faculty and students is much more complex and needs to be managed differently from a top-down, contractual role relation as it is expected in the case of business organisations.

Governance and Performance

The Agency theory of management and governance is based on the premise that separation of ownership from control creates better efficiency and productivity in corporations. This kind of separation has obvious advantages for owners of the corporation because it gives extra facility and space for owners to diversify attention and investment in different businesses, thereby reducing the risks in business.

Interestingly, the promoters and facilitators of educational institutions in India, also, invest in programmes from nursery to PG levels and sometimes have other businesses as well. Often, the promoters of family-managed educational institutions do not possess expertise and knowledge in the subject discipline, nor are they directly in touch with the day-to-day teaching and learning processes on campus. Hence, they appoint a director, principal, administrator, sometimes *CEO,* and *PR* managers who manage institutions on their behalf. In the framework of the Agency theory, the Promoter as the Principal delegates some decision-making authority to these Agents, that is, the director, principal, or *CEO,* in some selected areas like academics and administration. However, important decisions like admission, faculty selection, students, and financial management are often not delegated. As in Indian family businesses, the principal (owner) does not share finance and other critical functions with (Agents) professionals but only with their siblings and family members. Many private universities and colleges in India are family-managed and share similar features.

Agency, Principal-Agent Theory (PAT)

Often, *HEIs,* like corporates, are also engaged with achieving targets and completing projects where efficiency and productivity are relevant values. In an institutional rating scheme, the sum of the outcome or contributions of departmental tasks is taken as an organisational outcome. In the context of higher education, the curriculum and teaching-learning processes are connected and systemic and not to be conceived in terms of the efficiency of parts. For example, the vertical and horizontal levels of the subjects taught in the curriculum need integration in the sense that the content and learning of the previous courses support the subjects taken at the next level vertically. Hence, the coordination and collaboration of the faculty among subjects are of great importance. The dictates of the HoD, principal, or director cannot accomplish it. It needs a team structure where interdisciplinary collaboration is practised. It can happen when the vision and values of the institutions are consistent with the nature of educational structure and processes in *HEIs.* The team structure is not only a change in the top-down hierarchy but also a change in perspective, authority-power relations, and attitudes.

More specifically, in the context of public universities, central and state, it is the Ministry of Education, which is the central authority, appoints vice-chancellors as its agents. At the college level, the head and director assume the role of Principal, and faculty are in the role of Agent, though not formally, but in terms of role expectations. This formal and informal arrangement is made because of information asymmetry between the two levels of the higher education system. Ministry has less information about the competence and behaviours of the faculty or administrators and how they conduct classes and regulate. In this situation, manipulation of decisions for personal gains is always a possibility. The director may hide his full credentials while being selected for the post, or the ministry may select a vice chancellor who is favourable to the government in power. In both cases, there is a violation of ethical role boundaries, which results in serious damage to the institutional processes later.

When a wrong person is selected as principal or Principal or VC, it is a serious liability to the institutions till he or she is in the position (*Refer to the appointments of VC and faculty in Case Study Five, JNU: The Rise and Decline of an Academic Institution*). Ironically, the issue of who would monitor and influence the Principal remains a moot question. Also, the question of who would govern the Governing board or who would regulate the regulators is also asked. This is an area of ethics of governance and discretion in the use of power in the highest positions.

The ethical issues mentioned above go beyond the realm of administrative or managerial reforms and, in reality, cannot be resolved by using Technical Rationality *(TR)*, which focuses on parts rather than the whole for efficiency gains and indirectly impacts educational reforms. The *TR* perspective has no space for questioning ethical and governance issues. *TR* focuses on problems to be solved on a short-term basis but is silent on beliefs, values, and ethical perspectives that impact the situation in the long run.

Conclusion

The essay, a critique on the corporatisation of higher education, has argued that when the theory and practices of business corporations are applied to *HEIs*, it leads to serious conflicts on the use of power and authority to influence. In the process, the key stakeholders of education, such as parents, students, and faculty, are at the receiving end. However, it is also possible to avoid these pitfalls and develop governance and leadership norms that are conducive to strengthening institutional practices in terms of Principal-Agent Theory *(PAT)*.

The central assumption behind Agency theory, which is the basis of corporate governance, is that the goals of the principal and the agents are divergent and do not have a scope for convergence. The Principal in *PAT* wants efficient use of resources and surplus, and the faculty, as an Agent with an instrumentality, prefers leisure and would shirk from assiduous work. The assumption is based on stereotypes and biases and may not be realistic. Meaningful engagement with work remains attractive to conscientious faculty and students in an educational context. Hence, there is always a potential to develop a collaborative employment relationship between the agent (faculty) and the owner (HoD). Enlightened leaders in business and educational contexts in the role of the Principal initiate such collaborative processes at the workplace based on shared values and trust. It happens in union-management relations in industry and peer relationships among faculty, in which the Principal collaborates with agents in higher education institutions. Essentially, parts are not as important as the whole. In other words, the interests and goals of principal and agents should subsume in the larger goals of the institutions. Visionary leadership can also bridge the gaps in mutuality and trust in Principal-Agent relationships in the corporate sector and educational institutions.

REFERENCES

1. Chattopadhyay, S. (2018). *Neoliberalism and Freedom: Emerging Scenario, The Idea of a University*, Context.
2. Gerhard Barry and Rymes Sara. (2003). *Compensation: Concepts and Research*, Sage (explains Principal-Agent Theory (PAT)).
3. Yash Pal Committee Report (2009). Report of the Committee to Advise on Renovation and Rejuvenation of Higher Education.
4. Jensen, M.C., Mackling W.H. (1996). *Theory of the Firm*.

ESSAY FIVE

UNDERSTANDING BEHAVIOURAL PROCESSES IN HEIs

This essay describes a conceptual framework for building an academic culture and climate for improving institutional performance. It is presented in two parts. The first part explains how institutional structures and systems influence behavioural processes and how dysfunctional behaviours and attitudes necessitate appropriate changes in them. Understanding the top-down and bottom-up processes in institutions is important for building and influencing institutional behaviours. The second part of the essay focuses on the impact of academic performance management systems (PMS) on faculty attitudes, behaviours, and institutional processes.

PART ONE

Since the educational process is primarily a people-driven activity, interpersonal, group and intergroup relations and interactions among people and their behaviours are the most visible or tangible phenomenon in all institutions of higher learning. They are identified as behavioural processes of the collective that operate both at overt (visible) and covert (invisible) levels. From behaviours, one can decode the attitudes, thinking and feelings of the members. The main challenge in understanding institutional behaviours of people is to make sense of and interpret the behaviours by asking the question, 'Why do the people behave the way they behave?' so that it would explain the rationale of their behaviours at the workplace. In large organisations like universities or colleges, these questions can be better answered with the help of a theoretical framework of 'bureaucracy' developed by organisational thinkers like *Max Weber* (1947), which explains the efficient and widely used design of large-size work organisations.

The primary purpose of large-size organisations that follow the bureaucratic or Weberian model is to control and maintain power over operations so that results are achieved as desired. It is a model based on the principle of rationality, assuming that people working in organisations are driven by 'reason' to achieve their goals and fulfil needs. However, the intent and the avowed objective of the bureaucratic model and its outcomes do not always match, and the actions of those who wish to control the system would get some 'unintended consequences' like inefficiency in performance, apathy, indifference in attitude, and lack of initiative and internal motivation.

With the help of this theoretical framework of top-down authority and power structures, we can explain and interpret the causes of negative behaviours in educational institutions. More significantly, we can better understand why faculty, students, administrators, promoters of micro institutions, and even higher education regulators or apex institutions, such as *UGC* and *AICTE*, operate or behave in the way they behave/operate. Also, how far do these behaviours serve the institutional purposes? Are they functional and useful, or dysfunctional and harmful to achieve the primary tasks of institutions? This kind of inquiry or diagnosis would help institution builders in seeking solutions to dysfunctional behaviours in educational institutions. This essay tries to address these key questions on behavioural processes of institution building for coming to grips with the reality of institutional behaviours. Before that, let us note some of the features of bureaucracy as an administrative system because most *HEIs* are built on this premise.

Key Features of Bureaucracy as a Formal Organisation are:

(i) Bureaucratic Practices

- Paperwork
- Delayed actions on account of compliance with procedures
- Non-performance on account of failure to pin responsibility
- Preponderance of rules and precedents
- Redundancy in work
- Ascendancy of the administrative branch over other functions

(ii) Bureaucratic Procedures

- *Comprehensive:* covers all possible contingencies
- *Impersonal:* applicable to all equally
- *Non-discretionary:* a very small amount of discretion given to officers
- *Hierarchical:* supervisory layers over performing branches, reporting system
- Systematic and progressive conversion of personalised knowledge into the programming of procedures and redundancy, replacement of trust

(iii) Principles and Assumptions that Govern Bureaucracy

- *Rationality:* all activities in the organisation must be directed toward maximising the organisation's goals; individuals are rational in maximising their rewards and remuneration
- *Legal force:* Authority is legitimised through allegiance to some supreme principle and power to enforce decisions through means of coercion and legal action.

(iv) Perspective and Philosophy

- The world is an object of activity.
- Only task-centred relationships matter; there is no place for feelings
- People can be directed by the use of reason and logic
- Rewards and punishments, as well as authority and coercion, are useful in influencing people.

To understand the impact of bureaucratic authority and power on the behaviour of people in educational institutions at a micro level, it is necessary to know the structure of apex institutions such as *UGC, AICTE* and similar organs of the MoE at central and state levels and how they control universities and colleges through circulars and Government Resolutions (GR) to implement top-down decision-making processes.

The structure of bureaucracy relies on the division of work for better efficiency, and it is reflected in the separation of administration and academic functions, centralised financial disbursement through grants, filling up of faculty positions and even approval of curriculum design and structure of educational courses through GR. The structure makes faculty and staff of micro institutions dependent on the power centres at state and central levels. However, on the positive side, bureaucracy gives stability and continuity to organisations. It maintains a status quo for the power structure and thus explains why it is commonly used in all governmental organisations and even large-size privately owned organisations.

Some of the dysfunctional consequences of the bureaucratic model observed in educational institutions are

(i) Rivalry and distrust between the administration and academic wings
(ii) Imbalance in power between the regulatory organs and the universities, leading to vacant posts of faculty even though it is of utmost importance to processes of teaching and learning
(iii) An absence of professional values and respect for academic scholarship and research expertise, special knowledge by even those in positions of

power such as the vice chancellor, principal, and director, as evident in the *JNU* case study in the next section.

In short, the bureaucratic model, which overemphasises the rationality principle of formal structure, is an antithesis of the institutional model of robust system to accommodate the emotional dimension of informal systems within an organisation. This flexibility of permeable boundaries among formal-informal, rational-emotional, internal-external, top-down and bottom-up structures leads to organisation learning, innovation and change in ideas and behaviours. For example, many universities in India funded by the state fail to attract faculty from other states and countries. Often, the inbreeding of faculty from the same department leads to stagnation and mediocrity in the intellectual climate. It explains how rigid structures influence systems and processes of recruitment, which in turn impacts faculty attitudes and behaviours in universities.

Prof. *Rajén Harshe* (2023) has documented his experiences as faculty and HOD at *Hyderabad University* and later at *Allahabad University* as Vice-chancellor (2005-2010). He observed that the *UoA* faculty had little knowledge of the hard work in the context of the research process because they focussed on classroom teaching, which is emphasised in undergraduate colleges. Moreover, they were ignorant of changes in academic trends in the world. They did not read books written in the English language, and the library was underfunded to bring enough books. The point is that there was an absence of initiative and orientation for self-development. Is it a weakness of individuals or the system as a whole?

Theoretically, according to behavioural and organisational science, individual behaviours are largely influenced by institutional processes and systems. Only those with self-initiative break the barriers of negativity in the collectivity. It also means that knowledge about how people respond to formal systems and processes of institutions needs attention and diagnosis because, ultimately, it is individuals who change their own behaviours. The role of those who manage a formal system is to develop a better understanding of the parallel informal or 'living system' so that employees are helped to help themselves for better performance.

Prof Harshe also notes that the recruitment of faculty in both universities was driven by caste consideration and 'inbreeding' rather than on merit and academic competence. Above all, the faculty community lived in the 'past' glory of the university rather than the present conditions and ignored the poor quality of higher education. They compared Allahabad University to '*Oxford of the East*' because it was a residential university. However, in terms of academic climate and traditions, it was nowhere near it; in fact, faculty behaviours appeared to him rather pathetic, influenced by feudal values rather than professionalism.

Interestingly, the *AoU* faculty was influenced by the high court and politicians as the faculty moved to court for petty issues. They spent a large part of their work time filing queries in court under the *RTI* act, gossiping, taking undue interest in the personal lives of others, and petty politicking, among other things. In short, the city and its university campus breathed politics, and the professors, students and staff together kept the game of politics continuous and alive!

The above description of the bureaucratic system in Indian universities is embedded in a social-political context. It indicates an urgent need for change and intervention in the system in order to modify the structure and processes that sustain it. However, it cannot happen overnight, and without a systematic plan for change and development at an institutional level, it is unrealistic to expect change in larger systems at the national level. The right point to start the change process is in micro institutions because it is essential to reduce the negative impact on the behavioural processes in each institution before introducing change initiatives.

For clarity, consider Figure 1 for a conceptual understanding of the linkages between institutional aspects of Structure and its cascading impact on Systems-Processes-Attitudes-Behaviours of people at campuses of *HEIs*. The diagram explains the top-down sequence of *S-P-A-B* as levels of institutional systems and the impact of higher levels like structure (S) and processes (P) on the lower levels of people's attitudes(A) and behaviours (B).

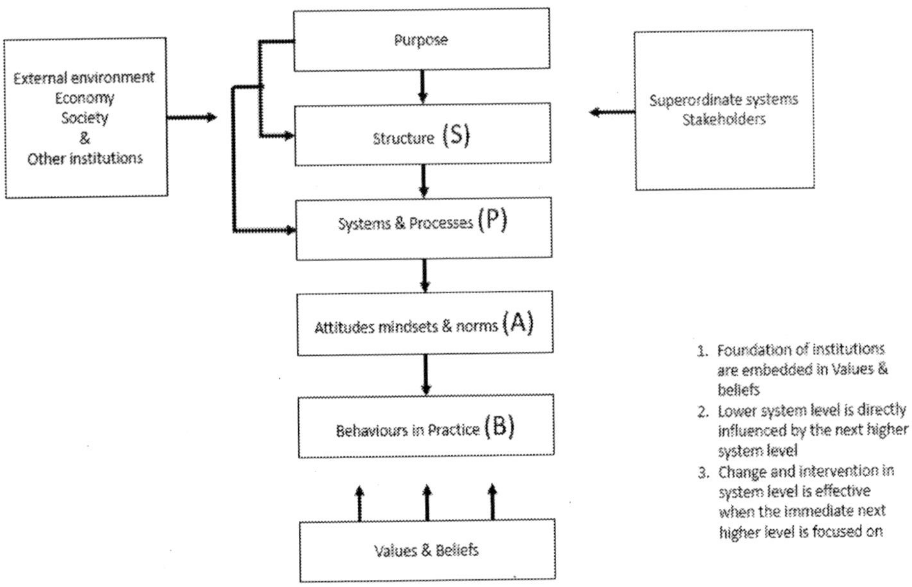

Figure 1: SPAB Model of Institutional Behaviours

The essay presents a broad framework for understanding the behaviours of faculty, staff and students on campuses of *HEIs* so that one can identify the levels and ascribe to the forces that influence behaviours. Institutional members are naturally engaged with tasks and other role-holders in the organisational hierarchy on a day-to-day level. They take action and express opinions and feelings. However, these behaviours do not occur randomly but result from collective norms that determine their attitudes, beliefs, and assumptions. Identifying these norms would help recognise the positive and negative attitudes that create a climate for the workplace.

As an instance, norms of academic quality developed internally by faculty groups in some reputed *IITs* in India determine how each faculty would assess the projects, whether to tolerate substandard output or insist on improving it. Any deviation from the norm or covert understanding by an individual faculty invites pressure from other group members to correct the deviant behaviours immediately. In contrast, consider a negative example of internal marks assessments in affiliated colleges of state universities by its faculty who tend to give maximum marks to get a higher percentage for their students. It is generally supported by an unwritten norm of collectivity in that specific college/institute wherein such dysfunctional behaviour is accepted as normal or acceptable because it benefits their college in competition with others in the educational market. It shows the negative power and impact of informal group norms on behaviours and how well-intentioned formal structures and processes of internal assessment may lead to dysfunctional attitudes and behaviours. Therefore, it is essential to develop a theoretical framework to diagnose and correct such systemic failures at the behavioural level.

In such situations, low-quality academic work gets sanctions from group processes and thus gets institutionalised. If we go deeper into interpreting behaviours, it is possible to decode, uncover, and interpret the norms and values that the institution holds collectively. In other words, the methodology of diagnosing or understanding campus behaviours at the workplace is a valuable tool to improve or correct dysfunctional behaviours and reinforce positive and functional behaviours with norms and values that are backed by the leadership of the institutions.

Below is a snapshot of typical faculty and staff behaviours in a university which is documented by a faculty member as a part of academic community on the campus. This would help us analyse the specific issues and problems to suggest ways to improve and change organisational behaviours.

This snapshot of typical daily routines of work culture in a university department in India, as described by a faculty member in a university-affiliated college, is presented below. It is followed by an initial analysis of why these behaviours happen, which would be helpful in taking appropriate actions and interventions for influencing institutional behaviours.

A list of typical educational routines on college campus:

> *'1. Classes are conducted, courses completed, 2. Students write for examinations, results are announced, 3. Rules for attendance, dress code, assignments, and research projects are announced 4. Conferences, seminars, and events are arranged for students and faculty.'*

This list of institutional routines may be longer, indicating a focus on activities rather than academic substance or direction.

The faculty mentioned in the above narration writes further that 'when the routine is repeated every year without a systematic procedure for review of performance, it results in wastage of resources, efforts and mindless duplication of work. For example, the topics of the research thesis are either too narrow or too broad, which makes conclusions less relevant. The fact is that there is no explicit criterion or guidelines recommended by the university on what makes a thesis original, except the fact that plagiarism check is conducted with the help of technology.'

'At PG level in professional courses, students repeat the project titles and adhere to the format prescribed by the system, but neither faculty nor students apply their minds to the purpose and outcomes of internship projects.'

Similarly, summer/winter internships for professional courses are designed to provide an opportunity for a live socialisation process to familiarise students with day-to-day operational practices and in natural work groups so that it does not remain merely a collection of data by conducting field surveys. However, it is perceived by faculty and students take it as an activity to fulfill curriculum requirements. The opportunity to have first-hand experiential learning and observations from internship experience in these live projects is totally ignored.

Hence, an internship is mistaken for collecting information from secondary sources and analyzing survey based field data, which does not need attention to the behavioural and technical-operational processes and reflections on it. For examiners, first-hand observations are merely subjective, biased data, but questionnaire-based survey data is considered objective data. Theory and concepts of learning and research methodology and evaluation criteria are rarely challenged in the university system because they would disturb the system's established routines that have become inflexible and bureaucratic, which is a sign of an anti-learning attitude.

There is an apparent disconnect between the educational routines reflected in behaviours of academic collectivity and the espoused objectives of higher learning. Academic routines are taken as a mandatory ritual for the completion of PG-level professional courses by students and faculty. Therefore, performing procedural routines without application of thought when producing a project report is considered as fieldwork. Ironically, the internship is expected to contribute to students' understanding of a professional discipline and applied knowledge at the end of the course.

The unintended impact of academic bureaucracy in converting academic performance into routine rituals without substance and relevance:

Similarly, other academic activities such as lectures, examinations, and student feedback are conducted as rituals so that they are rarely subjected to regular review and reflections by faculty and HOD. The double-loop learning model of experiential learning through feedback and reflections to reset objectives and methodology is missing in higher education processes. The mere physical presence of students in the class and staff at the workplace does not indicate a meaningful engagement with the task. Compulsory attendance is another manifestation of the bureaucratic approach to solving serious problems in teaching-learning. It is common to find that academic tasks like paper writing and presentations in seminars are used to make the right noises with appropriate jargon, and they have little to offer, which is significant and original contribution or insights.

Fear of failure and rejection, how it leads to cynical attitudes and dysfunctional culture on educational campuses:

In faculty and students, there is a deep fear of being original, which leads to avoidance of any risk due to the 'fear of failure' and rejection by the academic system. This attitude results in avoidance of out-of-box thinking because there is fear of rejection or ridicule by significant others like colleagues and those in authority positions. It happens because certain academic conventions and methods are legitimised by the system. Statistical tables and number crunching are considered the main evidence of objectivity and empirical facts. However, grounded, descriptive documentation or narration of lived experiences is considered subjective reality and not worthy of academic research. The dominance of the positivist-empirical approach to academic research, like Ph.D. research, is evident in universities. Innovation and creativity in curriculum, assessment, and academic administration are seen with suspicion and face hostility from the establishment, and it is justified on the grounds that there are no precedents to such practices in Indian universities. Inevitably, it leads to the premature death of good ideas and efforts in research and academic administration in *HEIs*. This happens because these ideas are not experimented with in a rigid academic climate of higher education institutions. Moreover, untested ideas are not welcome in a culture that prohibits any psychological, social or economic risk.

The linkages between academic structures-systems and behaviours-attitudes-values are apparent when one experiences an anti-learning mind-set and an attitude of cynicism that prevails in universities. The attitudes, assumptions, and beliefs that prevail in the academic culture of educational institutions in India can be summarised as: (i) College education and degrees are for paper qualification; teaching and research are for employment and careers. (ii) Writing academic papers and books and attending conferences and seminars are stepping stones for career progression.

Causal informal talk on campuses reveals some of the most damaging cynical utterances that negatively impact the identity formation of young faculty. Some examples are: *'Why do you take academics so seriously?' 'Sincere work for the institution would not change the system!' 'Nobody would reward faculty for better classroom teaching'; 'investing in student learning and institutional building-development does not benefit career progression'. 'Follow what we do rather than what we say or espouse.'*

These statements reflect toxic, cynical attitudes that distrust and discourage the possibility of authentic or honest behaviours in academic institutions. Cynicism prevails, and self-fulfilling prophecies of cynical beliefs become a reality since there is an absence of individual and collective intent toward the simultaneous development of the self and the system.

In state universities, parochial and feudal values drive faculty behaviours on campuses, and they negatively impact students and faculty from other states. 'Even senior faculty and HOD, though academically competent in terms of qualification and teaching skills, do not hold liberal and cosmopolitan values expected from the campus climate in universities. Students and staff unions are governed by identity politics that create distrust which is harmful for healthy interactions among faculty, staff and students.' (ref: *Rajén Harshe, 2023*)

Needless to say, transformation in values and beliefs would not occur by imposing formal rules and systems but by organisational learning and empowerment so that members take charge of the authority of self and collectivity. This is explained in the next Essay Six, on Theory and Application of *OD* and *ID*.

Human Resource Management (HRM) *practices in academic administration:*

Unlike corporate practices, where employees are held accountable for results and work, or groups and teams develop norms of desirable behaviours, academic administration in universities and colleges does not rely on collective norms developed within the group to regulate institutional behaviours. In fact, there is an absence of bottom-up, participative-collective decision-making, and its place is taken by top-down formal structures and routines. They are imposed by the apex regulatory bodies of higher education in the form of impersonal, standardised, bureaucratic rules in areas of admissions, classroom management, assessments and discipline, and they are usually disconnected from the ground realities and behavioural dynamics on the campuses of *HEIs*.

At a behavioural level, interpersonal relations and task-related interactions reflect a climate of lack of openness on the campus. As an instance,, faculty colleagues do not talk to each other or collaborate to solve problems and offer help and do not follow *'organisational citizenship' (OC)* behaviours. They do not chip in when administrative work is expected from an overloaded faculty, which is considered a sign of 'organisational citizenship behaviour'. They do not come to meetings on time and are not questioned for late coming, for not taking lectures on time and for not answering emails from the students or colleagues. Co-teaching and collaboration for interdisciplinary research are rare or absent; senior faculty refuse to mentor and coach new, young faculty. In fact, those in authority positions are suspicious of young faculty as a potential threat and competition for rewards.

Organisation climate survey is an effective tool used in the discipline of *OD to* locate and describe the emotional and thinking processes that are reflected through the behaviours and attitudes of employees. These behaviours are expressed overtly and covertly in the natural work setting at a day-to-day level. It depicts a behavioural theory-in-action of an organisation at collective level. Importantly, it is not an espoused theory or official version of the organisation's vision, mission, goals and values. The behaviours occur naturally and reveal conscious and unconscious beliefs and ideas of acceptable and desirable or unacceptable and undesirable behaviours in the collective. In a way, organisational climate and behaviours reflect attitudes, thinking, feelings and actions of those involved in the day-to-day engagement with work and related people.

Another snapshot of typical behaviours and attitudes of faculty is presented below. It is about the relations of faculty and staff with those in authority or management positions in *HEIs*. (*Farooqi I., 2018*)

'There is a predominant feeling of insecurity in faculty groups, which is reflected in behaviours of an 'active' cooperation between faculty and students. Faculty and students, as a community on the campus, are continuously engaged with academic routines of lectures, examinations, assignments, and conferences, but the outcomes and impact of these events are not directly visible, and no data-based documentation takes place on these academic activities for the benefit of institutional learning. Students organise seminars every year, but energy is spent on organising and PR work rather than on academic learning. The conduct of academic tasks of assessment, research, and lectures is done in such a way that its performance is more of a ritual rather than with the intellectual rigour of academic performance. In fact, 'What is an academic performance?' is rarely questioned or reviewed after the ritualistic performance has taken place. Student feedback is collected, but there is no analysis or interpretation of the data that can be used to make constructive decisions and take action to improve performance.'

Cooperation as a Means to Lower Academic Quality:

There is a lack of both a supportive and demanding climate for promoting quality of academic performance. Ironically, a supportive climate and cooperation between faculty and students are deployed to maintain the status quo and resist change. In this way, faculty, administrators and students collude to maintain an anti-learning climate on campus. The performance managing system *(PMS)* is not active or is absent.

Unintended Consequences of Academic Activities Conducted as Rituals:

Religious and social customs reflected in rituals have a symbolic value, and the purpose is to show deference to traditions and conventional practices. They are not productive in terms of progressive contribution to social behaviours. They are primarily meant to sustain conformity in behaviours to continue tradition. However, when ritualistic behaviours occur in an educational context, the difference between 'ritualistic performance' and 'productive performance' is exposed. For example, when faculty performance is measured on the basis of students' feedback, but the feedback data is not analysed and reflected upon, then this feedback mechanism is reduced to a ritualistic procedure. It would not help to improve faculty performance. Similarly, if students' performance is rated only in terms of examination marks, it does not help them improve their learning performance. In both cases, academic activities are conducted only as a ritualistic procedure, where symbolic meaning or optics take precedence over purposeful and productive actions.

Superficial and pseudo involvement is sufficient to complete ritualistic procedures, such as religious rituals. Psychological involvement or commitment is neither needed nor expected by the system because conformity, continuity rather than productive contribution or change and innovations are expected. The latter requires an attitude and climate of openness to question, reflect and modify practices. Similarly, in academic seminars or intellectual discussions, right noises, pet phrases, and clichés prevail, while the important, original and significant are lost in ritualistic gestures. A more serious point is that innovations in practices are encountered with suspicion and hostility in areas of research and pedagogy. These kinds of behaviours on the campuses originate from a climate of insecurity, cynicism and absence of independent thinking and openness to new ideas.

In short, individual attitude, orientation, perceptions and group norms influence behaviours in academic practices and impacts faculty-students realtions in the context of dissemination and creation of knowledge.

Impact of Cynical Attitudes on Institutional Climate-Culture

Cynicism stifles debates and kills eagerness to learn, question, and, more importantly, to share what one has learned while researching and teaching with colleagues and students. At a behavioural level, jokes and sarcasm are used to diminish and humiliate people and damage self-respect or divert serious discussion and critique, which are used as clever tactics to lower the quality of discussion in faculty rooms. Cynicism, which is a form of passive aggression in group dynamics, generates loneliness at a personal level and increases petty intrigues and politicking in groups, usually labelled as organisational politics.

Climate of nepotism: It is ironic that though the system of bureaucracy is supposed to bring impersonal authority in governmental and private institutions of higher education, it actually nurtures a culture of nepotism. Faculty and administrative positions are ensured for husband/wife, father/son, or relatives of the same family in power in privately managed institutions and, to some extent, in public institutions.

Nepotism is sustained by feudal values, where loyalty rather than an independent mind is rewarded, and positions of power are inherited. Entry of intelligent, independent minds is resisted, and tolerance of diverse views in academic culture is not an acceptable norm. The feudal mindset reinforces loyalty, conformity and obedience as supreme values that stifle higher learning and search for truth.

The challenge is 'how do we break the vicious link of cynical attitudes, a culture of nepotism and behaviours that generate negativity, lack of academic commitment, passive cooperation, lack of independent thinking and originality?' It can be best addressed using theory and practical insights from Action Research methodology and learning from best practices from national and international *HEIs*.

It is important to recognise that a climate of attitudes and behaviours in Indian *HEIs* has emerged from structures and processes based on bureaucratic, feudal and more recently, corporate values. It is evident in India and other university campuses the world over. *Gary Rolfe* offers an innovative solution to address the complex problem of dysfunctional academic climate and culture in his book *The University of Dissent: Scholarship in the Corporate University (2013).*

This imaginative solution is about ways to rebuild the university among ruins. More specifically, it is to "create a Para-varsity: a kind of phantom university within an existing institution, dedicated to fostering a culture of thought and collegiality that subverts market-related goals and research".

The author explicitly describes the foundational values of Para-varsity as 'valuable qualities for human existence and dignity'. "They are:

- It promotes excitement, wonder, restlessness, constancy and patience for open-ended understanding.
- It fosters a spirit of inquiry, collective effort and cooperation, constructive criticism, mutual encouragement and correction, inclusion and valorisation of diversity.
- It provides a space where one's individual and collective intellectual energies are sharpened and multiplied so that injustices are named and shamed, and alternatives may be imagined and thought through."

It is important to note that the most preferred option of many a conscientious academic in a university system the world over is for self-imposed '*internal exile*', i.e. disengagement from others. However, it is not an adequate strategy for maintaining an academic climate of freedom and intellectual values mentioned above. It is vital to create such a collective space in the context of *HEIs* because intellectual independence is under threat at the national level in India and the world over from those in power. The option of *Para-varsity* aptly reflects the notion that the creation of a subculture in the midst of the mainstream bureaucratic culture in a university system holds the potential to disrupt conventional values and processes. These deliberate, informal cultural shocks would possibly influence other subsystems towards experimentation, risk-taking, original thinking and heightened self-esteem and professional pride in academic work.

These innovative structures and practices would strengthen the building of robust institutions of higher education in India.

PART TWO
ACADEMIC PERFORMANCE REVIEW SYSTEMS AND ITS IMPACT ON FACULTY BEHAVIOURS

This section of the essay explains how Faculty Behaviours in *HEIs* are impacted by Academic Performance Indicators *(API).*

Historically, the written word was used to disseminate ideas and democratise knowledge. However, today, it is linked with *API* as a measure of performance to be considered for promotion. It has devalued the importance of passionate teaching in classrooms and of passionate writing to enlighten the readers. When academic production is equated with publication, it creates a sinister notion of ownership. One owns what she has written; in other words, the discussions, debates and research inquiry in and outside classrooms are considered less worthy in practical terms for academic careers. Only when the idea is published, one owns it officially. Unfortunately, the intent of publication has less to do with sharing and collaborating and more to do with owning and possessing.

The *API* informs that the evidence of performance is expected to be documented in tangible and, therefore, objective (read quantifiable) terms i.e. the number of projects, conferences, papers, seminars, books, and so on. Those who invest in making classroom teaching a vocation and consider it a sacred space for knowledge-sharing belong to a bygone era of irrelevance. What is more damaging is that 'critical' classroom teaching is under the gaze of those who are pro-establishment in the new regime. In a recent case (2021), a Goa University-affiliated college faculty in political science was threatened with agitation by students belonging to *ABVP*, a wing of *RSS*. According to a press report (*24 October 2020, Indian Express*), she explained in the class how views of *Manu-smriti,* stated in a Hindu text on women, used superstitious idealism as a tool of social control to suppress women. Fortunately, the faculty of many colleges in Goa stood by the assistant professor. They emphasised the autonomy and sanctity of college spaces where faculty has a right to express in debate and share readings of scholars in the field. Similar incidents have occurred in different states for organising talks that take a critical view of Indian history, identity and culture on university campuses since 2016. The point is that the quantitative measurement of academic performance overlooks the qualitative aspects of critical thinking and scientific inquiry in academic processes. Mediocre faculty, however, seems to be happy with the academic routines completed without being intellectually challenged. It keeps the higher authority happy and, hence, keeps their careers safe.

It is necessary to examine the consequences of the legitimisation of non-academic concept of 'ownership' in areas of knowledge production and faculty performance. It is a concept that goes against the foundation of 'universal' education in university since 'ownership' is the opposite of sharing and inclusiveness and the academic norms of how knowledge is generated and disseminated.

Polarisation generates a binary way of thinking in academic culture. It does not allow the notion of simultaneity of processes. One idea is pitted against another and is seen as mutually exclusive. Two examples of polarisation of ideas in higher education discourse are i) patents and innovation vs. understanding and critique, and ii) care and concern vs. individualism and self-interest.

The damaging impact of polarisation on the academic climate is that it weakens the culture of nurturing talent, mentoring young faculty, and collaborating with peers, along with a simultaneous discouragement for innovation and critical thinking. This is one of the prime reasons for the absence of interdisciplinary research and teaching in Indian universities and centres of higher learning. Such a culture is an outcome of polarised thinking models and, in the end, results in rigid structures and processes that are not questioned. It neglects both innovation and concern for others. Rigidity takes over fluidity in thinking processes. Yash Pal committee report to advise on Renovation and Rejuvenation of Higher Education (2009) highlights this point.

Emerging Issues and Questions on Academic Culture

A few critical questions on the purpose of education arise in the context of the prevalent norms of knowledge production and performance.

1. What is the space for teaching-learning processes aimed at facilitating lifelong learning, engaging with students for the sheer joy of learning and the magic of generating ideas through dialogues, discussions and debates?
2. What kind of quality of teaching-learning can be captured and inferred from the data of teacher-student ratio and timetables, schedules or prevalent *API* system of *NAAC* for evaluating the academic performance of faculty?

The result-oriented focus driven by an emphasis on efficiency in individual performance supported by rewards and promotions has unintended consequences. They negatively impact the purpose of higher education and the collaborative processes of the academic activities.

Value Shifts in Campus Behaviours

Significantly, traditional values and their meanings have changed and acquired new connotations in the 21st-century context. For example, competition as a value has replaced conventional feelings of jealousy and hostility. Collaboration and cooperation are substituted by co-option and silent elimination of dissent and independent viewpoint.

It happens in typical day-to-day operations of academic activities, specifically in the area of faculty relatedness with those in authority positions, students and colleagues. Subservience to those in power, considering students as consumers and colleagues as competitors are prevailing norms on educational campuses.

Below is an illustrative case incident on interpersonal and group dynamics on campus. (Farooqi I., 2018). The author, mentioned in the first reference, narrates his experiences as a young faculty member with incisive observations on academic ethos and the relationship between faculty and students, peers and those in authority positions. He writes,

> *"It is the ethos of managing relationships so that everyone is happy and conflicts do not take place. It is based on power equations, and interestingly, students as consumers influence faculty and authority. Decision-making is top-down, and very often, departmental faculty is informed about the decisions taken by higher regulatory bodies like MHRED, UGC, Executive Council and Academic Council and are only asked to follow the directions.*
>
> *"When young faculty who are not familiar with the system seek clarification and ask questions, they are told to ignore for practical purposes since it is futile and impractical to question top decisions. When departmental heads show such a conformist behaviour, young faculty are expected to learn the roles and follow the prevalent norms of 'non- dissenting' behaviours. It happens in many important academic decisions on criteria of assessment like credit system, multiple choice questions for descriptive and analytical subjects in social science, and literature in term-end examinations. Faculty do not question the merits of the new system or even engage in discussions on the impact on learning. There is a tacit understanding to not uttering a word or giving a personal opinion to arrive at a decision."*

The kind of cooperation mentioned above, the author observes, kills independent thinking and encourages faculty to focus on survival and narrow personal gains. It produces a culture of servility that damages the *IB* processes in the long run. Unfortunately, such a culture pervades from top to bottom in academic spaces and attendant environments. Unless, a department or university is autonomous in academic and both the academic and structural sense and are oriented towards exercising academic freedom to question and dissent at the behavioural level, the institutional culture will not be changed and will continue the status quo, despite incremental changes shown on paper and polices at national and state levels.

Not surprisingly, the same author also observes a similar behavioural norm of cooperation, which operates in areas that involve faculty and student interactions. It is generally expected that faculty cooperates with students in areas that do not go beyond helping students in studies, counselling, guiding, motivating and giving direction to career planning.

However, the faculty author further comments that students are helped in a way that makes them dependent on faculty by supplying notes and even dictating in class instead of expecting them to do essential prescribed reading as homework before the class. There is much talk of the use of technological tools and pedagogy of flipped classrooms. However, in reality, no demands are made on students to make them learn self-study material before lectures and develop the thinking skills needed for higher studies. Faculty expects good feedback from students that is relevant to his/her evaluation and career. Therefore, they do not push them to perform academically. It is as if both parties have tacitly agreed to maintain a status quo of mutual cooperation. Since such kind of 'cooperation' benefits both parties, it sets a culture of complacency and insensitivity that harms the quality of higher education in the long run.

The most damaging part of this academic climate of anti-learning 'cooperation' is in the critical area of assessment of students, where questions are asked to get memorised information rather than to test higher cognitive abilities like analysis and synthesis. Since question papers have little variations year after year, students copy from chits in pockets and, more recently, from mobile screens hidden under the sleeves. Faculty hesitate to take stern action so that the so-called norm of cooperation with students is not violated. The institution is more concerned with better results and no failures since that improves its ranking and brand image in the media to attract new batches of students.

The above analysis confirms the validity of the S-P-A-B model (Figure 1) to explain how faculty behaviours and attitudes are influenced and determined by the structures, processes (systems) and values of the *HEIs*. The moot point is how to change and intervene in dysfunctional institutional processes, which is the topic of the next Essay Six on 'Theory and Application of Organisation and Institutional Development'.

REFERENCES

1. Buchanan, D.A., Huczynski, A.A. (1985). *Organisational Behaviour*, Prentice-Hall International.
2. Farooqi, I. (2018). *Previsioning Academic Freedom: Reflections on an early career professional, The Idea of a University* (Ed. Apoorvanand).
3. Harshe, R. (2023). *Pakshi Unhacha: Inside the seven university campuses.* Sadhana Prakashan.
4. Nair, S. (2020, October 24). *Goa Law College stands by professor.* The Indian Express.
5. Orsimi, F. (2018). *Academic Un-freedoms. In The Idea of University* (Ed. Apoorvanand).
6. Padaki, V. (2020). *Organisation Development Revisited.* Management Review, IIM-B

ESSAY SIX

BUILDING INSTITUTIONS: THEORY AND APPLICATION OF OD AND ID

The essay first explains the perspective and methodology of Organisational Development (OD), which is a well-researched and tested methodology for developing all kinds of organisations. Both OD and ID belong to the Behavioural and Organisational Science disciplines and share many similarities but have distinctive features in terms of scope and perspective. The perspective and methodology of OD, when applied to a higher and inter-organisational systemic level, is the domain of Institutional Development (ID). An illustrative case specific to ID in higher education is given to highlight the key issues and challenges in the macro-level institutional development of HEIs in the Indian context. Tools and methods used in OD and ID, like diagnosis, intervention, empowerment, and team-building, are suitable for building educational institutions because they are based on egalitarian values.

Historically, within the perspective of the welfare state, education, along with the health sector, has been considered an integral part of social institutions. However, only in the last few decades, with rapid economic and technological growth, the importance and relevance of higher education to the development of human capital in terms of skills and abilities are recognised and calibrated as a national priority in India. Higher education and public health services are now considered critical sectors of the national economy, along with industry, agriculture, banking and others.

For a better understanding of *HEIs* at the conceptual level, it would be relevant to recognise them as having a twin purpose, social and economic, so that we can apply an appropriate methodology to build and develop them. It implies a simultaneous focus on the social and economic objectives of higher education institutions.

As an organisational theory, the open systems perspective has not only contributed to the understanding of the complexities of institutions but has also led to the development of applied management disciplines like Organisational Development *(OD)* and, more recently, Institutional Development *(ID)*. *OD* offers a coherent package of theoretical perspective + a methodology + tools + skills for building and developing institutions. In contrast, though it has potential in the contemporary context, *ID* is still at a nascent stage of development as a theory and methodology for application. However, the most critical part of the two applied disciplines is their underlying egalitarian and democratic values of building and managing organisations. These values are very relevant for institution building in India since it is the largest democratic country with problems of equity, access, and uneven quality of higher education.

OD focuses on systemic development within the boundary of the organisation, whereas *ID* aims at 'trans-organisational' collaboration, which is an essential process in the theory and practice of developing macro institutions. In *ID*, the institution is conceptualised as an umbrella institution or 'organisation of organisations' that is held together by a set of values and norms which the constituent members or organisations adhere to without giving up their individual goals, pursuits and interests.

The institution-building process at the micro level of higher education, that is, at the university, college, or institute level, can benefit from the insights and methodology of *OD*. It is a multidisciplinary perspective focusing on engaging with simultaneous individual and collective improvement. It uses concepts from various social sciences like psychology, sociology, anthropology, economics, political science, and management. Moreover, it is not restricted to the conventional positivist approach of management science and quantitative research methodology but is open to and uses Action Science, Reflective practice, Ethnography and Phenomenological approaches for institutional inquiry, research and organisational interventions.

In the context of top-down or hierarchical structures and management of higher education at the macro level in India, *OD* offers an alternative of bottom-up or participative approach in diagnosis and intervention for institutional improvement at the micro level so that change and innovation can be planned and implemented effectively. *OD* is based on participative and democratic values because it views any intervention to change and develop an organisation as an ethical responsibility. Therefore, without a mandate from stakeholders and their willingness to accept the change intervention, *OD* should not be initiated by those in power. OD requires the support of those at the top but needs the involvement of people at all levels. In this sense, it is a non-manipulative, open and transparent perspective and methodology that is deployed by institution builders, internal and external change agents or facilitators.

OD is also a normative, re-educative strategy of institutional improvement. Members of the institutions can examine, question, modify, and discard behavioural norms and replace them with more effective norms. Through the Action Learning methodology it minimises the coercive influence of authority and external experts. It is driven by generating grounded data on the day-to-day realities of institutional life to design interventions based on a grounded diagnosis. Stakeholders participate in action learning groups.

OD also offers an empowerment model for individual and organisational change for development. It is based on the assumption that 'people at the workplace and society have a natural capacity for problem-solving and self-development that they have somehow lost due to the conditions in which they operate and exist'. However, they can regain their lost capacity if they learn to build a 'process sensitivity' towards recognising how the situations, either self-made or imposed from above or outside, have shaped or conditioned their attitudes and behaviours that are sometimes functional or dysfunctional. This process of awareness-building propels them to change themselves and the circumstances around them. In overcoming the blocks of attitudes and behaviours to empowerment that are self-imposed and system-driven, they are facilitated to work on systemic, hard and soft aspects of the organisation with the help of an internal or external consultant facilitator.

However, the *OD* methodology of 'sensing-diagnosing-intervention' does not initiate mindset change in the initial stage of inquiry or diagnosis. For example, merely changing the attitude of a faculty or HOD who is a 'difficult or problem person' may not be a solution when the root cause of the problem may lie in the design of roles and structures of the organisation. Therefore, *OD* methodology moves away from conventional management, which focuses on individual and role change. It works on larger and more complex systemic levels of groups, teams, structures, and cultures, as explained in the *SPAB* model (Essay Five). It helps organisations maintain sustainable problem-solving processes wherein organisational problems remain solved and are not repeated subsequently. *OD* emphasises helping people to help themselves and learning process skills to diagnose and solve problems and improve their systems.

In order to come to grips with the systemic reality of micro *HEIs* like universities and colleges, the top academic, administrative authorities and promoters must be involved in the organisational processes. The reason is that the involvement and support of the top management signal to the collective of human resources that there is a continuing commitment from the top to the long-term process of *OD* for change and development.

OD focuses on engagement with interpersonal, group and team processes but limits itself within the boundary of an organisation. In comparison, *ID* goes beyond the organisational level and works on partnership management with other subsystems and institutions because solutions to many problems of micro institutions need inter-departmental and inter-institutional collaboration at a higher or macro level. Educational institutions operate in the context of the state, bureaucracy, market, and society at large; hence, these interfaces also need planned engagement.

At this stage, more clarity and discussion on the theory and methodology of *ID* is pertinent. *ID*, as a distinct but emerging discipline, is at an early stage of development in its theory and application. *ID* is an extension of *OD* and has an overlapping body of knowledge with *OD*, which is a tested and well-researched discipline at the group and organisation levels. *ID* is a theory and practice on inter-organisational transactions and relationships through partnership and networking. However, compared to *OD*, it is a less researched discipline where theory is less developed with grounded evidence on application. *ID* has taken a few baby steps in its application in *HEIs* of India. An illustrative case of the Education Promotion Society of India is presented in this essay as an experiment in *ID* in the context of *HEIs*.

In essence, *OD* is about building organisational culture, values, and identity, whereas *ID* focuses on developing trans-organisational relationships at the systemic level so that *OD* processes of several micro-level institutions are further strengthened and sustained. (*Padaki V, 2003*) Not much documented knowledge and practices are developed in this area, which has the potential to address some serious limitations of application of *OD* with its focus on developing teams and brand-identity of a micro institution as a competitive strategy vis-vis other institutions. This approach, in reality, has restricted the healthy growth of the larger higher education system at the macro level in India. *HEIs* have a collective need to develop processes of influencing policies, coordinating, and managing resources to sustain the developmental process in the larger socio-economic context of the Indian higher education system.

Need for *ID* in the Context of Higher Education in India

Due to its scale of operation and complexity, higher education in India at a macro level faces enormous challenges that sometimes appear insurmountable. National Commissions on Education (2015, 2020) have created relevant and ambitious policies on higher education. However, its implementation is an important task, and India has a dismal record of reforming higher education at the macro-national level. The main reason for this failure is the absence of a sound theory and a political will to introduce interventions at a systemic level of higher education. These interventions, if designed carefully, hold the potential to facilitate the implementation of national policies at regional levels wherein micro and micro institutions of higher education are designed and developed for collaborative synergy.

In the perspective of *ID*, higher education at the macro level is also an institution. It has a meta-organisational entity, which has the potential to become 'purposeful to the extent it facilitates the effectiveness of its constituent organisations'. For example, the apex bodies or regulators of higher education in India, like *UGC*, *AICTE*, and *AIMC*, are expected to perform 'institutional functions' in the interests of constituent organisations like universities, colleges, institutes, etc. However, in the contemporary context of India, they act more like agencies of the State and MoE and focus only on monitoring and controlling micro institutions rather than facilitating inter-institutional processes. In fact, building collaborations at the inter-institute level is not on the agenda of these regulatory bodies. Therefore, there is a need for a meta-institution to perform facilitative functions. It highlights the need for a theory and practice of *ID*, which is rather scarce or absent.

It is also important to recognise that the distinction between macro and micro institutions gets blurred. As an instance, in agricultural research, multiple institutions have been created in the field of preserving microbes. It is initiated by the Indian Council of Agricultural Research *(ICAR)* and many state-level agricultural universities. Such duplication of work wastes public resources and funds and needs one umbrella institution to perform the role of coordinator to facilitate collaboration among institutions. This kind of institutional role can be played by macro or micro institutions as well.

The pertinent point of the essay is that the one-dimensional focus on the development of micro-organisations/institutions is not only dysfunctional but may also be a barrier to the development of the meta-institutional processes. For example, some institutions get more resources at the cost of other institutions, as it happens in the case of elite public institutions like IITs and IIMs or central universities;

they are funded disproportionately by the central exchequer at the cost of resource-starved state universities and colleges in India. There are 459 active state universities and 11,816 affiliated colleges in India (*UGC, 2020*).

A substantial portion of resources spent by *MoE* are given to elite institutions like IITs, which in turn neither share it voluntarily nor are asked to share their facilities and knowledge with average universities and engineering colleges. Therefore, developing an inclusive macro-institution of higher education should be an important objective for the long-term, sustainable development of higher education in India.

The National Knowledge Commission *(NKC)*, as proposed in *NEP (2020)*, is a similar attempt to create a higher education institution to address the issues of improving the quality of higher education and making it relevant to the socio-economic goals of nation-building. However, it is envisaged more as a regulatory body to command and control rather than to facilitate the development of under-resourced micro-organisations like universities and colleges. This has also happened in the case of the previous reports and recommendations of past commissions. In addition, the issue of the ownership and implementation of the recommendations have remained unanswered mainly because the task of *ID* calls for a foundation of a theory-methodology platform. It means that the conventional tools and techniques of developing organisations used in *OD* or national planning would not be effective for the *IB* process at the macro level.

All attempts at higher education reforms have given more power to apex institutions and have made micro institutions powerless or incapable of exercising autonomy in academic matters, and it is the root cause of the low quality of many public and private universities and colleges in India. This paradox of excessive powers bestowed on apex institutions created by *MoE* and the powerless universities, institutes and colleges makes *HEIs* drift from the primary purpose.

Focussing on the task of aligning the vision, mission, strategy and goals of both macro and micro institutions is an essential first step. This would enable macro institutions to facilitate collaboration among different and diverse micro institutions, that is, universities, institutes and colleges, for a common purpose or programme. Without an integrated theory and methodology of *ID,* efforts to add and build more micro institutions *(HEIs)* would not benefit the primary purpose of higher education as envisaged in the reports of the Education Commission, the most recent being *NEP (2020).* Building micro institutions of excellence, for example, more IIMs or IITs, would lead to sub-optimisation of the higher education system where some units benefit at the cost of the whole system.

A recent example of the Education Promotion Society of India *(EPSI)* established in 2005 with the initiative of the private universities in India is a testimony of the impact on how a macro-level institution is built to gain more advantage for private universities and colleges and, therefore, could weaken the public universities and affiliated colleges, that need more resources and attention from the State or *MoE*. *EPSI* is an interesting case of a collective institutional initiative taken recently to represent and coordinate five hundred micro institutions operating as private, autonomous management institutes and universities offering *MBA* and *PGDM* courses.

EPSI: Illustrative Case of Institutional Development *(ID)*

The Education Promotion Society of India *(EPSI)* was established in 2005. Its mission and focus are resource sharing, joint action and lobbying to influence national policy and business corporations favourably on behalf of private universities and institutes of higher education. It needs to be clarified that the two terms, institution building *(IB)* at the micro level and institutional development *(ID)* at the macro level, are used in the context of higher education in the book.

ID functions at the macro level, wherein institutions are 'overseeing bodies' or 'umbrella organisations' and 'organisation of organisations'. In this context, "institutions are held together by a set of values to which the constituent members/ organisations adhere without giving up their individual pursuits or interests." (*Padaki V., Vaz M., 2003*).

EPSI is one of the few examples of ID in India as an 'organisation of organisations' that collaborates and shares resources to influence problem-solving in inter-institutional and inter-sectoral areas. The case describes the mission and activities of *EPSI*. Also, it discusses the main challenges that macro institutions in higher education must address to develop as umbrella-like macro institutions and as an 'organisation of organisations'.

Case: The *EPSI*, established in 2005, is an umbrella body at the macro-level of over 500 higher education institutions such as *XLRI-J*, *MDI-Delhi*, and *Ashoka University*. The mission of the society is mentioned below. (*EPSI website*)

1. to promote, expand and develop the education sector,
2. to cooperate with the government and various other organisations in the country and abroad with a view to further the promotion of education,
3. to be and act as an apex body of institution/agency/unorganised sector in the field of education.

The Society explains its context and purpose as follows:

> '*We (*HEIs in India*) have no agency on behalf of the academic world, for the industry interface or taking up issues with the government. It is the need of the hour to facilitate the academia, industry and government...to face challenges within and abroad... In the challenging environment, enhanced expectations and no effective coordination between the regulator, operators, and acceptors, we have failed to see opportunities in the internal demand in R&D, engineering, design, medical consultation, legal service, HRD, and large employment and education opportunities.*'

The note on the website of this institution concludes with the following words,

> *"Our education system must have a lively interaction, even if it is on business principles, with the rest of the world."*

Also, the note makes references to WTO and affiliations with international universities as well. As the socio-economic context of higher education in India has changed in the first fifteen years of the 21st century, the need exists for macro-level institutions for coordination among the *HEIs*, the State, and MoE with the higher education market that constitutes industry, employers and competing *HEIs*. The terms used in the *EPSI* manifesto are 'regulator, operators, and acceptors.' These are very revealing from the perspective of higher education as a system, wherein *HEIs* are considered operators, which connotes a machine and business metaphor. The role of the state as regulator is to regulate and supervise, and the students and parents are seen as 'acceptors' with the implication that they have no choice but to accept what the regulator and the market of education have to offer.'

In other words, the value premise and perspective of *EPSI* are more consistent with the trend of corporatisation of higher education in India, where a macro institution is created to fulfil the demand of *HEIs* as business operators. Without debating the appropriateness of the perspective, the fact remains that about 500 private universities, professional institutes and colleges have joined the society as members. Hence the need for a macro institution exists to function in the emerging market of higher education.

However, the reality of *HEIs* in India is that, so far, collaborative macro institutions for publicly funded universities and affiliated colleges have not been created where the need is more urgent to create employment opportunities for their students in order to survive in the growing competition from private universities which are supported by policies of the state. They need to ensure secure jobs for their faculty and staff, and above all, need to improve the quality of higher education and human resources. Macro institutions are very much needed for private and public universities in India to facilitate the development of *HEIs* affiliated with state universities, not merely as regulators but as legitimate providers of education and to provide access for those students who need it. Moreover, they should create a system that involves students and faculty as participants in the higher education process and not as passive acceptors of the inputs delivered in classrooms.

In short, the orientation of an *HEI*, both at the micro and macro levels, is reflected in the mission and values guiding its operations. The role of the facilitator of macro *HEIs* is more serious than that of liaison because it responds to the needs of the constituent members and other stakeholders like the state and market. If it is one-way acceptance, then it may benefit only a few institutions and a section of students.

Larger Context of Access, Equity, Quality in Higher Education and the Role of Macro Institutions

EPSI website informs that it conducts seminars, conferences, and workshops on contemporary themes of higher education and works as a national catalyst agency for policy advocacy. It holds discussions and activities in areas of quality improvement, accreditation R&D and consultancy in higher education.

In this context, it is essential to recognise the contradictions in *EPSI's* mission, goals and tasks it intends to undertake and has undertaken or conducted as published in its newsletter. It appears to protect the interests of mainly non-governmental private universities and institutes and has the potential and power to act as a pressure group to influence policy decisions of the State and *MoE*. This reflects that *EPSI* has a limited and narrow vision, which is inadequate to address the deeper and critical problems of higher education at the macro level in India, such as access, equity and quality, along with a shortage of material and faculty resources.

More importantly, *EPSI* has not disclosed its perspective and methodology on how it plans to develop itself as a macro institution. For long-term purposeful sustenance and development, it is essential to have a theoretical perspective, values and a methodology to build an integrated vision, mission, values and practices. The *AR* methodology of simultaneously taking action and research (Action Learning) is more suitable for *ID*. In other words, when a macro institution has an articulated strategic plan of institutional development in terms of its specific processes and learning methodology, it would help sustain its development as a macro institution or an 'organisation of organisations' in the long run.

However, using the methodology of micro institutional development, such as *OD*, with emphasis on team building, identity, culture, and shared internal values as practised in elite private universities, would be dysfunctional in the context of higher-level macro institution building. It is more likely that in the case of *EPSI*, the collaboration and network among private institutions in higher education would pose a threat to public or state universities in the market and impact the latter negatively. The reason is that *ID* at the macro level should not be equated to the cooperation of a selected group or cartel to compete with the rest in the higher education market. The values on which macro educational institutions are built and developed should be broader, developmental, and different from those of micro institutions with private self-interest. The vision and strategy of collaboration should be more inclusive and address the central issues of quality of higher education and human resource development at the national level rather than forming an opportunistic collaboration only to act as a pressure group vis-a-vis the government to get a competitive advantage in the growing higher education market in India in the post-liberalisation period.

Considering the implementation of *NEP 2020*, it appears that the implicit agenda of the national policy is to strengthen the private sector in the higher education market and reduce the resources and grants of public universities by way of providing finances for building a few more *IITs* and *IIMs*. The policy supports the entry of private universities with a brand name as a mark of quality enhancement.

As a result, macro institutions like *EPSI* may not contribute to the vision of the *NEP 2020* document, with its mission to generate collaboration among its stakeholders, because the state policy is not favourable for collaboration between public and private universities. Hence, it is unlikely that macro institutions in higher education in India will develop with the perspective of *ID*, which is built on systemic robustness that remains purposeful in the long run. In simple words, the vision and values that guide macro institutions determine their practices and outcomes.

In short, the main challenge and the gap in the higher education system in India is institution development (*ID*). There is an absence of *ID*, both in terms of theory and practice, due to the promotion of the neoliberal perspective and policies of the Indian state and the subsequent trend in the corporatisation of education. For example, *Ashoka University*, Haryana is one of the many private universities and institutes that are members of the *EPSI*. A well-known faculty and scholar-thinker of *Ashoka University*, *Prof Pratap Bhanu Mehta*, had to resign for his writings in the press, as they were critical of the government in power. An academic of repute neither got support from the institution where he worked nor from other

HEIs in his crisis. It is ironic that the academia of several US and European universities showed solidarity with *Prof Mehta*. It shows how a liberal intellectual academic finds it hard to work in a non-liberal academic and political environment in India.It also undelines the importance of of building robust macro institutions based on *ID* processes.

Similarly, a large section of faculty at Delhi University and its affiliated colleges works on a contract basis of employment for more than a decade without being confirmed. Since such issues cannot be resolved at the individual or micro-institution level, there is a strong need and an emergent requirement for macro-institutional support to address these issues. This is more so in the context of substantial reduction in the power and independence of other social institutions like trade unions of university teachers and media.

Other Challenges of Macro Institutions in India

The micro institutions of higher education are caught between the power play of the state and the market. Both power centres command overt and covert influence over faculty and students of micro institutions because their promoters and management fail to protect them against any injustice. In such a situation, addressing these issues at systemic and structural levels via a well-developed macro institution is the only option. However, it is essential to build such macro institutions on a robust theory and methodology based on research, structures, processes and practices of *ID*. Newly established institutions like the *EPSI* should work towards this goal and expand their membership to public universities and institutes where their services are also needed.

As deliberated upon, at the beginning of the *EPSI* case study, the institution building process necessitates focusing on the purpose of higher education in India in the context of new equations between the state, regulators, and the higher education market. In other words, the vision and mission of a non-governmental macro institution should be based on scanning or analysis of the educational environment in India so that collaboration of some institutions does not lead to unhealthy competition with other institutions. Public universities and affiliated colleges need to be strengthened to realise the larger purpose of access, equity, quality and inclusiveness in higher education at a systemic level.

New Structures and Strategy for Institutional Development

Improving the quality of higher education at the national level depends on ensuring an academic culture and also the self-esteem of the individual faculty members of each *HEI*. Many micro institutions need adequate financial and academic support from the apex institutions like *UGC* and others to focus on their distinct mission and identity, which is under pressure from state control and its market-driven policy.

The task of designing and building collaborative macro-institutions for higher education requires serious attention from the main stakeholders, such as academicians, researchers, administrators, promoters of private universities, local communities, and policymakers in India. Also, it would need redefining their roles for the purpose and creating new structures for macro institutions *(ID)* while retaining the membership of their roles in their respective micro institutions *(OD)*. In other words, they would compete at the micro-institutional level, collaborate at the macro-institutional level, and consider competition and collaboration as complementary forces for survival and growth.

Old and new roles of stakeholders: The transition in taking and making new roles by the stakeholders from micro to macro levels would not happen automatically but only through process sensitivity on 'how things are done' to the day-to-day transactions among different parts configured for the purpose of macro institutions for *ID*. Process sensitivity of top management, faculty, and staff can be built using the *OD* methodology. Also, new multilateral structures need to be replaced in previous unilateral leadership structures of micro institutions. Flexibility in dual roles would occur with process sensitivity, and all stakeholders would be required to learn it while engaged in practice. Action learning of *OD* is an essential methodology for developing process skills.

Two questions: What are the value assumptions in a neoliberal perspective and *ID* perspective? What is the difference between the two value assumptions and their consequences on the *IB* process?

The former relies on the premise of self-interest as a primary motive and competitive spirit as a basis for the progress of effective micro-organisations. Inter-organisational effectiveness in *ID* depends mainly on collaborative behaviours across affiliated members' organisations. It is observed that when the work culture is egalitarian, and the leadership process is based on multilateral structures rather than unilateral structures, there are more chances for collaborative behaviours to occur. For institutional effectiveness, reliance on democratic social structures rather than authoritative leadership, is more conducive. Also, a collective interest is preferred over the self-interests of member organisations. In other words, these value premises need to be accepted formally in the institutional character, though the actual behaviours and attitudes would take time to allow consolidation of the value assumptions in the *ID* process.

On Competition and Collaboration in *HEIs*

Conceptually and thematically, it is significantly vital to comprehend the two behavioural processes as complementary rather than mutually exclusive. Competition brings innovations in policies and practices that usher change, and collaborative behaviours bring continuity and stability. It is important to recognise the pitfalls of oppositional thinking in terms of either-or and polarised thinking. If a balance between competition and collaboration is not maintained in the IB and *ID* process, institutions will face the problem of sub-optimisation. As an instance, problems would emerge from too much competition, leading to interpersonal rivalry and too much cooperation, resulting in 'group thinking' or conformity due to the absence of critical-independent thinking. This would damage the health of the overall higher education system. Similarly, too much of cooperation would stifle innovative ideas, originality and individual initiative. It would be the role and responsibility of the leadership to support continuous 'institutional learning' to maintain the balance of complementary processes of completion and collaboration, which are erroneously seen as opposites and polarities in the popular management discourse of institutions and organisations.

Commitment of Members of Macro Institutions

Unlike organisational membership, macro institutional membership differs in terms of stake holding and affiliation. Organisational membership is often captive in the sense that members are expected to conform to the rules, regulations, standards, norms, and values. In contrast, institutional membership differs in the level of involvement, commitment and degree of stakes. It is an open and flexible membership. Therefore, institutional membership depends more on a value system that needs to be consciously articulated, understood, shared, and reinforced.

In such a situation, the rhetoric of cooperation would not produce collaborative behaviours automatically but can happen only when there is interdependency between the members and the institution. 'When the needs of the member organisation can be fulfilled only through the achievement of institutional goals and when the goals of the institution can be achieved by the fulfilment of members' organisational needs to belong and contribute.' (*Padaki V and Vaz Manjulika, 2003*).

Since institutions are primarily rooted in collectivity, they evolve organically, with a bottom-up process to sustain the purposeful behaviours of the community members. Institutions set up by an external agency like the state or promoters follow a top-down approach and tend to exist to the extent the external agency supports it. They have less capacity for internal survival and development and rely on hierarchical structures and powers to govern members' behaviours.

Institutional Leadership Process

There are two types of leadership roles in institutions: Expert leadership and Facilitative leadership. They require two contrasting working structures. Most educational institutions, both micro and macro, require facilitative leadership and multilateral structures. Problems arise when expert leadership with unilateral structures is imposed on situations where facilitative leadership with multilateral structures is needed. These multilateral structures are suitable to deal with decision-making at multiple points. They require high interdependence and complementary skills.

Summary and Conclusion

The essay describes the theory and application of two disciplines of organisational development (*OD*) and institutional development *(ID)*. The methodology of application has similarities and differences as well. Both focus on empowering institutional members. *OD* is more suitable for strengthening micro institutions such as colleges, institutes, and university. In contrast, *ID* is primarily designed as a collective to synergise the strengths of each institution for a positive impact on society, the economy, and the education system as a whole.

The essay also highlights the limitations of *OD* when its methodology is extended to the macro institutional development of *ID*. Collaboration at the trans-institutional level would need shared values of collaboration and interdependence without giving up the individual identity of each institution. However, both disciplines focus on initiating interventions for change and development at the structural, process, attitudinal and behavioural levels. Compared to *OD*, *ID* as a discipline is an emerging field of theory building an application but has a significant potential to overcome the negative impact of dysfunctional competition among institutions that do not benefit the key stakeholder's students and faculty or improve the quality of higher education at the national level. Institutional development (*ID*) is, therefore, essential to overcome the problems of sub-optimisation of the higher education system in the contemporary context, which is reflected in lopsided development in terms of access, equity, and quality of higher education in India. The essay suggests multilateral structures and facilitative leadership for building robust institutions, which is the theme of the next Essay Seven on Leadership Styles and Processes.

REFERENCES

1. Deshpande, M. (2023, April 28). *Crucial Juncture of Institutions.* Maharashtra Times.
2. Education Promotion Society for India. (n.d.). Retrieved from EPSI website.
3. Hindustan Times. (2019, January 25). All India Survey on Higher Education.
4. Mehta, P. B. (2021, March 19). *Resignation letter of Pratap Bhanu Mehta.* The Indian Express.
5. Padaki, V., & Vaz, M. (2003). *Institutional Development in Social Interventions: Towards integrating inter-organisational effectiveness.* Sage, Delhi.
6. Padaki, V, 2010, *Organisation Development Revisited, Management Review, IIM-B*

ESSAY SEVEN

LEADERSHIP STYLES AND PROCESSES IN HEIs

'Education is all about building bridges' – ***Ralf Ellison***

This essay is presented in three sections. The first section explains the concept of leadership. The second section discusses leaders' styles and their impact on institutional stakeholders. The third section examines the 'social-psychological' theory of organisational leadership. Essentially, leadership is a quality of mindfulness, which is important for top leadership positions and executive roles in educational institutions.

SECTION ONE

In the context of discussing leadership in *HEIs*, it is important to describe the role of a leader and explain the concept of leadership. The distinction between the two terms, leader and leadership, is often blurred. A formal leader is a person with formal authority, such as the principal of a college, *HOD* of a department, or Vice Chancellor of a university, because they carry out special responsibilities to give academic direction and implement the mission of the institution. On the other hand, the concept of leadership includes all persons with executive roles who are engaged in executing the decisions taken at strategic and operational levels. They are executive leaders spread across the institution at all levels and in different functions.

Leadership is therefore a generic term utilised deftly to describe the decision-making process and its implementation at various locations and levels of organisation/institution. It shows that the formal leader holds responsibility on behalf of her team of executive leaders, and as such, she is only first among equals who perform various leadership roles. Hence, leadership operates in a multilateral structure where team members work as a collective and are engaged with tasks of leading and implementing. A formal leader in this context is 'first among a group of peers' as mentioned above, but also a part of her team. This is called the 'collegial structure' of leadership, often followed in innovative academic and research organisations that are less hierarchical, unlike conventional, bureaucratic, top-down structures.

However, it is a fact that Indian universities have a centralised leadership structure with affiliated colleges around. In practice, these institutions rarely use the structure and processes of team leadership. Due to this rigid, unilateral structure with downwardly distributed authority and communication, wherein the leaders remain at the centre of the hub, and the role boundaries are impermeable, collaborative decision-making is not possible. The case study of Ravi Mathai's leadership at IIM-A clearly explains how the director had to make a special effort to build a network and structure of interdependent roles in the institute so that it enabled the faculty team to use the autonomy of the institute for designing innovative academic programs and its effective execution. This is an excellent example of a shared leadership model initiated by a visionary leader like Prof *Ravi Mathai*. (*Case Study Two on 'Leadership and IB'*)

For this to happen, it is necessary to acknowledge the value of leadership potential in persons at all levels of an institution so that the synergy of collective leadership can be deployed to achieve the purpose and mission of the institution. In fact, all those who are in a position to influence internal and external stakeholders are considered part of institutional leadership.

Therefore, it is essential to recognise that leadership is not limited to individuals but inclusive of collectivity. The role of the formal leader is catalytic and facilitative so that the expertise available in functional leadership roles is collaboratively utilised for the larger goal of building institutions.

To appreciate the dynamics of leadership in an institutional context, one must first recognise the distinction between two sides or dimensions of all work organisations:

(a) *Hard:* Concrete, structural aspects, and
(b) *Soft:* Human, cultural dimension.

The hard aspects are manifested in structures, systems, and tasks, whereas the soft elements are revealed through people processes of meaning-making, choice-making, relatedness with others, leader styles and organisational culture. Since organisations are purposeful entities, they are expected to deliver products and services. However, their stakeholders are humans. For example, a building office is a physical part of the organisational structure but lacks self-awareness, which is entirely a human quality. Buildings would not be able to say, 'I am getting old; therefore, paint me now.'

Therefore, the role of the leader is to sense the needs of the structure, systems, purpose of the institution and respond appropriately. Hence, leadership roles in organisations go beyond functional expertise and technical competence. They are essentially facilitative roles. At the highest level, leaders also require a visionary perspective that goes beyond the tasks and expectations of the present, which happens to be a rare but essential quality of institutional leaders.

It is important to ensure that when top positions of public and private institutions are filled in, the criteria of such appointments should be whether the person selected would take the institution forward and give direction to its stated purpose and mission. The fact is that, sometimes, the competence of the person and role requirements do not match. It is observed that a faculty of an elite institution like *IIT* is sometimes appointed as director of a reputed university or as a director of research institutions, which are essentially educational institutions rather than technological institutes. Unfortunately, in recent times, selection criteria are based on questions like 'who belongs to whom' or the ideological leanings of the person. More worrisome is the fact that most appointments for top positions in *HEIs* are delayed, in positions of *VC*, Director and Principal. Therefore, important decisions in institutions are not taken or delayed, and hence the careers and morale of young faculty members are negatively affected. Thus, problems in leadership in educational institutions in India are often linked to the apathy of policymakers and those in power.

Developing Faculty Leadership in *HEIs*: Learning Reflective Practice

If leadership is more of a role rather than a position or office, then it is possible that faculty and staff of an educational institution would be able to take personal initiative to slip into this role while being engaged with the tasks of teaching and administrative functions. Those involved with teaching and administrative roles in educational institutions can benefit from applying the methodology of Reflective Practice *(RP)*, which is often used in the context of faculty and teacher development programmes in many countries (*Dymoke Sue*, *2009*).

Essentially, *RP* is about asking searching questions about experiences at offices, classrooms, activities and interactions on campus. It is conceptualised as a state of mind and an ongoing behaviour. This means that teachers and administrators would examine their personal experiences at the workplace in an open but safe environment, supported by senior colleagues and the top management in educational institutions. It is a psychologically useful tool to maintain the well-being of employees. It is more useful for deeper learning because the work experiences in schools and colleges are embedded in the larger political and social structures. Moreover, *RP* also helps develop a consciousness of one's personal and professional identities.

The point is that the above-mentioned 'soft' aspects of developing consciousness of 'being' in the workplace depend on the human capacity for self-awareness, consciousness, and sensitivity towards self and others. Those who are in a leadership position need enough maturity to contribute and make up for the inevitable gaps in material or human resources, structures and systems. They are the tangible aspects of organisational design, primarily oriented towards the efficient performance of tasks that are mechanical or routine processes. In other words, institutional leaders need to have the capability to overcome the deficiencies of rational and technical dimensions of the hard system. (*2×2 diagram on Four Dimensions of Institution in Essay One*). Human or soft dimensions go beyond the usual bureaucratic and reactive styles of leading, which are reinforced by the technical rationality of work organisations. This kind of shift in style is possible only when the leaders remain sensitive to their 'self' and others, so that they are not overly preoccupied with personal anxieties and insecurity. The processes of leading depend on the development of human consciousness of the collective at the workplace and it can be learned through Reflective Practice methodology.

Unfortunately, in Indian educational institutions, it is observed that those in positions of authority and power, from vice-chancellor to professors to lower operational levels, many are seen to be preoccupied with their insecurity and anxiety about the present and future of their careers. It deprives them of developing a precious human quality of interpersonal sensitiveness, simply about 'whatever I grant to myself and value, I shall grant the same to others', which is rather absent. Self-preoccupation and insensitivity make a person either 'reactive or passive'. As a consequence, these leaders show a tendency to hoard, over-control and micro-manage. Above all, such a person loses his/her capacity to listen and engage with colleagues, staff and students.

Institutional leaders need sensitivity and pro-activeness to add value to the collective processes because self-centred leadership is the antithesis of building an institution to face the present challenges and work for a future vision.

A TYPOLOGY OF LEADERS' STYLES

Other variations of dysfunctional leadership styles and behaviours on educational campuses are analysed in depth by a senior management consultant and education advisor, *Raja Krishnamurthy.* It is a typology of leaders' styles that distinguishes various shades of leader behaviour and its impact on others and organisations.

Mr. Krishnamurthy (2003) observes that the main distinction between an organisation and an institution is the quality and type (style) of its leadership because even a well-managed organisation may not be able to reach the status of an institution due to the absence of leadership which is an essential factor in institution building process.

Many potentially capable organisations remain bureaucratic or focus more on procedures and hierarchy but are less concerned about other dimensions of institutional leadership. These qualities are about behavioural orientations, such as quality of self-awareness, sensitivity to self and others, proactivity, principle-centeredness, and regeneration.

These mental and behavioural dispositions of leaders bring maturity and higher quality to the institution-building processes, which is the central theme of *IB*. To understand and anticipate how different combinations of positive and negative leader qualities impact each style in terms of behavioural consequences in organisations, a typology of styles given below would be helpful to the readers. These styles or behaviours positively or negatively impact key internal stakeholders of educational institutions like students, staff, parents, and faculty; external stakeholders like competing institutions, society, and industry. Therefore, it is necessary to explain the main dimensions of leadership styles that can serve as a guide for leader development.

Five attitudinal orientations of leadership are:

(a) Proactive, or Reactive, Passive
(b) Over concern for self, under concern for others, or simultaneous concern for self and others
(c) Coercive, Controlling or Facilitative, Collaborative
(d) Having an attitude of commentator, cynic, and judgmental expert
(e) Self-awareness, sensitivity with action orientation for problem-solving

Let us consider and calibrate in a detailed manner, the opposing side or counterpoints of each dimension and its perspective. The opposite of the first dimension, which is proactivity, is reactivity or passivity. When the reactivity is low, the leader shows sensitivity to self and others. An open and positive outlook helps institutional transformation because the leader simultaneously owns the responsibility towards herself and the system. However, when the leader is high in proactivity but more self-preoccupied rather than having concern for others, it leads to a coercive and controlling orientation. Hence, even when the leader takes many initiatives and shows a high level of action orientation, it has a negative impact on others and organisations in the long run.

Contrarily, in the case of those (leaders) with a high level of sensitivity but a low level of proactivity, it leads to the stance of an expert commentator of life. They are more consultants than leaders due to a lack of active involvement and ownership. Those with a high level of reactivity, but, possess intellectual clarity tend to remain *eternal critics* of the system but fail to provide any positives. Leaders without conceptual or intellectual clarity remain *cynics* and join the common '*cribbing clubs*' in many organisations. They pass judgment and irresponsible comments toward others, stay in the role of 'spectator, commentator' and sometimes even become *spoilsport or cynics.* It is relevant to refer to Essay Five on Understanding Behavioural Processes in *HEIs* in this book to get concrete examples of cynics, spectators, opportunists and commentators in many faculty groups of state universities in India.

To summarise, the four leadership styles that emerge from behavioural combinations are:

(a) Philosopher – leader
(b) Dictator – Controller
(c) Expert – Commentator, and
(d) Spectator

When the three opposites or negatives of high reactivity, high passivity, and high self-preoccupation coexist, the fifth leadership style emerges – the *Eternal cynic, w*ho tends to pollute the climate and culture in organisations and is quite prevalent in many universities and affiliated colleges in India.

The essential quality of institutional leadership is *principle-centeredness*, or being a *Drashta,* who holds the detached attachment of a 'Seer', balancing short-term and long-term goals. This leadership attitude emerges from a conviction in basic human values that depends on one's ability to witness life experiences with detachment. It is a level of self-awareness that operates on conviction in principles or values rather than convenience and opportunism. It enables the person to give and contribute to the system rather than exploit the institution for personal benefits or remain an eternal consumer rather than a giver or contributor.

To synthesise elements of leadership typology mentioned above, one would find some casual connections in these qualities:

(a) High sensitivity and low proactivity lead to an '*expert commentator.*'
(b) High sensitivity and reactiveness lead to '*eternal critic*',

However, the most common leadership stances in educational institutions are:

(a) A *spectator and eternal* cynic, which is a combined outcome of reactivity, passivity and high self-preoccupation.
(b) Controller and opportunist orientation without principle-centeredness.

Both the stances have a similar and negative impact on institution-building (IB) processes.

Governance and Leadership

In the Indian context, *HEIs* badly need leaders who are investors and creators rather than mere bureaucrats or careerists. However, educational institutions sometimes get principle-centred leaders with a deficit mind-set. They are the best bureaucrats or administrators, particularly VCs in universities, but they fail to replenish or transform the higher education *system*. They execute changes in systems and procedures in admissions, examinations, teaching-learning, and research, but they tend to act from the point of convenience rather than conviction. In the long run, self-centred and bureaucratic leaders damage institutional processes because they focus on the next career opportunity. Good governance without vision has a limited impact on institution building. An example of the submission of resignation letter by the director of *NAAC* to the chairman of the *UGC* exposes the weak governance practices of the apex higher education institutions. *NAAC* (1994), as a regulatory body, is expected to maintain high quality standards and credibility for all *HEIs* in India. The director had alleged that affiliated colleges and institutes get higher grades in quality evaluation at *NAAC* by illegal and corrupt means. (*Maharashtra Times*, 6 March 2023) It shows the relevance and urgent need for good governance practices to control and maintain accountability at the top level of the regulatory body.

However, whether the Director's resignation can be considered a step towards good governance practice is a moot question. Though a resignation may be a morally correct response, it is debatable how the root cause of malpractice in institutions is located and squarely dealt with. In an informal discussion, the director revealed that he had made a yearlong effort to reform the system but could not succeed. Moreover, he informed the press that his letter was wrongly taken as a resignation letter by the higher authority, then chairman of *UGC*. To cut the long story short, it appears that he had to relinquish his position because he exposed the grave lapses and lacunae in the system. An opportunity to reform the system by an insider was lost in the process which would damage robustness of the institution in the long run

Good governance practices and leadership behaviours are also dependent on a larger ecosystem of higher education in India. Building a climate for good governance is a real challenge so that top leadership can focus on the primary task of higher education. This would help confrontation with challenging issues and corrupt practices without pushing them under the carpet to protect vested interests.

In other words, individual leadership as a chairman of *UGC* or VC of a state or private university would require a courageous and visionary orientation to transform *HEIs* in India towards good governance. Interestingly, it is also observed that many top leaders of *HEIs* in India had complained about poor governance practices only at the end of rather than during their careers. However, rarely can we find leaders at the top of national institutions who are ready to protest publicly and, at the same time, transform the system from within during their tenure. Top leaders of educational institutions may not necessarily be tall leaders! Also, the macro socio-economic and political environment in India fails to nurture or sustain quality leadership at the top. This is a serious challenge in robust institution building for higher education in India.

The larger ecosystem of higher education is transformed by such ethical practices of leaders in all fields. Needless to say, the climate of poor governance practices remains entrenched in India even though individuals at the top have the potential for visionary and transformative leadership.

Role of Collective Leadership

The above description and analysis of limitations of individual leadership qualities and styles highlights the fact that collective wisdom and leadership are as essential as individual leaders for institution building. When an individual leader shows common behavioural weaknesses, such as reactivity, insensitivity, deficit mind-set, and passivity, it is the role of the collective leadership in institutions to take the initiative and compensate for the deficiencies or intervene in processes. However, the presence of collective wisdom is dependent on how macro-level national leadership, micro institutions and society as a whole have nurtured democratic and egalitarian values in family, judiciary, industry, media, bureaucracy and government. When collective and democratic leadership is a norm in community and national culture, it permeates the social, economic, and educational institutions of society.

Historically, institutions in corporate and educational sectors have several examples where collective leadership within and collaboration with other stakeholders have saved many Indian institutions from misuse and degeneration. For example, the leadership style of *Dr. Verghese Kurien*, founder and chairman of NDDB from 1965 to 1998 *(AMUL)*, transformed rural India and made India the largest producer of milk. He set up a cooperative structure wherein the organisation is not owned by an individual but by all producer members who are the stakeholders and decision-makers at every stage. (*DNA, 2019*). As a leader, Dr. Kurien is remembered for personal integrity, honesty and commitment to the values of cooperation and protection of farmers' interests at any cost. His professionalism and search for excellence faced challenges from politicised cooperative organisations in the later years of his career. This is an example of how an institutional leader can withstand the pressures of macro institutions and political bosses. However, these leaders had to pay the price for their courage, conviction and values.

The case of *AMUL* highlights the need for institutional robustness of systems, values and strong leadership that truly represent the composite collectivity to survive and replenish. Social institutions can adequately face challenges when institutional robustness help them maintain flexibility to survive and grew during changes in socio-economic and political environment. The future of our institutions and democracy hinges on such amalgamation of the collective wisdom and leadership, which need to be nurtured by all concerned citizens for a better future of Indian society.

SECTION THREE
SOCIAL-PSYCHOLOGICAL THEORY OF LEADERSHIP

Research on organisational studies and social psychology, has, enriched development theory and related concepts on leadership processes in all kinds of work organisations. These studies and research have been conducted for decades on data on community behaviours to explore social and psychological processes in groups. They help explain how social-psychological processes affect the behaviour of those who take the role of a leader and also those who work with them or follow them. These studies provide valuable insights into the minds of those who are in leadership roles and the emotional, intellectual and ethical challenges that they face. In the context of *HEI*s, leadership sub-roles are shared at various locations of the institution, from the board of governing council to principal and faculty, from vice-chancellors to heads of various departments in the university system. These sub-roles provide information and generate learnings to support the leader in making choices and facing challenges in the development of leadership.

When leadership is considered as a role rather than a position, then entry into and performance in this role is defined by leaders' emotional, moral, intellectual, and behavioural orientations. In this sense, leadership demands the best human capabilities in terms of thinking, feeling, action, and moral judgement. However, one must conceptually distinguish a leader from leadership to understand the leader's role; a leader may be appointed as the head but may not perform leadership function and role. On the other hand, without formal office, one may influence the institution and perform the role of a leader informally. The position of leader makes the individual accountable, but leadership as a role focuses on individual and mutual accountability. Leadership is essentially a shared responsibility spread over the institution and a collective phenomenon. However, the top leader is accountable for leadership functioning at all levels and dimensions.

According to *Theodore Mills* (1988), who conceptualised leadership roles from a social psychological perspective, there are four key features of leadership roles, specifically, from a theoretical perspective of the sociology of group behaviours. The theory is based on concepts of social-psychological processes in work groups. It highlights the subtleties and complexities of cognitive and emotive processes in the mind and behaviours of those in leadership or executive roles at the top.

The theoretical premises of the social-psychological perspective are:

(a) A role is not limited to parts, levels or subsystems, and the responsibility of the role is to the total dynamic configuration of a person in an organised group within a changing environment. It is similar to the role of parents in a family life situation and the role of the head of government in a historical situation. It includes all experiences like routines of interactions, interpersonal and intergroup attachment, animosity, feelings of trust or mistrust, confidence or anxiety, elation or sadness, also the implicit and explicit beliefs and values. The leader's role is concerned with these multilevel and differentiated but interdependent configurations. They are processed in the leader's consciousness. Hence, consciousness is the seat or location wherein experiences, feelings, and interactions are synthesised for meaning-making.

(b) As a consequence of the above feature, the leader identifies with the meta group of the institutions and is concerned about the process of 'becoming' and has to make choices with and for the group. Since the process of 'becoming' is unpredictable and complex, the choice-making in a leader's role cannot be guided by a simple set of formulae or rules like those used in limited, bureaucratic roles. Choices are made at process and interaction levels.

(c) Disowning or de-committing from old roles and taking new roles are critical in leadership roles as the leader has to advance from an instrumental, task-focussed role at the operational level to a transformative role at higher levels of consciousness. It is his/her responsibility to evaluate alternative goals and to change the current goal if needed. In a maintenance role, the leader is concerned with questions like who sets the rules, how they are set and, if necessary, how their legislation might be changed. In an expressive role, the leader is concerned about not only the expression of feelings but also how those feelings are expressed or suppressed, whether they present possibilities for exploration or place limits upon what the group can understand about itself and what it can do with it. In brief, the leader assumes the role of what the group 'might become' rather than what 'it has been' so far.

d) From a psychological point of view, a leader is both an insider and an outsider in the group or community. A leader's stance vis-a-vis social system is comparable to the role of the ego in the Freudian (psychology) framework of the structure of the mind and personality, which has three layers of the mind conceptualised as Id, Ego and Superego. The ego manages forces both from within and from without and must maintain its dual orientation if it is not to collapse with a loss of identity. These processes are internal and invisible processes that are internally experienced by the person and reflected in the behaviours of the leaders. Maintaining identity at individual and collective levels is the key task of a leader.

(e) The social systems theory of leadership makes a distinction between leader as a person and leadership as a shared or collective phenomenon. Hence, it is helpful to conceptualise leadership as a social 'system' and 'process' rather than as a person in a specific role. In an institutional context like a university or college, the leadership system means a set of all leadership orientations and processes that are distributed across all levels, organised and performed by the members of the institution in different locations. In fact, any member, regardless of position or office, who performs a role in an executive system or undertakes any executive act, whether normal, routine or unique, that resembles the performance of the leadership function is recognised as a part of the leadership system.

The 'system of leadership' is also concerned with how it monitors behaviours, emotions, norms, beliefs, goals, and organisational processes of the institution. For that, the system requires a feedback system of assessment and performance review so that decision-making and learning take place. In short, a leadership system is a 'set of orientations and processes' that are distributed and maintained among members across institutional space.

Two Challenges in a Leadership Role

1. *Theodore Mills* (1988) emphasises the depth of awareness of 'self and situation' as an essential quality of leadership role. The first challenge in taking this role is in the area of knowing about the collective consciousness. A leader is concerned about increasing group capabilities in terms of what the group is and also what it can become. However, there is a serious limitation to getting complete information on self-awareness and development of each individual and the group at any moment and on the ongoing activities. This is because the consciousness of any human group cannot be fully realised to have access to complete information. Therefore, a leader has to accept the invalidation of her assumptions and evaluation of others and the group with an attitude of humility. Creating spaces in collectivity for generating valid data and testing it openly, formally or informally is essential for a reality check so that the danger of untested/uncontested assumptions and decisions is averted. Hence, a leadership role demands a readiness on the part of leaders to revise and unlearn past knowledge that they have acquired. In this situation, the leader has to screen and select information with some frame of reference or thinking frames to distinguish what is relevant and important from the unimportant and insignificant in a context. It is vital to use a theoretical/conceptual basis to take a parodic, critical review of the data and actions taken.
2. The second challenge for the leader is in the area of doing or changing the group behaviours and status quo. Leadership in all domains, such as political leaders, social reformers, and poets, have to face these challenges when they attempt to reform collective consciousness. When they realise that it is beyond their powers to modify and rejuvenate, they have to be humble and imaginative to design interventions that may not radically disturb the present state but use minor interventions that have the potential to trigger a larger impact. Leaders can achieve better results in organisational performance when they can diagnose with a perspective or a theory that helps them distinguish between the cause and the symptoms so that they can select a feasible and ideal solution.

The analysis of *Theodore Mills* ends with a conclusion on the most essential leadership competency as mentioned below:

> *"The most important ability for those in leadership roles is to work with limited information and limits of personal consciousness. No one can be omnipotent but the leader is placed in a situation that demands access to all variables in the situation and therefore has to rely on the unique human abilities of a) learning how to learn and b) learning how to intervene."*

The above conclusions implies that leadership competence depends on a consciousness of the subtleties of meaning-making processes, a domain Phenomenology, which is discussed in detail in Essay Eleven, which delves upon 'Qualitative Research for Change and Transformation'. It is possible to fine-tune these skills by asking questions that require judgement, for example, 'Which elements are of critical relevance? Which are important combinations of the elements? And from the many alternative actions which are strategic with impact?' Though individual judgements demand complete and intuitive familiarity with the situation of the group or organisation, the leader would benefit from a framework of thinking about the dynamics of group behaviours at workplaces based on Mill's theory of leadership behaviour.

Leadership Roles in *HEIs* Context

The essay concludes with a note on academic leadership in the context of educational institutions in India, wherein hierarchical structures of bureaucracy and expertise-based leadership are the norms that govern the practices of the system.

Generally, in hierarchical structures of organisations, a leadership role requires a design that is highly differentiated, with specialised functions, so that work is performed independently and efficiently. The output in such structures is additive as it adds and coordinates the outputs from other roles. The leader is a subject expert who holds a single point of decision-making. Manufacturing organisations in a stable environment are structured on such differentiated leadership roles.

In contrast, educational institutions need another kind of leadership because they require dynamic and flexible roles since the environment, either internal or external, is not static, and circumstances keep changing. In the field of higher education, the dynamic part of the environment constitutes a) the inflow of students with new aspirations, b) changes in knowledge leading to changes in curriculum design and delivery, c) the interdisciplinary nature of research and learning, and d) market competition to attract faculty and students. Therefore, leadership roles and academic, research and administrative functions become interdependent, and the end output is expected to be synergetic for maximum impact. This requires 'facilitative' rather than expert leadership, and many academic leaders are not prepared for it because they come with a background of functional expertise or subject expertise. For example, the skills needed for top positions like VC in universities are complex and demanding. Usually, senior professors, as faculty, who are subject specialists, are not exposed to these roles.

To illustrate the unique features and demands of a leadership role in the educational context, one can examine the role of the vice-chancellor of a university, a director of a regional or national level institute of higher education or a member of a board of governing council in order to analyse the kind of leadership behaviours desirable for these roles.

Two roles at the top level of managing higher education institutions are: (a) Academic administration, and (b) Academic processes.

Academic administration involves managing human resources and financial management as well. It includes functions like staffing, selection, appointment of faculty and staff and deciding on the promotion criteria. It also involves allocating funds and generating other funding sources along with tuition fees and determining the proportion of official and private work like consulting, research projects, etc. Both areas of leadership need critical decision-making and accountability. However, the level of discretionary decisions is higher in the area of academic processes. Therefore, accountabilities need to be internal professional values and norms to ensure that operations and decisions are implemented in a fair and proper way. Therefore, academic leadership requires behavioural and value-based competencies explained in Section Three on Learning Resources.

Since an institution is a collective of people, leadership is a collective phenomenon; each decision must be based on clear reasons and good justifications. In a university system, leadership is accountable to the senate and the society at large, and leadership is expected to demonstrate fair and firm adherence to the norms without fear and favour. Academic leadership require a facilitative leadership style, which can be more effective in multilateral rather than unilateral structures.

In contrast, professional expertise can best perform administrative roles in specific functions, such as law, finance, human resources, and education. It also requires structural and centralised authority, but many of the decisions need broad consensus among stakeholders. Therefore, the leader in an administrative role also requires, to some extent, competencies to nourish collective leadership at all levels. Hence, it would be wrong to conceptualise leadership in educational institutions as the job of a specific leader that requires only functional expertise in her subject or discipline.

Synthesis

The concept of leadership comprises individual and collective behaviours that shape *IB* processes. The effectiveness of leadership in *HEIs* depends on multilateral, decentralised structures so that initiatives for decisions and actions can be taken at multiple locations at all levels. Development of leadership qualities would require knowledge of phenomenology, reflective practice and soft or human skills, which are different from technical skills. It shows that problems and issues in higher education and its institutions cannot be resolved only by using information technology-enabled services. Leadership needs multiple competencies, conceptual and behavioural. Above all, executive minds need to be anchored in professional and ethical values to offer visionary leadership for *HEIs*.

REFERENCES

1. Agarwal, P. (2009). *Indian Higher Education: Envisioning the future.* Sage India.
2. Datar, S., Garvin, D.A., & Cullen, P.G. (2010). *Rethinking MBA: Business Education at Crossroads.* Harvard Business Press.
3. Dymoke, S., & Harrison, J. (2008). *Reflective Teaching & Learning.* Sage.
4. Krishnamurthy, Raja. (2003), IMDR. *Proceedings of the Second Pulin Garg Memorial Symposium on 'Institution Building'.*
5. Maharashtra Times. (2023, March 6). *Editorial, Question on NAAC.*
6. Mills, T. M. (1988). *The Sociology of Small Groups.* Prentice-Hall of India.
7. Pareek, U. (1981). *Beyond Management.* Oxford & IBH.
8. Thompson, Q. (2018). *International reflections on university autonomy and freedom. In The Idea of a University.* Context, Chennai.
9. Vaz, M., & Padaki, V. (2003). *Institutional Development in Social Intervention.* Sage.

Essay Eight

Institutional Purpose: Vision, Mission, and Strategic Planning

"Without vision, we have no context for feedback; we are just responding to what someone else values or wants. We fall into the trap of trying to become all things to all people, meeting everybody's expectations, and we end up eventually meeting nobody's, including our own. But with a clear vision and mission, we can use feedback to help us achieve a greater integrity." – ***Stephen Covey***, (1989).

This essay explains the relevance of an articulated vision, mission, and values statement with examples of three reputed institutions of higher learning. It also explains the method of strategic planning in order to achieve the purpose and goals stated in the vision-mission (V-M) for the survival and growth of an institution.

The purpose and avowed objective of higher education stated at the national policy level and the purpose-in-action of micro institutions of higher education are distinct and different. The former focuses on broad idea of the purpose of university education as 'search for knowledge and truth'. In case of micro-institution, vision-mission is conceptualised in terms of the specific regional, socio-economic and historical context. Hence the vision-mission of an institution is meant tomobilise its internal stakeholders such as faculty, staff, promoters, board members, and students. Since the mortality rate of new organisations in business and non-business sectors is relatively high, it is vital to have a long-term vision and mission for institutions, more so for an educational institution, because it is responsible for building the future of the young generation and consequently of the nation.

Therefore, *HEI*s are expected to commit and contextualise themselves to a statement of purpose in terms of a vision-mission. In this process, they benefit from initiating a process of strategic planning to ensure that the vision-mission statement is periodically reviewed to keep the institution on track. Strategic planning aims to come to grips with the reality of the institutional context through an environmental scanning exercise so that the vision mission does not remain merely on paper but is implemented. In other words, the purpose of an institution is articulated in its vision and mission statement, which in turn is implemented through a systematic process of strategic planning.

According to the viable systems perspective of organisation theory, the long-term goals of work organisations are sustainability, growth, and development. Institutions of education also have multiple stakeholders whose expectations extend beyond 'profit maximisation' for shareholders, as in the case of business and industrial organisations. However, thanks to the neoliberal policy of the state, in the contemporary context, both business and education institutions operate in a competitive environment with multiple players in the market. This necessitates a consciousness about the purposiveness of their organisations. Vision, mission and strategic planning are valuable tools to keep the organisational focus on the primary purpose for both business and educational institutions.

The reality of higher education in India shows that although there is growth in the number of colleges and institutes, not all institutions are able to survive. Akin to small and medium enterprises (*SMEs)* in industry, the mortality rate is relatively high for unviable organisations in both industrial and education sectors. For example, in the last two decades, it has become evident that not all colleges and institutes can survive and sustain themselves in the competitive market in India. In other words, like the high mortality rate of the *SME* sector in industry, many engineering and management colleges and institutes have applied for closure in *AICTE* in recent years. They are unable to survive for various reasons, particularly in terms of the quality of courses and the reputation of the institutions in the market.

Therefore, organisations in all sectors, both business and non-business, are compelled to work on a systematic strategic plan (*SP)* for future direction with a purpose to remain viable and sustainable. One of the key elements of the strategic planning exercise is to develop a '*vision-mission-goals*' flow chart to get necessary feedback on the institutional performance that would help in course corrections.

In other words, the vision of an educational institution informs 'where the significant institutional stakeholders aim to be, as a collective.' Moreover, the mission highlights 'what they do' and 'What makes them different from others'.

The common point between vision and mission is that both help clarify the purpose and identity of an educational institution.

The function of the vision statement is to focus on how the institutional stakeholders see themselves some years from now. It inspires them to give their best because it is generally developed in a participative and collaborative process. The mission statement generally lists broad goals and aims for which the organisation is formed. Its prime function is internal, that is, to specify key measures or success criteria to achieve targets and performance. It is meant for all those who contribute to the outcomes: employees, students, faculty, staff, project teams, advisors, and the governing board members.

More precisely, the mission focuses and addresses the questions on '*What do we do, and why do we do what we do?*' It also specifies, '*For whom do we do it and Why?*' The mission is a combination of institutional goals and values as well. It distinguishes an institution from others operating in the field or the market because it specifies its target group and the values that drive institutional members to engage and commit to the goals they have set for themselves. These values define the unique identity of the institution.

Since the vision and mission enumerate the primary purpose and values of the institution, no drastic change is introduced in these statements in the course of any institutional change and evolution because they are embedded in its identity and values. Based on the socio-economic, technological and cultural changes in the environment, institutional goals may change in the course of its evolution to keep the system viable and sustainable. However, any change in the vision and mission of an institution would require careful consideration so that its primary purpose remains intact and is not compromised.

In times of crises or loss of direction in the growth and evolution of the institution, revisiting and reflecting on the vision and mission prove imminently useful in finding out the deviation and its impact on performance, values, and stakeholders.

Some organisations specify *values* and *norms* that would guide the behaviors of internal stakeholders. They define deeply held beliefs and principles that the organisational values. Identifying the values that covertly govern organisations is an important step to articulate vision and mission.

"Service before self" is a value statement of the Indian Army, and "We respect our customers; fellow associates" is a revised value statement of the State Bank of India (*SBI*) in the context of competition in the post-liberalisation period. Both are large institutions of repute. However, organisational values are also expressed unconsciously through behaviors that are not formally announced. An interesting example of how values are expressed without management intervention or expectations is of the Indian Hotels in the 26-11 attack in Mumbai. The staff of Taj International Hotel showed exemplary behavior in allowing the customers in the restaurant and suites to be evacuated first by the rescue operators, and the Taj employees were the last to leave the premises. When the then chairman, *Mr Ratan Tata,* was asked to explain the reasons behind the exemplary behaviour and how it happened, he was candid enough to say that he was unable to offer any rational explanation since the management neither mandated it nor was any formal training on disaster-appropriate behavior was given to them. Hence, it can be inferred that the only possible explanation is in the beliefs and values embedded in the institutional culture and collective consciousness that Taj employees expressed spontaneously in a crisis.

Let us also discuss a few examples of vision-mission statements of *HEIs* in India and show how they highlight the distinguishing features of identity, purpose and values of these institutions.

Three examples of *HEIs* are mentioned below: a) *TISS, Mumbai, b) IIT, Mumbai, and c) IMDR, Pune.*

Example 1: *Tata Institute of Social Sciences (TISS), Mumbai (1936)* is an autonomous institute of Mumbai University, managed by Tata Trust.

Vision of TISS: 'To be an institution of excellence in higher education that continually responds to changing social realities through the development and application of knowledge towards creating a people-centered, ecologically sustainable and just society that promotes and protects dignity, equality, social justice and human rights for all.'

The vision statement focuses on the purpose 'to be an institution of excellence' and also informs on the means of reaching it by i) continually responding to changing social realities, ii) development and application of knowledge, and iii) creating a people-centred, ecologically sustainable and just society. It also makes institutional values explicit, such as promoting and protecting human dignity, equality, social justice and human rights for all. In short, the vision statement constitutes 'Purpose + Values'.

The mission statement of TISS articulates the guiding principles of institutional goals of teaching-learning processes, and governance for faculty, staff and management. Interestingly, the mission consists of 'guiding principles' which are embedded in institutional values.

Guiding principles mentioned in the mission of TISS:

(a) Accountability and transparency in work matters
(b) Decision-making in management and organisation processes which is collective, participatory and non-hierarchical
(c) Pedagogy, which is participatory and experiential, fostering dialogue, mutual learning and critical reflection
(d) Freedom of expression and cultural, ideological and intellectual diversity.

In summary, the vision, mission and values of TISS are:

Vision: To be an institution of excellence, continuously responding to changing social realities and creating a just society.

Values: Dignity, equality, justice, freedom, transparency, human rights for all

Mission: Teaching-learning through workplace values of TISS: transparency, participative, non-hierarchical climate, and freedom of expression.

Example 2: *Indian Institute of Technology (IIT) Mumbai.*

Vision: To be the fountainhead of new ideas and innovations in teaching and science.

Mission: To create an ambience in which new ideas and creativity flourish and from which research, scholarship, leaders and innovations of tomorrow emerge.

Core values: Integrity, Merit, Academic freedom, Excellence, Innovation

The vision-mission statement of *IIT Mumbai* also mentions specific goals as a part of the mission statement as under:

(a) To provide the best possible educational facilities for training bright students for careers in technology and science
(b) To provide research, development and consultancy that will promote contact with and be of service to industries, government and civic organisations
(c) To provide leadership in curriculum design and development

Example 3: Vision-mission and values of *Institute of Management Development and Research, Pune (1974); The first self-regulated, autonomous B-School in Pune.*

Vision: 'IMDR is a learning community that strives to be productive, creative and open. Here, every member, staff or student has sufficient freedom to pursue his own interests while meeting common interests.'

Mission: (i) to prepare professionals for down-to-earth performance, (ii) to develop students into thoughtful and sensitive professionals, (iii) to prepare professionals who examine and modify their own practice for short-term and long-term effectiveness, (iv) students focus on personal, professional and social domains of development

It is interesting and insightful to find similarities and differences in the values and mission of the three institutions, which reflect each institution's identity. For instance, the vision of *IIT Mumbai* focuses on new ideas, innovation, merit, bright students, professional integrity and excellence. Hence, the focus is on individual contribution towards excellence. In contrast, *TISS's* vision is to reach institutional excellence by responding to changing social realities and contributing to developing a just, equitable, eco-friendly society.

IMDR's vision and mission strive to maintain a balance in personal and community interests, short and long-term goals, and personal, professional and social development through education. Its mission is 'to prepare students as down-to-earth professionals' and thus distinguishes itself from other institutions by focusing on rootedness in professional practice. As a strategy for teaching, learning, research and placements, it focuses on management practices of medium-sized organisations that contribute significantly to the Indian economy and industrial production. In other words, the missions of the three institutions mentioned above have identified a distinct space for themselves. More importantly, the vision and mission statements of the three *HEIs* mentioned above articulate their distinct institutional identities and values.

The larger thematic point is that, the, mission and values remain at the core of *IB* and the development process. More importantly, they provide motivation, guidance and satisfaction to the internal stakeholders on a long-term basis. In the contemporary context of promotion of the higher education market, corporatisation and brand building, the relevance and importance of the mission and values of *HEIs* cannot be underestimated. However, the critical point is the process of strategic planning at the level of each institution, which has the responsibility to make the vision and mission a reality so that the vision mission statements do not remain on the *HEIs*' entrance walls or used merely as a public- relations material.

Strategic Planning Process

It is essential to have a strategic planning process in place for an institution to realise the purpose stated in the vision-mission charter. In order to formulate a strategic plan, some basic preparation is necessary. This section of the essay addresses the following questions on Strategic Planning *(SP):*

(a) What is the process of *SP* ?

(b) What is the relevance and significance of *SP* for building educational institutions?

(c) What is the role of strategic human resource development (*SHRD)* in institutional building?

The essential step before taking up the *SP* exercise by *HEI* is to build a consensus on values, vision, mission and goals among the key members of the institution; in the case of educational institutions, the faculty, students, staff and management should be involved in the process. If not done so, the vision mission will remain disconnected from the ground-level reality. Consequently, there would be an incongruence between stated values and values in action or behaviors in practice.

The methodology of *SP* is to facilitate and channelise the implementation of the purpose, vision and mission of the institution. It involves the participation of key stakeholders to assess the internal and external environments of the institution. It helps give direction and continuity to the organisation for a sufficient period of time. One of the strategic planning techniques is a *SWOT* analysis, which charts the features of internal and external environments in terms of strengths, weaknesses, opportunities, and threats. In a way, it is an application of viable systems theory that remains relevant for all man-made living systems, including industrial and educational organisations.

However, the strategic planning approach in *HEIs* would be somewhat different from that of business organisations. It would be an assessment of the external environment in terms of the education market, competition, regulatory systems, state policies and control, political, social and economic trends, and recent developments in the field of technology and research. The internal assessment would be in terms of the development of human resources, funding, academic processes like teaching-learning and research, capacity building, strengths and weaknesses of the institution in key areas.

The process and quality of strategic planning depend on the sources of data on internal and external environments. The data and information relevant to educational institutions are often scattered, unreliable and superficial. Paradoxically, the purpose of strategic planning is to come to grips with the environment so that the mission and vision of the institution can be actualised. The quality and rigorousness of strategic planning would determine its outcomes and effectiveness in its implementation. For instance, at a macro level, the National Education Policy (*NEP 2020*) provides a vision and plan for higher education in India. However, there is no clue on how it would be implemented in the specific context of institutions like universities and colleges in different states of India.

Moreover, each institution operates in a specific historical, geographical, social, economic and global context, which would determine how mission of *NEP* would be implemented. Therefore, each micro institution needs a strategic plan and process to implement it. Otherwise, like many good reports on education policy prepared earlier in India, it may remain another grand vision document without much impact on the ground level.

A few suggestions would be of guidance in developing a robust strategic planning process.

(a) Identify and document the key features of the Indian, local, and global environments in which the institution is embedded.
(b) Reflect and review the features with data collected from the actual, grounded experiences of the participants in the planning process.
(c) Use research evidence rather than personal impressions or feelings on the dimensions of the environment.
(d) Strategic planning is a participative process that converges multiple experiences and research findings.

The main purpose of *SP* is that experiences, data, and reflections are meant to shed light on internal and external realities so that the implementation of the institutional mission becomes a reality. The discussion on the plan is to be used as a basis for further exploration and analysis in the field. It is not a final word but an effort to discover the essence of the institutional environment: its internal strengths and weaknesses and threats and opportunities externally. However, it needs to be taken as a process of comprehending environmental realities, not an absolute truth.

Most importantly, the *SP* process is based on insights from actual experiences and episodes of those involved in the professional practice. It also uses research-based evidence rather than personal feelings about the phenomenon. It is a data-based approach to building robust higher education institutions.

Synthesis

Institutions are manmade, purposeful systems and hold the potential to sustain them for a longer duration. Some Indian universities have survived and evolved for over one hundred years in India, and a few universities have survived for six centuries in Europe. Institutional purpose connects it with the internal and external needs and expectations of the stakeholders. Management theory has designed tools for vision-mission statements and the *SP* process, enabling organisations to navigate the ever-evolving process of building institutions. This essay has presented key ideas of these tools and processes designed to facilitate institutional building of *HEIs* to keep them focused on the purpose, vision and mission.

REFERENCE

1. Padaki V. and Vaz M. (2005), *Management Development in Non-Profit Organisations,* Sage Publications, New Delhi.

Essay Nine

Human Development in Higher Education: A Humanistic Perspective

This essay is contained in two parts: The first part explains the concepts and ideas of Prof R Ackoff and Dr Amartya Sen on human and economic development and its relevance to the primary purpose of higher education and developing abilities and capabilities of humans. The second part discusses the psychoanalytical theory of Wilfred Bion, a researcher at Tavistock Institute, London, which focuses on the psychological perspective, that is, conscious and unconscious processes in groups and collective behaviours. This theory offers valuable insights into group dynamics that are immediately relevant for understanding institutional behaviours and leadership processes in small and large groups. The essay provides foundational concepts in human development for effective Higher Education and robust group processes for Institutional Building.

Part One
Humanistic Perspective of Development

Dr Amartya Sen has proposed a theory of economic development where he establishes a connection between development and freedom. He argues that unless freedom is available or created, humans will not reach the stage of development because the level of liberty defines human development. In other words, the goal of economic development needs to be achieved through the means of freedom; thus, development and freedom are interdependent. This essay attempts to establish a connection between economic development and human freedom. Needless to say, it is a conceptualisation that combines economic and human development and is relevant to the discussion on the institutional development of higher education. (*Sen, Amartya, 2000*)

Before we discuss and dwell upon the concept of economic and human development further, it is equally necessary to establish a connection between processes of academic learning in schools and colleges and the development of capabilities of human resources and society at large.

The concept in *cognitive learning* that has impacted teaching-learning in education at all levels in contemporary times is the theory of '*constructivism*' or the focus on the process of 'how the learner builds knowledge in her mind'. The theory is a major deviation from the conventional emphasis on memorisation for examinations in formal education. It facilitates a conscious change and transformation in the thinking and behaviours of not only the students but also the orientations of teachers and faculty towards learning processes. The theory reminds us that the aim of higher education is not merely to provide information but to develop students' cognitive ability to comprehend, apply, observe, and make decisions based on facts. In higher education, the focus needs to be on higher-order thinking and reflections on actions to solve problems intelligently. The ultimate purpose of higher education is to make learners independent, capable of using available resources, and develop intellectual and emotional capabilities so that they can contribute to building a healthy and developed society and nation. In short, the 'constructivist' approach to educatio*n* is in sync with the ideas on human development of thinkers like *Dr. Sen and Prof. Ackoff*, which are presented and discussed in this essay.

In the theory of human development, proposed by *Prof R. Ackoff (1984)*, which is based on a systemic perspective, he makes an important distinction between two concepts: growth and development. Growth implies the addition of more parts or resources to individual and man-made living systems like work organisations and nations, but it should not be equated with or taken as criteria of human development. As an instance, when a middle-class person purchases more amenities like white and luxury goods, when a government of a developing country gets more funds for poverty alleviation programmes from the World Bank, or when an educational institution adds more books to the library, these are instances of an *addition to the existing parts of the system*, home, country, library and signify its growth rather than their development. Therefore, having more goods, amenities, and funds should not be equated with the development of nature-made or man-made systems like persons, organisations, or economies of developing countries. According to *Prof. Ackoff*, "Development has less to do with '*how much a person has*' and much to do with '*what a person does with the available resources or what she has*'."

In other words, human development is about building the capabilities of individuals. Moreover, the process of human development is also about acquiring higher-order needs and desires, which go beyond basic needs.

Prof. Ackoff further explains the concept of growth and development in terms of the evolution of a living system made by nature or man:

> *"We, as humans, have similarities with others in terms of stages of physical growth like childhood, youth, middle and old age, but we, as individuals, are dissimilar in terms of degrees of development or levels of maturity at these stages. On the other hand, social institutions also go through phases of growth through the acquisition of physical and human resources and the addition of functions and departments. However, each institution as a system is different in terms of the level and quality of development because of how the addition of parts and resources are utilised for the development of people and the purpose of the institution. These processes determine a system's development, and they are distinct or different for each system."*

Thus, human and institutional development needs to be seen primarily as a process rather than an end state because the potential for the development of living systems is limitless and cannot be predetermined. Possibilities for the development of people and institutions are never fully exhausted. It is influenced by several factors, such as the natural evolution of living systems and their history. It is also determined by human intentionality, conscious planning, change initiatives, and other interventions for the empowerment and development of human collectivity. Therefore, research-based knowledge and methodology to study organisational and institutional processes are essential to diagnosis and plan interventions for development.

Three related disciplines relevant to Institutional Building *(IB)* include *Organisational Studies (OS), Organisation Development (OD) and Institutional Development (ID). OS* is a multidisciplinary research activity that combines concepts and methodologies of social psychology, anthropology, and other social sciences. *OD* uses applied behavioural and human sciences for diagnosis and interventions at organisational levels of individuals, groups and large communities. *ID* is an emerging discipline that focuses on inter-organisational and institutional processes of conflict resolution and collaboration to reach common goals.

In addition, according to *Prof Ackoff*, the development of individuals is also reflected in an '*increase in a person's needs and desires.*' For example, professionals like doctors, lawyers and engineers try to acquire knowledge and skills through formal education to develop competencies in professional practice. The behavioural, ground reality of this developmental process is that though the motivation for professional development is reflected in the acquisition of these abilities and skills, it is primarily driven by an individual's unique desires and activation of her inner needs to do better and excel. The inner need for excellence and achievement is an essential part of self-developmental motivation.

Since a person is a sub-system of a larger system of community and society, as the General Systems Theory (*Bertalanfy L., 1950*) states, individual development is about acquiring legitimate needs and desires for self and others. A person has the liberty to develop herself without obstructing the right of others to develop. Moreover, developmental needs and desires are not inborn but acquired through a process of socialisation and learning from role models, from primary organisations like family and later at workplaces. Educational institutions are essential in making these role models available to the young on their campuses.

In other words, it is necessary to recognise that human development occurs in a larger social context, where the legitimate needs and desires of others must be considered. Any attempt to restrict the legitimate needs and desires of others would be damaging to human development for all in the long run. Hence, a '*simultaneous concern for self and others' development*' is an important social and ethical dimension of human development. In the context of higher education policy at the macro or national level, it is expected to be inclusive and equitable so that some sections of society are not deprived of access to higher education.

In General Systems theory, the problem of inequity is called sub-optimisation, wherein a sub-system grows at the cost of other parts and hampers the overall growth of the total system. For example, higher education has benefitted the middle class but has not reached tribal and socially disadvantaged communities. This tends to disturb the system's equilibrium at the regional and national levels. General and open systems theory principles apply to all kinds of man-made living systems, such as family, social, business organisations, and educational institutions.

In the context of higher education in India, a large portion of the young population does not have access to it for socio-economic reasons. More recently, with the increasing use of online education, many students from low-income families have lost opportunities for school and college education. Such a situation would also restrict the development of even those with access to education in the long run because such changes would result in social tensions, unrest and under-employment of these sections of society who are deprived of higher education. It is observed that underdevelopment due to the denial of better and higher education to people leads to a rise in the rate of crime and corruption. Hence, there is a viewpoint to make education free and accessible to everyone as a right to education, an essential policy in a welfare state that is in the society's interest. Education is a primary means of human development, and it is argued that it should be considered a part of public goods rather than private goods, which are available only to those who can afford it.

Nobel laureate economist *Dr. Amartya Sen* (2000) has refined the theory of economic development by integrating it with human freedom. (*Chattopadhay, S., 2012*) In relation with that purpose, he makes a finer distinction between *physical capital and human capital* since both are considered as categories of capital. Physical capital plays an instrumental role in increasing the productivity of economic activity. In contrast, human capital is more important for individuals because it is not merely used to get more output, such as physical capital in factories or for generating goods and services in the industry. In fact, employing human capital as an input promotes the feeling of dignity and self-respect for the workers. It is essential to recognise that human capital can be a means for attaining production goals, but it is also an end in itself in terms of its worth and value. This is the main difference between physical and human capital, which *Dr. Sen* emphasises in his theory.

The implication and relevance of the above distinction is that the purpose of higher education would not be restricted to its capacity to enhance productivity and efficient use of resources as suggested by the 'human capital theory', also implied in the mainstream economic theory. Therefore, it is vitally significant to recognise and calibrate the differential between the concept of human capital in economics as a social science discipline and its implications for human development, particularly in the context of education. It must be noted that essentially, human capital, per se, is embodied in people and, hence, should be considered important and valuable in itself without being attached to an instrumental role, as implied in mainstream economic analysis.

Human capital, in essence, is not just a means but an end in itself. This kind of conceptualisation by *Dr. Amartaya Sen* clarifies the connection between human capital and human development, which is not implied in conventional economics but is crucial for defining the primary purpose of higher education.

According to *Dr. Sen*, human capital is developed in educational institutions and through '*on-the-job learning*' at workplaces, such as traditional crafts. It empowers people in many known and unknown ways by providing formal and tacit knowledge for productive and socially useful work. Moreover, such productive work of crafts gives satisfaction to the person for a longer period of life in terms of appreciation of life and beauty, which is also a higher level of aesthetic need. It gives a sense of dignity and self-respect because it liberates the person from social and religious taboos and enables her to make decisions independently. Such a person, who has invested in her own development in terms of human capital, can then exercise her 'freedom of choice', which is not dependent or linked with a person's ability to earn money.

Looking at it again and delving inside it, *Dr Sen's* theory has conceptually delinked 'development as freedom' from the conventional idea of the purpose of higher education as acquiring abilities and skills to earn a living. Hence, it has challenged the dominant policy perspective that higher education has to play only an instrumental role, mainly as a supplier of workforce to the economic engine of nations for competitive advantage. They are considered as primary expectations from higher education underlying the theory in human resource management, human capital theory in economics and management, and, more recently, in the National Education Policy (*NEP-2020)* in India.

Capability and Human Development

Educationists and institutional builders would be able to appreciate the role of higher education in the broader context of human life and society in the light of Dr Sen's theory of 'human development as freedom'. The perspective is elaborated further by him in terms of the 'capability approach' to development. These two ideas can be understood better when contrasted with options offered in welfare economics, such as i) free education and ii) distributive justice, such as admission quotas based on low income or lower castes. Both options mentioned above are based on assumptions of liberal political economy. However, assumptions of the welfare state fail to come to grips with the essence of the purpose of education. In contrast, *Dr Sen's* 'capability approach' has much to offer on the developmental role of higher education beyond liberal economics.

He emphasises development as a function of 'what people are effectively able 'to do' (becoming) and, equally important, 'to be' (being) with their capabilities. A related concept of 'functioning' is associated with 'capability', which implies that 'a person manages to do or be or the state of the person.' 'Capability' reflects a person's ability to achieve a given function of 'doing' and 'being' as well. In contrast, the development of 'abilities' mentioned by Prof. Ackoff earlier focuses on 'doing' and productive skills. It ignores the role of 'being', the state of a person, and how she experiences the meaning of her existence, as implied in Dr Sen's concept of human capability development.

It is significant that *Dr Sen* includes the state of 'being' of a person as an equally important aspect of human development. This point needs to be underlined because the contemporary discourse on the purpose of higher and professional education focuses mainly on 'doing' or action abilities and is totally silent on the state 'being' of the learner and the educated professional. It is observed that one of the prime causes of 'burnout' cases in educational and business organisations is not due to overwork but because of the failure to find 'meaning' in work. Without access to one's 'being', professionals and knowledge workers are disconnected from the purposefulness or meaningfulness of work life. Over-focus on doing and success in professional education is a myopic perspective of education and professional work and is also reflected in the widespread corrosion of institutional, professional and societal values.

Dr Sen further analyses the role of entitlements in human development. In the context of political and economic policies at the national level, human capabilities are closely associated with 'entitlements', which refer to a set of commodity bundles that a person can command in a society, using the totality of rights and opportunities that he or she has. (*Chattopadhyay, S., 2012*) As an instance, education and health facilities are a part and parcel of entitlement that help a person overcome his or her deficiencies in income. Moreover, entitlements are related to the opportunities a person gets, which depend on three factors: a) availability of social institutions like schools, colleges, and hospitals, b) a political system that supports it, and c) family traditions and cultural norms. In the context of recent political discourse on freebies, *Dr Sen's* ideas throw light on its relevance. Socio-political and cultural factors determine whether a person can convert entitlements like free benefits or 'quotas' in education into 'functioning' so that they can impact his or her social and mental structures. Therefore, in *Dr Sen's* conception of development, a few crucial questions emerge such as:

(a) 'What does one do with the opportunities or availability of consumption goods?

(b) Do they go beyond mere consumption of goods and services, aspire to live with dignity and seek to achieve a 'state of being'?

(c) How do people relate to entitlement and opportunities offered by liberal and welfare economics?

Answers to the above questions in the Indian context would depend on the vision and effectiveness of the education system, particularly higher education. This is the link that Dr Sen establishes between 'freedom, capability and human development'. In short, Dr Sen's theory of human development constitutes three related concepts: i) human capability, ii) socio-economic development, and iii) individual freedom to make choices.

The economic perspective on development of *Dr Sen* is rightly described as a *Humanistic* approach, which considers the purpose of education is '*to enable people to have a sense of the future for themselves, for their families, and communities, provide them with a kind of choice, open up new vistas of life and extend the horizon of life*'.

Thus, the *Humanistic* approach to development sharply distinguishes itself from the modernist theory of Human Capital, which considers higher education as a means to provide the raw material of workforce and knowledge workers to industry and economy to compete in global markets. It assumes that preparing students for employment is the primary purpose of university and college education. Human capital enhanced through higher education is a means to the goal of growth of the economy and industry, according to this perspective.

In contrast, the theory or perspective of development proposed by *Dr Sen* proposes that the process of economic growth depends on the expansion of human capability. Therefore, economic development also depends on simultaneous structural changes and freedom to question existing inequalities and unfair socio-economic practices. Hence, the agency and intentionality or consciousness of people nurtured in a climate of freedom are more important than mere access to commodities. Individuals are expected to be actively involved in determining their destiny rather than being dependent on the developmental programmes of the state. The policies of the state, as well as the purpose and values of *HEIs*, would play an important role in the application of *Dr Sen's* humanistic approach to national development in India.

Thus, it is vitally significant to note that education is central to the 'capability approach' to economic and social development. Education not only enhances wellness and freedom of the people but also triggers social change. Social structures can be either barriers or emancipatory variables of developing capability, and education institutions are a part of these structures. Though economic growth contributes to the expansion of human freedom, mere growth does not ensure a secure sense of 'self-worth' for individuals. The Humanistic perspective considers people as an end in themselves rather than as a means of economic growth, as envisaged in the Human Capital (HC) approach in mainstream Economics. Recognising the potential of human intentionality or the ability of self-determination is the essence of *Dr Sen*'s humanist theory of development.

One of the sincere implications and reflections of the above-mentioned '*capability approach*' to human development is that merely widening educational opportunities in higher education to all who need it would not lead to an expansion of human capabilities because social or institutional processes within the education system may also act as barriers to human development. In this sense, educational institutions are a sub-system of the larger social-political and cultural system. Therefore, it is crucial to ensure that institutional or community processes in education at school, college and university levels, should, facilitate the development of capabilities. For instance, one of the main causes of suicides of reserved category students in *HEIs* is due to the discriminatory treatment given to them by faculty, peers and administrators on campus, as evident in the case of *Rohit Vemula* (*Refer to Case Study Four in Section Three*) and others who could get admission to professional courses in *HEIs* for the first time in family.

This significantly deeper connection between the development of human capabilities and socio-cultural processes in educational institutions justifies the relevance of the systemic perspective of Institution Building for higher education, particularly in the context of socio-cultural inequities in India.

Synthesis

A subtler point in *Dr Sen's* conceptualisation of '*capability as freedom*' is the importance he has given to human agency for its ability to distinguish 'needs from wants'. Higher education and its socialisation processes play a supportive role in developing human intentionality that makes a person work on inner, developmental needs rather than on pursuits of satisfying wants through acquiring goods and commodities. With intentionality, the person would like to develop her capability to be in charge of the situation rather than be driven by the 'wants' artificially stimulated by the market. The person uses his or her 'freedom' to think independently and maintain one's autonomy and self-esteem, which is also a manifestation of human intentionality. In other words, related values of socio-political freedom and institutional and personal autonomy are central to *Dr Sen's* concept of capability as freedom. His conceptualisation of human freedom and development adds a broader, socio-economic-cultural dimension to the institution-building processes of higher education.

PART TWO
PSYCHOANALYTIC PERSPECTIVE OF HUMAN DEVELOPMENT IN GROUPS: WILFRED BION'S THEORY OF GROUP BEHAVIOURS AND DYNAMICS

Apart from the socio-economic-cultural perspective of human development, it is also necessary to attend to deeper psychological processes that influence the behaviours of work groups and learning communities. A theory of group dynamics is relevant to our understanding of the psychological processes of group development, which are influential factors in the institutional building process. It is conceptualised as a continuum of 'dependent group' and 'work group' by a reputed organisational psychologist. (*Wilfred Bion, 1961*). He has developed a psychoanalytical framework to understand developmental and regressive processes in work groups. This psychoanalytic framework highlights two distinct mental states that exist in all kinds of groups and organisations in industrialised societies.

They are a) Basic assumption mentality and b) Work group mentality. Both mind-sets influence and determine the ability of the group members to relate and engage with the primary purpose of work or deviate from it.

Bion's findings from the study are documented in his book '*Experiences in Groups*'. They are about the effectiveness of the life of a group in engaging with tasks. It depends mainly on the extent to which its members can manage their shared tensions, anxieties, and relatedness to the primary task and to 'use its capacity for realistic hard work'. (*Bion, 1961*). In contrast, the 'basic assumption' mentality influences the group negatively and is taken over by strong emotions—fear, hate, love, anger, guilt, and depression.

Moreover, the members of the group dominated by the '*basic assumption mentality*' lose touch with its purpose and become stagnant because they are caught up in 'unconscious group collusion' with members to deviate from the primary task. The group projects its leader as a saver or messiah who can protect them in crisis without being engaged with hard work of coming to grips with the primary task of the group. It lives in an as-if or illusory state of the collective mind and loses touch with reality. This is an instance of dependent group with a leader who is elevated to a higher position as if he has extraordinary powers. Members are hypnotised because they consider that tasks will be achieved magically by the leader and they do not have to learn and engage with the reality of the here and now.

It is important to recognise that two mentalities operate simultaneously in all kinds of organisations: educational, business, political, and spiritual. The insights of Bion's theory on two types of mentalities in a group's emotional life and behaviours-in-action are relevant for understanding the processes of *IB* and leadership. It would be revealing to recognise the symptoms of the *Basic Assumption* group in many religious sects and political parties in India. The leader is much above everyone and possesses supernatural powers. Furthermore, members lose the ability to reason and learn from experiences. They live in a make-believe world; needless to say, the mind-set of such groups is anti-science and anti-learning. It also highlights the importance of the Work group mentality in achieving the primary purpose of the organisation. *Bion's* insights are important for *IB* process, and they show the pitfall of deeper psychological dynamics that often occur in all kinds of work organisations.

Bion explains the behavioural processes of groups in the following way. Every group, whether formal or informal, meets to 'do something'. In this kind of 'work group' mentality, thought is developed into action and is always in a time frame. However, in a 'basic assumption' mentality, the group holds the 'as if' characteristic. It is caught up by an 'assumed to be' mental state as more real than a purposive action on the ground in a time frame. It is in a reverie state of mind, engaged with the past and future but rarely with the present situation. In contrast, the Work group tries hard to remain in a state of vigil so that it can engage with the 'work' and the purpose of the group.

Bion also clarifies notions of 'reality' and 'truth' in his analysis of dynamics in his book *'Experiences in groups'* (1961) because, at an existential level, "human beings were aware of the painful and often the fatal consequences of having to act without an adequate grasp of reality and therefore they were aware of the 'need for truth' as a criterion in the evaluation of their working."

In other words, the reality also refers to the 'emotional truth' or 'psychological reality' of the group task. Important decisions and actions are based on 'truth' recognised by the internal register of individual and group consciousness, mainly because it is often difficult to fully grasp the factual and rational reality of a group before action.

Bion's experience in research on applied work of clinical psychology is driven by a 'search for truth'. He found that the search for 'truth' is growth-promoting and an anti-truth stance is psychologically regressive. Healthy mental growth depends on subjective truth for engaging with existential reality, just as a living organism depends on food.

The Work group mentality tests itself simultaneously against truth and reality even when it means postponing pleasure and accepting pain; it also includes capacity for understanding or consciousness' (*Bion*, 1961). However, the *Basic Assumption* mind-set resists the new insights that arise from exposure to truth. It is threatened by any new idea that demands the development of the psyche.

Bion further affirms that the *Work group mentality* is precisely a developmental achievement; in contrast, the *Basic Assumption mentality* is rooted in 'resistance to development'. It represents a hatred for developmental processes, '...a hatred to learn from experience and a total lack of faith in the worth of such kind of learning that values 'truth' in the absence of a full grasp of reality.' Mahatma Gandhi referred to his internal register of 'conscience' or inner voice when making important decisions and taking action when he was in a dilemma.

The most important observation of *Bion* is that the '*Work group mentality*' is ready for and has the capacity to confront psychic realities of group purpose and membership. It acknowledges the tension between shared intentions and individual differences in the group. The primary inputs for developing Work group mentality are 'people or members with minds who can transform their experiences; and the resulting outcomes are insights, understanding, learning and development.'

(Lawrence et al., 1996). In simple words, the development of the Work group depends on its members and their capability to learn from experiences or 'learning to learn', which is a quality of productive groups. In essence, 'work groups' are a medium of human development. Educational institutions that are engaged with the *IB* process are expected to provide an ambience for a 'work-group' mentality to its members.

In short, group behaviours at workplaces are determined by the capacity of its members to negotiate consciously and unconsciously the tension between developmental push and regressive push of two opposing mentalities such as a) new and transformational thinking and b) a mental activity dominated by platitudes, dogmatism and tendency to be in a comfort zone which stagnates members' psychic development. The members of the second category show pseudo-vitality, an 'as if' feeling of purposefulness that is accompanied by a motive to avoid the experience of pain in the developmental process. The Basic Assumption mentality is regressive since it does not demand any painful sacrifices and, therefore, can be prevalent in workplaces because it provides a false sense of security and protection to its members who are dependent on the leader. However, essentially, it has an anti-learning and anti-development orientation to work and living.

The essence of *Bion's* theory on the development of the human psyche lies in its potential to throw light on the unconscious undercurrents of human interactions in groups and the capacity of individuals and groups to overcome the regressive forces of 'as-if', basic assumptions mentality where people lose a sense of purpose and the focus on the primary task. In contrast, a work group mind-set demonstrates a capacity to contain emotional tensions that groups engaged with tasks usually encounter. However, they are expected to take purposeful action in the presence of these tensions. *Bion's* theory addresses the problems in managing these two opposing forces faced by all formal and informal groups engaged in purposeful action. They must confront the reality and psychological truth of working with such group dynamics and focus on purposeful action.

Experiential learning in work groups holds potential resources for human and institutional development. Therefore, the psychoanalytic theory of individual and group development has direct relevance for building robust educational institutions from within as an inside-out approach approach of organizational learning with process awareness.

Synthesis

The common theme that runs through the two theories mentioned above of human development is that they bring individual, group and societal dynamics at the centre of the developmental process. Prof. *Ackoff's* conceptualisation cautions us on the conventional view of planners and policymakers that confuses growth with development. Growth is the addition of parts to the system, and development is the integration of parts into all kinds of living systems. His approach is holistic rather than a mechanical or arithmetic summation of parts or resources. He also refers to the ethical dimension of growth and development and proposes a balance between freedom and responsibility.

Dr Amartya Sen adds a critical factor of 'human intentionality' as a feature of the developmental process because the true sign of human development is a person's capability to exercise choice and determine her destiny.

Bion's emphasis is on the role of the work group wherein members can contain the negative emotions emerging in group dynamics that divert the members' attention from the group's primary purpose, which is a dysfunctional mentality. He explains the behavioural aspects of a developed work group with reference to its 'capacity to learn from experiences', understand reality and have the ability to recognise the subjective 'truth', even when complete information on reality is unavailable. These psychological undercurrents in the group have the potential to give a direction to the psychic energy of the group members in both constructive and or destructive ways therefore needs self-regulation by institutional members with a work group mentality.

REFERENCES

1. Chattopadhyay, S. (2012). *Education and Economics.* Oxford University Press. New Delhi.
2. Bion, W. (1961). *Experiences in Groups.* Tavistock. London.
3. Sen, Amartya. (2000). *Development as Freedom.* Oxford University Press. New Delhi.
4. Ackoff, R., & et al. (1984). *Mechanism, Organism and Social Systems.* Routledge.

Essay Ten

Quality of Higher Education: Measuring Institutional Performance

'Quality is achieving or reaching for the highest standard as against being satisfied with the sloppy or fraudulent.' – ***Tuchman***, 1880

'Quality is not a problem to be solved but a competitive opportunity.' – ***Gavin***, 1988

'Institute a vigorous programme of education and self-improvement.' – ***Deming, W.E.***, 1986, ***Quality Guru***

The above quotations are from reputed thinkers on quality management in business and industry. In the context of this essay, complex issues of quality of higher education are presented in four parts:

(a) The first part discusses key issues in the quality of higher education and conceptual frameworks to address the challenges in improving the quality of academic courses and the institutions that offer them.
(b) Two frameworks for evaluating institutional performance are presented and compared for insights into the process of improving quality.
(c) Experience-based insights on the ground-level issues and problems in Indian universities are discussed in the third part.
(d) The last part of the essay deals with underlying linkages among capability development in institutions, talent management and quality improvement processes at the institutional level.

In the process of initialising discussion on quality of higher education, it is necessary to clarify a few misconceptions about the deterioration of the quality of the higher education system in India. Four misconceptions need special attention.

The most commonly held perception is that the rapid increase in the size of higher education, mass education or the so-called mushrooming of engineering colleges and B-schools has deteriorated the quality of higher education. This is only a half-truth because, in principle, the education system can maintain good quality even though there are more enrolment of students and more colleges if adequate infrastructure and qualified human resources are made available to the system.

In 2014-15, engineering institutions, according to the *All India Council for Technical Education (AICTE)*, had 3.2 million seats. It came down to 2.32 million in the year 2020-21. The response of the Chairman of *ACITE* appeared in the press given below, reflects the official perspective towards the problem;

> *"The number of engineering institutions had grown exponentially, leading to overcapacity and a large number of vacant seats. The recent trend of engineering colleges shutting down or reduction seats will lead to consolidation and ensure sustained quality in the years to come."*

It confirms that the access and quality of higher education are affected by the state policy of liberalisation and the absence of planning at the top of apex institutions. It is apparent from the above response that complex and interdependent issues of quality, access, and employment in higher education are left to adjustments in market mechanisms, with a naive belief that markets would solve these problems. It explains why malaise of low quality in higher education persists for decades in the absence of willingness to properly diagnose and offer systemic solutions in terms of appropriate changes in policy, structure, process and systems.

The second misconception evident in the policy decisions of MoE is that by providing more financial resources for higher education, the quality of education can automatically improve. A recent example of such an attempt is to increase the number of *IITs* and *IIMs* at the pan-India level with an untested assumption that it would expand access to and improve the quality of professional education. However, the critical ingredient of quality in higher education is investment in institution building *(IB)*, which is not considered in this situation. It includes the development of faculty and learning resources to build a conducive academic climate. Both cannot be manufactured by the state fiats to establish institutions of excellence. Therefore, neither a brand name nor material resources are essential conditions for ensuring quality education.

Despite the availability of more *IIMs* and *IITs* and the availability of more seats, the fact remains that quality institutions in technology and management remain limited to those initially established, such as reputed institutions like IIM-

A and IIT-Mumbai. It explains why an investment in developing soft or human aspects of institutional capabilities is more important and relevant in the Indian context.

The third misconception is that quality is an administrative problem that needs to be solved by a better regulatory system to control and inspect. The state university system has a department called 'quality assurance' and regulatory macro institutions like *NAAC and NBA* to inspect and control the quality of higher education programmes and institutions. However, its impact on quality improvement is not substantial at the national level. Moreover, the main weakness of the higher education system is the neglect of traditional universities offering conventional courses because they are not on the priority list on the agenda of *MoE.* The painful reality is that unless the states provide essential human and financial resources like faculty and grants, the quality of university education will remain rather uneven or low. For example, in July 2021, 6500 faculty positions were vacant or not filled in for the last five years in state universities, despite promises made in Parliament by the education minister.

It is near to an impossibility to improve the quality of higher education when faculty positions in undergraduate colleges are low-paid and work on a contract of clock-hour basis teaching. These are contractual jobs, and infrastructure facilities are not upgraded for years. Neglect of quality in *HEIs* is a topic that goes beyond the realm of institutional management at the micro or college level. It only shows that the issue is related to the supply and demand aspects of the higher education market. The supply of adequate funds as input and the demand for employment opportunities as the output are the factors that matter. However, they are not under the control of the unit-level institutional management. For example, when Delhi University in the country's capital cannot fill 600 faculty positions for some years, it is difficult to expect it to happen in remote parts of state universities in India.

The fourth misconception on quality is related to a common perception that admission to elite institutions is a mark of higher merit since a few students are selected. The fact is that in a competitive market of higher education in India, the merit of a student is measured by his or her selection to a few elite institutions like the *IITs*, *IIMs* and other institutions of reputation. In reality, selection in a competitive admission test is tougher and challenging because the seats are very few compared to the number of aspirants in the Indian context. Hence, merit is only a relative term, and those not admitted were not of low merit; they were merely below an arbitrary cut-off point. The real reason for rejection in such cases is that India does not have adequate resources to admit those not 'meritorious' students, who are rejected mainly because available seats are limited. Privatising universities to create more seats is not an answer because it would create problems of 'inequity' as many with academic merit would not afford to pay high fees. Issues of quality, access and equity form a vicious circle that the higher education system in India finds most challenging to break.

Demand and Access to Higher Education in India

In the last decade, there has been an increasingly augmented demand and clarion call for higher education due to the rising aspirations of the young generations and a crisis in the agricultural sector. No significant provision has been made in budget allocation to higher education in recent years, and the NEP-2020 is conspicuously silent on the financial allocation to the higher education system, which is essential to implement the policy vision presented in the document.

The above discussions and deliberations suggest that higher education and the public health system remain two necessary foundations that need immediate attention since they sustain the developing economy of India. The irony is that though privatisation of education has definitely made access to education possible, as it is evident from the fact that 70 per cent of enrolment in higher education is in private universities, the quality of private and state universities is a question mark for various reasons. These include profit motive and neglect of soft or invisible aspects of *IB,* like capability development of faculty and staff and nurturing an academic climate-culture on campus, even though private universities make substantial investments in infrastructure development.

Similarly, when profit-making is not a legally acceptable objective of public or private institutions in India, a cost-plus formula of charging fees prevails in private universities and colleges. Generally, their fees are much higher compared to state-aided colleges. Moreover, either officially or informally, a provision is made to accommodate management quota seats to create additional funds in colleges. Seats are sold for a few lakhs in private colleges with a cynical justification by the management that it is an alternative to the subsidies available to government-aided colleges. What is overlooked is that the entry of students via management quota distorts the academic climate in classrooms and campus, indirectly affecting the quality of education negatively. It is important to recognise that the issue of quality at the micro-level of *HEIs* is mainly related to the academic and administrative processes conducted on the campus—how teaching, learning, admission, assessment, and recruitment of faculty are conducted. It is an issue of good governance practices. However, priority is given to achieving the enrolment target and filling up the seats. Access to higher education gets a priority at the macro policy level, while issues of financing and branding are given importance at the micro institutional level. Good governance practices and sources of funding in institutions are essential conditions for improving the quality of Indian higher education.

Campus Culture and Quality of Education: An Illustrative Case Incident

It would be relevant to contextualise and mention the real-life experience of a well-known management consultant, Mr *Sharu Rangnekar*, when he conducted a seminar at a B-school in Delhi. He has narrated a real-life episode that he had experienced to illustrate so-called 'Menace of management quota in B-Schools'. (*Samada, MCCIA, Pune 2012.*)

> *Mr Rangnekar's lecture was arranged for about 100 students and half a dozen faculty members. Interestingly, the faculty members were standing at various points in the class. Mr Rangnekar asked the organisers to get the faculty members to sit down, but he was told that in order to keep discipline in the class, the faculty had to stand and personally supervise students. There was applause when the speaker was introduced; however, about 10 to 15 students kept clapping even after others stopped the applause. The faculty members then went from row to row to stop the claps and get the meeting to order. Thereafter, whenever there was applause, this group would prolong it to disturb the class. Later, when a management film was shown, the students began cross-talking because the lights were off.*
>
> *When the speaker, Mr Rangnekar, discussed the problem with the faculty after the lecture, he was told the following reasons for the lack of discipline in the class.*
>
> *Management quota students have limited interest in management films and take advantage of darkness to gossip.*
>
> *They cannot give any breaks during the lectures because students who go out do not come back promptly and keep entering over a period casually, disturbing the class.*
>
> *It is difficult to make them study the curriculum. Management quota students do not accept failure because they have paid double the fee that normal students pay. Their parents consider an MBA degree as a return on this investment. In case of failure, they complain to the director, and the director blames the faculty for not teaching well enough. As a compromise solution, the question papers in examinations include some questions that are very easy to write on.*

In a manner, management quota students are well connected and get jobs in family businesses, but they fail to get employment in industry, which affects the placement record of the school. They are then absorbed as course coordinators at nominal salaries in the same institute to keep a 100% record of placement of the institute to attract prospective students.

> *Mr Rangnekar makes one more pertinent point to conclude his article, which is closely connected with the issue of quality of education in institutions of higher learning. He comments that we hear a lot about the lowering of the quality of education in India due to the low calibre of students of SC/ST/OBC in society. However, problems created by management quotas are never publicised anywhere. He also observes that though reserved class candidates with lower marks are given 27% admission, they try hard to succeed. If they fail, it is due to their deprived socio-economic background. But most of them do very well as they realise this is an opportunity to improve their capability. The recruiters also find that they do come up to the general standard.*
>
> *Contrarily, the management quota ranges from 15% to 50% based on the financial needs of the institute, and the seats are given on auction at more than double the price. These students do not consider it an opportunity to learn but as some special privilege since they have bought it at a higher price. Many of them are pressurised by their parents to take admission for the course, as in some states, a management degree fetches better dowry value and the higher fees can be compensated later. They do not attend classes and have a nuisance value over which neither the faculty nor the director has control.*

Mr *Rangnekar's* experience indicates that the quality of higher education is also connected to a larger socio-economic inequality in the Indian context, which is further aggravated by recent neoliberal policies promoted by the state. Those who have money to buy management quota seats get access to higher education, and others from deprived sections of society who cannot afford fees are out of the employment market for better jobs, in future forever.

To sum up, the present system of admission and fee structure appears to benefit the promoters of educational institutions and also the coaching classes that prepare the students for admission tests. They do not benefit other significant stakeholders such as faculty, society, industry, and students who are affected by the general quality level of higher education, which has deteriorated rapidly.

Merit and Quality: Are they different?

The concept of quality in the context of education raises questions of specificity, such as (a) the quality of inputs like the content and design of curriculum, as well as (b) the quality of performance outcomes and results. These are relevant questions because marks and grades received in assessments are taken as a mark of merit in the Indian context. Similarly, grades given by *NAAC* in institutional rating are taken as a mark of merit and quality. Technically, comparative and longitudinal performance analysis in specific areas of academics, administration, management of finances, research output, faculty and institutional development need to be conducted. Ideally, the institutional rating should be based on data collected internally and continuously to recognise the level of excellence in the quality through students' performance and the development of faculty and the institution. In the current scenario, such a system does not exist in *HEIs*.

In this situation, it is not surprising that a movement called '*Save merit, Save nation*' is launched in cities of Maharashtra state by middle-class parents and students, who have so far relied entirely on good education as the only option to make future careers. This group had protested publicly against the proposed increase in reservation seats to the Maratha community that would go beyond 50%. However, they do not consider the hidden reservation through management quota for those who can buy seats at higher fees. They hold a genuine fear, though, that further reservation would bring gross inequity in socio-economic progress through education for future generations in India.

At the national keel, it would be a difficult proposition to have merit in the strict sense of the term in higher education when a significant part of the national income of India is in the hands of a few families, businessmen, industrialists and so-called educational entrepreneurs who are unconcerned about the issues like quality of higher education or serious investment and commitment to education. In other words, the quality of education in the Indian context should not be discussed at academic or institutional levels only, but it would require a socio-economic and political analysis at a macro level as well.

However, as the above discussion suggests, the issue of the quality of higher education is intimately connected with academic and institutional performance. It, therefore, needs a Performance Management System *(PMS)* at the institutional level. An integrated perspective and value attached to quality consciousness are equally important. Also, the criteria for measuring quality needs a conceptual framework so that more attention is given to the strategic role of quality issues in the delivery of courses and the impact of the quality of students and research on industry, society and nation-building. As discussed in *Essay Two* on techno-economic perspective, the quality of higher education depends on the quality of students as an input of the input-process-output system through the admission process.

When education is considered a service industry, and if it is indeed so, it is a unique service where every student is an input and output, in contrast to other services like airlines or hotels. In the service industry, the customer is a receiver of the service and not a producer. In contrast, the education process requires faculty and students as inputs, who are also an integral part of the output of knowledge and skill creation. More importantly, the motivation and intent of the student and faculty are the key factors in maintaining the quality of education. The time taken and efforts made in the teaching-learning process by the students and faculty together and individually, supported by the staff and management, would determine the quality of academic output. The commitment of faculty and administration and time spent on improvement in the quality of academic processes of teaching, learning, research and industry-academia projects are critical factors.

In management parlance, as the second quotation by *Gavin* at the beginning of the essay suggests, quality should not be taken merely as a problem to be solved but has strategic importance for the competitive advantage and reputation of the institution. A long-term perspective of process of maintaining quality of education is crucial to plan strategically.

However, in the present structure and culture of many educational institutions, members of the faculty community, who are directly engaged with the teaching-learning process day in and out, do not have a say in the admission process, curriculum design, or assessment system. They have to accept the expectations of management and students to compromise on quality standards. In fact, they are at the receiving end of the education market with the rising expectations of students and management on the one hand and the regulatory system on the other, which are the power centres that determine the rules and performance indicators of the higher education system. Students are considered primary consumers rather than learners, and educational institutions and faculty remain service providers rather than knowledge creators.

Faculty academic behaviours in *HEIs* are controlled by numerous circulars on revised rules sent unilaterally by the apex bodies of higher education like *UGC* and *AICTE*, and they must adhere to them without raising questions or showing resistance. In case of low quality in delivery or academic performance of students, blame goes to faculty and colleges. However, the key decisions on admissions, faculty development, learning resources, compensation, tenure, and funding depend on both the state regulators or top management and promoters of institutions.

It is important to note that in the present context, managing quality in higher education depends on a top-down strategy wherein apex bodies give direction to the *HEIs* and supervise and control them. However, ideally, it requires a bottom-up process of engagement of key stakeholders in educational processes and the involvement of board members to monitor the quality of courses, which should to be an essential part of *IB* and governance.

Measuring Quality of Performance: Two Approaches

In the context of quality improvement in the Indian education system, let us consider and enumerate the approach of quality control used by apex regulatory bodies like *NAAC* and *NBA,* wherein accreditation procedures and quality rating are used as a part of the regulatory system rather than as a part of the institutional building process. This approach to quality performance distinguishes the Indian perspective on education from the approach of the American *Baldrige* system.

The impact of regulatory bodies like NAAC and NBA is that they have made *HEIs* dependent on them for quality certification, which is considered a licence, though it is an optional choice of each institution in the present situation. The espoused purpose is to help *HEI*s operate in the higher education 'market' with a mark of official credibility. The current process of how accreditation is administered, however, ignores the institutional need for empowerment of internal stakeholders such as faculty and students and capability building of institutions for future needs. Also, it does not recognise the importance of the distinct identity and mission of each higher education institution, which needs to be considered an integral part of the quality of an institution. This is a grave flaw in the conceptual framework of the Indian system and perhaps the leading cause of the low quality of *HEIs* in India.

Theory and Practices of Total Quality Management: Lessons from Industry

The above discussion on the management of quality in *HEIs* indicates that it has become a one-dimensional improvement programme with procedures and rules of quality assurance. Learning from the theory and practice of Total Quality Management *(TQM)* in the industry, one has to recognise that it is a comprehensive approach to institutional practices based on a philosophy towards institutional change and transformation.

Educationists and institution builders can immensely benefit from the contemporary theory and practices on quality improvement in industrial and business organisations using the concepts of *TQM.*

W. E. Deming (1986), considered a management Guru of quality, affirms that improving quality can decrease rather than increase costs, and it can effectively help in the achievement of goals.

- *TQM* focuses on customer needs and perceptions. Unfortunately, in the educational context, though students are considered as customers now, they have no say in the education processes and are taken for granted regarding their needs and expectations.

- *TQM* emphasises accountability for poor quality by the key role holders who, in turn, are given training and education to perform for better quality output. Accountability for quality is the missing point in the educational context of India.
- Teamwork and collaboration across functions facilitate quality improvement. *HEIs*, in contrast, are governed by top-down structures and curriculum of with subject specialisation without interdisciplinary focus.
- Above all, *TQM* reiterates that change, continuous improvement and organisational learning are encouraged so that employees/staff/faculty can aspire to go beyond the current state of quality to the next stage. Hence, it is similar to the processes of institution building *(IB)*, which is the central theme of this book.

Interestingly, at a conceptual level, the *TQM* approach has many similarities with the systemic approach of institution and organisational development (Essay Six), with a focus on change in individual and collective beliefs, attitudes, and behaviours at the workplace. The change has to be 'total' and radical, and everyone in the company/institution must share the basic philosophy.

The most important feature of quality management in industry is that it has moved further in the evolution of theory and practice from equating quality only with inspection and control of outgoing products. Instead, it focuses on all facets of the organisation—customers, employees, processes, collaboration, teamwork, vision, mission and leadership at all levels of the organisation. It is an example of applying the General Systems Theory (*GST*), wherein the whole is more than the sum of its parts, that connects all subsystems in interface with the dynamics of both internal and external environments.

At this stage, it is important to mention that though *TQM* procedures used in industry have more robust technologies like Statistical Quality Control *(SQC)*, sampling and process control procedures, they cannot be mechanically transferred to educational processes for obvious reasons of the difference between nature of industrial and of educational services and products. The quality issues in *HEIs* can be addressed more effectively by qualitative and phenomenological research methods, as explained in the next Essay Eleven, from a human science perspective, since the core of *HEIs* is its people processes and not products as objects. However, the main benefit of applying the *TQM* methodology to educational institutions is that it takes a systemic perspective of institutions and has flexibility for combining it with a developmental perspective of *OD* and phenomenology.

Some of the ideas of *W.E. Deming* (1986), in his famous 14 points for managing quality, have direct relevance for *HEIs*, as they focus on action initiatives such as i) to nurture human skills, abilities and knowledge base, ii) to engage in non-competitive activities internally among employees, iii) to focus on means, processes and not merely on results, and to continuously improve, iv) to improve satisfaction and commitment of people, v) to have customer-driven focus to satisfy their needs.

Perspective on Quality in Education: Measuring Quality Performance in HEIs

It is important to recognise that the above-mentioned action steps for quality improvement are also used as criteria to measure quality performance in the *Malcolm Baldrige National Quality Award (MBNQA)*, established by the United States government in 1987, to recognise and stimulate quality improvement in the US industry and later, in educational institutions as well. A comparison between the criteria of the *NAAC* and *Baldrige* model is presented to highlight the difference between the two approaches and their potential impact on quality improvement practices. A Diagram of concentric circles based on the Baldrige model is given below:

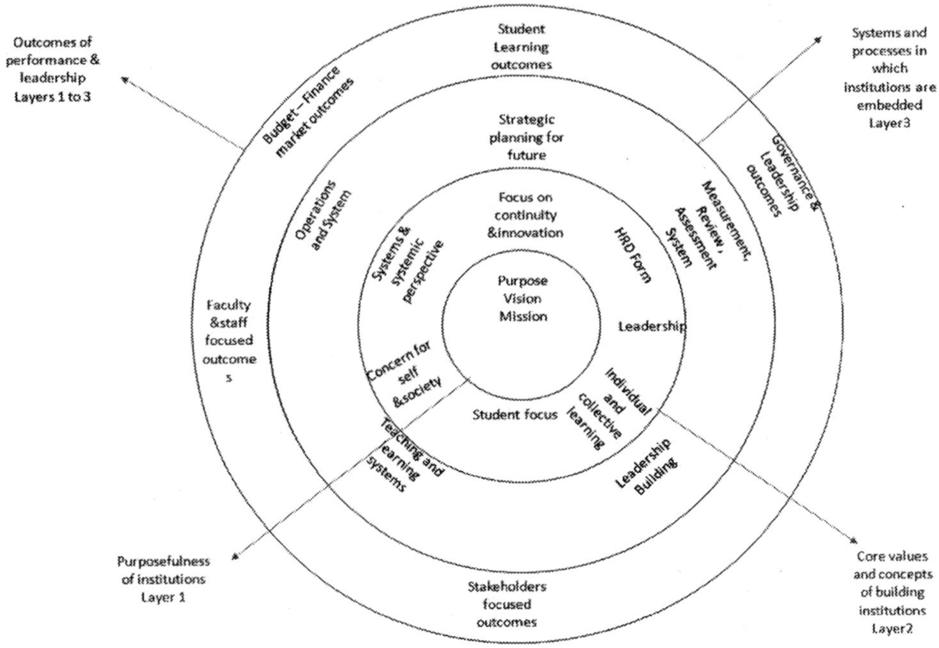

Figure 2: Model of Institutional Performance

Note: Adapted from Baldrige Model of Performance Excellence.

This framework is designed on the premises that though the individual components of the quality framework are essential for evaluation, the overall effectiveness of educational institutions and management systems depends on how these components relate to one another and operate synergistically,

The framework is conceived as three concentric circles of a systemic perspective of institutional quality and excellence that consist of (i) the innermost circle of *core values,* (ii) the outer circle of *processes and systems* and the intermediate processes, and (iii) *management systems* to reach *results* in areas of *leadership, governance, workforce, student learning* and *academic processes, budget, market* and *strategy.*

However, unlike the Indian framework of *NACC* and *NBA*, it emphasises the critical role of shared values and an understanding of the core concepts like a) *values* such as ethics and transparency, valuing people, societal contribution delivering of values and results and b) *concepts* like organisational learning and flexibility, visionary leadership that is strategic and long term, student centred excellence management by facts, management for innovation.

The message embedded in this model of performance excellence is that without the foundation of core professional values and beliefs, such as accountability and integrity, institutions of education would not go to the next level of management process in areas of leadership, strategic planning, student learning, measurement, analysis and management of workforce and operations. With professional values, management systems and processes, an organisation can get results to reach high performance. The results are in the areas of student learning, governance, market response, and outcomes related to faculty, staff and stakeholders.

The quality of higher education is an outcome, or a consequence of academic and institutional performance. It is also related to the purpose and mission of each institution so that it remains purposive with a focus on its unique mission. In other words, there cannot be a standard template for quality improvement for all kinds of institutions, even in specific subject domains such as sciences or humanities. However, a common conceptual framework can be used for guidance and application, as is the case with the *Baldrige* Quality framework, which is particularly designed for educational organisations. It provides guidelines and concepts for approaching the task of quality management, rather than recommending a rigid procedure for supervising and control by the regulators such as *UGC, AICTE* and IMC, as it occurs in the case of *NAAC,* NBA accreditation templates given to *HEIs* in India.

In essence, the *Baldrige* model of quality excellence in performance is a 'non-prescriptive framework' that does not provide ready to apply solutions to problems and bottlenecks in the quality of courses and institutional performance. However, it does provide a set of questions and orientation that guides leaders to think about the organisation and its functions in depth and generate data that is helpful in arriving at solutions to problems. It provides insight into the strengths and weaknesses by exploring the institution-specific territory in the concentric circles in the framework. Thus, the model works like a conceptual map to encourage new ideas to improve performance and practices. This approach to measuring institutional performance is best suited for all kinds of *HEIs* since it is an open-ended, holistic and rigorous framework that does not make institutional stakeholders dependent on an external evaluation system but instead encourages and strives for the local initiatives for self-regulation. The catch is that it presupposes the values of integrity and professionalism.

The framework is not to be expected to be perceived as a process to acquire a license or certification on quality. The model is not meant to supervise or control performance from an external agency but to give direction and guide the quality improvement processes; it has no centralised ownership over the process but is delegated to institutions for self-regulation.

In contrast, in the Indian approach of quality regulators, the commitment to improve quality is not an essential condition for the top management and administrators within the institution. It is considered more as an external inspection, conducted periodically, but is not an integral part of the institutional processes and values that necessitate the involvement of all relevant stakeholders. Consequently, the outcomes are not visible in performance and behaviours, and it breeds further cynicism about quality initiatives from regulators for institutional change and development. The participation of *HEI*s in the *NAAC* and *NBA* process has been much below expectations for more than a decade despite efforts to propagate its benefits.

The main reason for this failure of quality regulation in the higher education system in India is poor consideration of the mission and purpose of educational institutions to make them a unique and integral part of the *IB* process. The real question is that the institutional identity of *HEIs*, mainly affiliated colleges, is not emphasised since they perform the function of service providers of state universities with standardised courses. In the prevalent process and design of university-colleges setup, the possibility and freedom is minimum for designing curriculum, pedagogy, teaching hours, selection process, and student welfare for the institution, which are in accordance with its mission and strategy. This freedom or genuine autonomy with self-regulation is essential because quality improvement would occur only through the empowerment of and collaboration between management, faculty, students and staff.

The reality is that the prevalent view of regulators is that there would be malpractices in institutional processes if academic freedom is given. However, ironically, the significant deviations in the systems had occurred mainly due to interferences from the state and other vested interests in appointing persons to top positions and faculty in elite institutes and universities funded by the central and state governments. The issue is about the use of power. It, therefore, is connected to the issue of governance, which needs attention since it directly and indirectly affects the quality of higher education. As explained in Essay Five, the attitudes and behaviours of institutional members is influenced by systems and processes of governance. The real work of quality improvement begins with forming appropriate values and attitudes for quality performance.

Returning to the guiding principles mentioned in the *Baldrige* framework of quality assurance, one can see that though it uses distinct criteria for evaluating quality performance, they are designed to be considered in totality as an integrated system. Thus, the conceptual model underlying the Baldrige framework is organic-flexible rather than mechanistic-rigid.

Essentially, the *Baldrige* framework mentioned earlier in the diagram is for quality improvement in academic and institutional performance rather than for quality supervision, audit, appraisal or certification. The data collected on seven key criteria of the quality framework can be applied further for improvement with flexibility. For example, in order to work on the criterion of analysis, data collected on other criteria can be used for identifying organisational strengths and opportunities. This process is also relevant for strategic planning in terms of analysis of the environment at external and internal levels in order to locate areas of improvement, gaps and blind spots. Since the data collection is to be carried out by institutional members, it would have a diversity of opinions, observations, and facts, which are collected by formal and informal methods. It would give insights into the strengths, weaknesses, threats and opportunities for the institution. The diversity of views and experiences would help analysts arrive at realistic conclusions as compared to the limited view of a few members of the board of management. This methodology is similar to systemic *OD* and *ID* (Essay Six). Some specific benefits are given below.

(a) Data collected on each category can also be used further for individual and organisational learning.

(b) Leadership data can be used for peer development or inter-disciplinary team development programmes; it explores all aspects of leadership at different levels rather than focusing on leader development.

(c) Data on operations and administrative processes can be analysed to improve management practices and performance.

(d) All criteria are suitable for diagnosis in developing an internal in-house programme of organisational development (*OD*) for different types of education institutions.

The performance results mentioned in the above model indicate performance data in the following areas. This data is relevant for internal and external stakeholders:

> *(a) Leadership and governance are considered, but they are conspicuously missing in the* NAAC *and* NBA *evaluation schemes. (b) The performance of student learning, academic process, workforce, student and customer orientation are evaluated as they are important for external stakeholders of an educational institution. (c) Performance in areas of budget, market, and strategy are studied as they are essential for managing finance, marketing, and strategic planning functions.*

An Insider's Diagnosis of the Quality of University Education in India:

An incisive and pithy analysis of the deficiency in quality education and causes of low quality in the Indian university system is made by the former vice-chancellor of Gujarat University, *Pankaj Chandra* (2018), in his article on '*Questioning Academic Freedom*'. The key points and arguments made in the article are summarised below:

The purpose and objectivity of a University is lofty and broad, which is not matched by any other work organisation. 'A country's progress is measured by the advancement of its universities.' They build perspectives on intrinsic values, judgements, and skills for the present and the future. It can also connect with the masses and go beyond the boundaries of the ivory tower. It teaches and practices important democratic values about engagement, compassion, fairness, and justice.

Dr Chandra laments that university faculty, who are expected to be 'thought leaders' have given up their commitment to values of autonomy and freedom in terms of a) deciding what constitutes learning, b) how it is to be delivered, c) how engagement with and between students is organised, d) how rules of assessment are defined, and e) how learning would take place.

To cut the long story short, all critical choices in academic processes mentioned above are disowned by the university management and faculty. Hence, students in the university system do not build the ability to question, are not able to distinguish good from not-so-good, make ethical judgements, learn to be compassionate, courageous, self-critical, and independent-minded and yet ready to collaborate. As the abdication of responsibility in key academic processes by university authorities and faculty has impacted the development of the capabilities of students and ultimately degraded the quality of higher education.

Abdication of responsibility by university authorities to shoulder demanding role expectations from the university system has led to a campus climate where the academic administration of universities does not tolerate freedom and autonomy for students and faculty. Instead, values of efficiency and control replace the above values through standardised courses. Unfortunately, this approach of the *MoE* is not questioned or resisted by vice-chancellors, heads of departments in universities. It kills the spirit to try alternative approaches, views, and interpretations. Instead, the apex bodies recommend a model 'one size fits all' curriculum. There is no space for a culture of critiques and debates, and they are sometimes curbed by state intervention as anti-national behaviours. (Refer to the Case Study Five on *JNU, Rise and Decline of an Academic Institution)*

As discussed earlier, it is essential to recognise that quality improvement in education cannot be precisely like a process of quality management of products because the medium and means of education are not material but human resources, particularly faculty and students. At the same time, student performance, which is limited only to curriculum subjects, would not be an adequate criterion to measure the quality of students since it does not evaluate the whole person but only subject knowledge and technical skills. In this context, co-curricular activities like sports, debates, discussions, fine and martial arts, community work, and other areas that express the individual talents of students are equally, if not more, important for the growth and development of students as persons. In this sense, it is wrong to mark a student as a 'product' of a particular college or university because individual talent can be nourished in all settings if an egalitarian climate and support are provided. This is an issue of talent development and capability building in higher education for better quality.

Capability Development for Quality Performance

Capability signifies and reflects the potential of each student, and therefore, it is not always visible. Human potential only indicates a possibility that needs to be experimented, tested and nourished by each person and the educational system. As an instance, fifty students of a secondary school run by an NGO in a district of Bihar performed a one-act from the play of Shakespeare, *Julius Caesar* (*ET*, 2018). Significantly, the parents of these children did not know the English language, nor could they even benefit from school education. It shows how the hidden talent of students can be nourished by a supportive climate and values created by teachers, community workers, and the school. It demolishes the myth that quality is possible only in selected institutions and a social class of students. The above example also points to the process of identifying and nurturing individual or collective capabilities and talents.

The issue of quality improvement linked with capability and talent development brings us to the selection of an appropriate pedagogy to create a conducive campus climate of care, concern, and encouragement for development, as well as a culture that demands improved individual performance. However, it is made possible by peer support and collaboration. Hence, there is no space for interpersonal competition based on jealousy and bad faith. Individual talent, to begin with, is an outcome of a person's mind-set, attitudes and self-beliefs. They are explained below more specifically.

Six key sub-concepts in capability development are *Mindset, Self-efficacy, Self-acceptance, Capability, Growth, and Development.*

Mindset: It is a person's attitude or way of thinking about something: self, others, objects, qualities. It is often seen that people's mindset about their capabilities, intelligence, and talent is the biggest obstacle to their own improvement.

For example, if a student's belief or mindset is that her intelligence and capabilities are inborn and fixed and cannot be changed, it is called affixed mindset. However, individual mindset, intelligence and capabilities can change over time by working hard, seeking help and feedback, and it is called a 'growth' or development mindset.

Self-efficacy: It is self-belief and behaviors that help a person to realise their potential. Each person is born with an untapped potential to do several things and is not restricted by the specialised education undertaken later in life. Many are not likely to actualise even a small part of it in one's lifetime. However, some people discover and apply more of their potential, while some do not. The reason for our underutilisation of talent or potential is that we are not fully aware of our inner resources and hidden talents and are not ready to accept ourselves.

Self-acceptance: Self-acceptance of one's positives and limitations influences an individual's ability to prepare, act on plans made and utilise the untapped resources, which are important for growth. It is a paradox in life that the more one accepts oneself with positive and limiting qualities, the more one is ready to change and grow.

Developing Individual Talent of Students and Faculty: Overcoming Institutional Barriers

Factors that positively contribute to talent-capability development are:

(a) **Exploratory orientation**: The more you do or apply, the more you know about your talent. Such a person takes the initiative to do things before being asked to do so, is not afraid of making mistakes, takes moderate risks, and is open to change. Capability is not developed by contemplation only. It requires action first and then reflection for learning.

(b) **Self-disclosure:** When you communicate with others, you learn more about yourself. The person shares opinions, feelings and knowledge with others.

(c) **Receptivity to feedback:** Feedback from others tells us about our blind spots, allows us to learn from the impact of our actions, and learn more about our strengths and weaknesses.

(d) **Sensitivity and Emotional Intelligence:** It is important to be aware of our feelings and those of others. Such sensitivity balances our efforts to develop ourselves by learning from others.

The duo of hypocrisy and the attendant irony of the education system apparent among the top leadership of universities and in the *NEP-2020* is that though regulators announce and give autonomy and academic freedom to colleges, these values are neither demanded by nor granted to faculty and students. It unveils a hidden agenda behind the demand for autonomy and freedom—to serve the vested interest of those in power, and is certainly not for educational purposes. Autonomy to *HEIs* is for those in power who run institutions rather than for the key stakeholders like faculty and students.

The actual meaning of academic freedom is evident, when a faculty is free to offer courses around her passion and expertise, determine the syllabus, manage the evaluation process and make collective decisions to build a shared vision of the Institution. The reality is that faculty in affiliated colleges, due to the rigid hierarchy, is reduced to the role of executives or office staff to implement decisions taken by the apex bodies in Delhi rather than as originators of key academic decisions. The power of governance is interpreted as control, centralised in the top position, vice-chancellor or principal, who usually remain in the same position till they retire. The system leads to a monopoly of set ideas, nepotism and favouritism. The board members of governing councils are interested in decisions of resource allocation for vested interests, and these are rarely done transparently through participative and collective decision-making. In this kind of structure, climate and values, an independent-minded faculty has no choice but to become either compliant or cynical or remain a cribber forever.

A critical analysis of the Indian University system given above indicates that (a) Improving the quality of higher education needs change in attitudes, processes, structures and values of the system at all levels, (b) major structural reforms are needed to impact anti-learning values and culture of complacency that breeds shoddy quality in university education.

Dr Pankaj Chadra, who, as Vice-chancellor, had experienced the legal hurdles in university administration, has recommended an important change in the legal structure whereby "each University Act has to explicitly state that what universities teach and research and how they do it is to be determined by the university because it is they who know it best, and sometimes better than the regulator. They have to be protected by the judiciary and ombudspersons. Academic freedom should percolate down to all faculties of academic administration as well to bring decentralised decision making".

Synthesis

Quality management is one area in which education institutions can learn from studies on industrial and business management. A good theoretical base like *TQM* is available to guide the implementation of quality improvement programmes applicable to other domains of institution building in higher education. The chasm between theory of technical and social systems can be bridged by an integrated theory of Total Quality Management *(TQM).*

It is pertinent to remember that quality improvement in education is not merely a tool for inspection and detection of errors or fixing problems but a part of a strategic intervention to focus on the competitive advantage of the institution by working on its identity, unique proposition to students, faculty, industry and society at large. It goes beyond the standardisation of programmes and procedures but can also focus on the needs of the students and faculty, who are an essential part of the process of generating learning and knowledge. The most important principle is that quality improvement is the responsibility of the top management and is expected to be percolated down to everyone. In this sense, it is an integral part of *OD* and *ID.*

Along with the conceptual understanding of the *Baldrige* quality framework and *TQM* principles, it is equally important to take cognisance of the ground-level reality and learn from the experiences and thoughts of those in leadership roles like of VC and HOD in the Indian university system.

To sum up the discussion, the quality of higher education is not simply a matter of improving the quality of courses and programmes since they are not industrial or consumer products. It requires some deeper-level interventions in the structures and processes of institutions to make university education vibrant and relevant and contribute to nation-building.

REFERENCES

1. Chandra, P. *Questioning Academic Freedom,* Apoorvanand (Ed.). (2018). *The Idea of a University*. Context.
2. Chhokar, J.S. (2011). *OD and the Quality Movement.* S. Ramnarayan & T. V. Rao (Eds.), Organisation Development. Sage.
3. Deming, W.E. (1986). *Out of Crisis,* Cambridge, MA: MIT Center of Advanced Engineering Stuides.
4. National Institute of Standards and Technology. (2019-20). *Baldrige Performance Excellence Framework Education Criteria Commentary.* Retrieved from https://www.nist.govt/baldrige/publications
5. Ramnarayan, S. (2011). *Enhancing Capability for Improving Performance.* S. Ramnarayan & T. V. Rao (Eds.), Organisation Development. Sage.
6. Rangnekar, Sharu, Sampada, MCCIA (1012). Pune.

Essay Eleven

Qualitative Research Methods for Personal and Institutional Change and Transformation

'While educating the mind of our youth, we must not forget to educate their hearts'. – ***Dalai Lama***

'The whole purpose of education is to turn mirrors into windows'. – ***Sydney J. Harris***

This is an elaborate descriptive note, rather than an essay, comprising of three parts on Qualitative Research methods. Qualitative methodology is a more appropriate device for pedagogy, teaching-learning processes and institution building. The note discusses (a) Phenomenology, (b) Reflective Practice and (c) Action Research. Together, they provide guidance on methods and tools for initiating change and transformation at individual, group and institutional levels.

The first part of this note is on Phenomenology that distinguishes itself from the features of conventional academic research done in most Indian universities, which is based on a positivist perspective. It explains how the phenomenological approach to research and pedagogy differs from the conventional one as it is embedded in a systemic perspective of reality and institutions. According to *Krizanits J* (2009), 'There is no objective truth; the observer (researcher) is a part of the observation.' It explores the layers of 'reality', and focuses on how humans experience reality. It does not artificially separate subjective and objective, internal and external dimensions of perception of the reality.[1]

Let us first understand the context of academic research of higher education in India.

Context: Personal and professional growth and development of key stakeholders, that is, faculty and students, are crucial for the quality of teaching-learning at the higher education level and the Institution Building *(IB)* process. Academic institutions like universities and colleges are engaged with teaching-learning in specific disciplines. Hence, the research carried out in universities is discipline-oriented, though in different domains, such as sciences, literature, social sciences, commerce, etc. In professional colleges, the focus is on applied research in engineering, management, medicine and so on. The most common approach and methodology followed in academic research are positivism and empiricism. A qualification in PhD research is often mandatory for appointment for faculty positions in *HEI*s, and it is regulated by UGC and similar apex bodies. This kind of research is conducted in domain-specific studies and follows empirical and experimental methodology towards building hypotheses and testing hypothetical conjecture for verification in relation to the empirical reality. It uses statistical tools and techniques of data collection and analysis with experiments, field surveys, observations, structured or exploratory interviews, and case studies.

The central premise of academic research is rooted in the positivist approach, which does not claim direct access to the actual reality in the field, nature, or society, as the case may be. Therefore, this research only assesses the correspondence between the data collected on observed reality through questionnaires, interviews, and participant observations. It analyses the data by conducting tests on the conjectures or hypotheses about the presumed reality, which is built based on theory already available and developed in the subject discipline. In other words, this kind of research is both empirical and contributes to theory-building in specific disciplines as well.

Consequently, academic research heavily depends on concepts and theoretical premises built by earlier research. These domain concepts are helpful in conducting research and teaching-learning in academic disciplines as they facilitate the description and identification of various aspects of reality. Moreover, concepts also define the main features of the phenomenon in the real world, which brings clarity and a common language for understanding and building new knowledge, which is the ultimate purpose of research in higher education.

In short, conventional academic research *assumes* that there is something called an '*objective reality*' in the external world and, with the help of conjectures or hypotheses about presumed reality, uses quantitative and statistical tools to collect and analyse empirical data that the researcher had collected. Moreover, this approach to research separates the observer, that is, the researcher, from the observed world and tries to maintain a rigour of not allowing subjective bias or orientation to the observations as an essential feature of scientific discipline. This is recognised as a 'positivist' approach to scientific research.

However, this kind of scientific study and research is primarily conducted on nature-made systems. When used for man-made social systems, it separates subjective and objective, internal and external reality, assuming it is possible to reach and discover the 'actual reality' with positivist research methodology and logic. However, the reality in man-made systems such as social and educational organisations, unlike nature-made systems, constitutes a combination of tasks, technical systems, and human and social processes. This combined reality is also created by the human process of *experiencing* and individual *intentionality.* In such a situation, '*there is no objective truth; the observer is a part of observation*'—generally known as a *constructivist* approach, which is a counterpoint of the positivist approach of academic-scientific research. Constructivism is an alternative perspective of social and human sciences, that remains the foundation of phenomenological research methodology.

Qualitative research methods based on phenomenology can play and important role in individual and institutional change and transformation, which is presented in three sections. Each section explains a specific qualitative research method and describes its salient features to bring about internal and external change and transformation in persons, collectivity and institutions.

SECTION ONE

Section One focuses on Phenomenological Research (*PR*), which is designed and conducted on man-made social systems and persons. It is based on the assumption or premise that '*reality cannot be seen in an objective way and is always seen as constructed by the observer.*' Therefore, in *PR,* it is necessary to discover the meaning-making processes and narratives humans make on their view of reality, which is emphasised in qualitative research. The assumption of *PR* has far-reaching implications for research and development activities conducted at individual, social, organisational and institutional levels. It provides a deeper dimension of human reality and gives insights into how social reality is built simultaneously by '*meaning-making*' processes deployed by persons and collectivity as a part of lived experiences.

The constructivist perspective of reality is a common factor in Phenomenological Research *(PR)*, Reflective Practice *(RP)* and Action Research *(AR).* These three qualitative methods hold an untapped potential to bring about profound individual and organisational change and transformation. They are designed and oriented towards the 'empowerment' of the human system by activating 'human intentionality'. The three methods mentioned above deploy and facilitate active engagement of the researcher as a participant-observer of the phenomenon with an assumption that reality is essentially created by people, and they give meanings to it and act on it. In other words, organisational or institutional 'reality' is dynamic, unfolding, and influenced by human perceptions and intentions. In the research process, the observer and researcher remain an integral part of the observed reality. Unlike academic, positivist research, phenomenological research does not use so-called detached observer stance of the researcher. However, it actively uses its potential to impact and change the researcher herself, as well as the participants and the external organisational reality she is engaged with.

Phenomenology focuses on the person and meaning-making processes that impact individual and collective behaviours. Reflective Practice *(RP)* is relevant to the professional development of academic faculty and students, whereas Action research (AR) is an effective tool that combines research and action to improve practices at the workplace, and focuses on small and large groups of students, faculty, staff and other stakeholders. *AR* methodology is a well-researched and powerful tool in organisational diagnosis and interventions for change and development (*OD)*. It is also a tool to empower people, which is applied by *OD* consultants and social workers engaged in purposeful actions and projects for institutional and social change.

PR method has good potential both as a learning resource and research tool primarily for faculty and students of *HEIs* to conduct academic and activity-based projects. The pedagogic methodology is mainly derived from the seminal work of *Max Van Manen (1990*) on phenomenology and experiential learning in collectivity.

The contents of the first section of the essay are based on a paraphrase and synthesis of Mr *M.V. Manen's* insights and observations on the relevance of *PR* to pedagogical processes at school and college levels of education. *Manen* first clarifies the distinguishing features of 'phenomenological research', which makes it fundamentally different from 'Positivist' or so-called objective research. The latter is used extensively for academic and doctoral programmes in natural and social sciences at universities in India, Europe and the US. However, with the exception of courses in education, knowledge of the theory and practice of *PR* is scarcely shared or deployed in research institutions and universities in India. It could be because of the prevalent assumptions and premises about '*objective reality*' or refusal to acknowledge the '*subjective truth*' by the academic community. Some unique features of PR are presented below to clarify common misconceptions and emphasise its relevance.

(a) The human phenomenon is essentially mental, social, and historical and, therefore, is different from a natural phenomenon, which is physical, chemical, or behavioural. This is so because human phenomenon primarily requires interpretation and understanding, whereas natural phenomena involve observation and explanation. "*We explain nature; humans must be understood.*" (*Manen*, 1990)

(b) Phenomenology is a part of human science that is distinct from natural science, which studies 'objects of nature, things, natural events' and the way those objects behave. Human science, in contrast, studies 'persons' or 'beings' that have 'consciousness' and that act 'purposefully' in and on the world by creating objects of 'meanings'. They are expressions of how human beings exist in the world. Phenomenology, as a human science, studies persons rather than subjects, individuals, or respondents, as it is normally done in social science research. Meaning-making is a distinctly human process rather than a mechanical or merely a behavioural outcome. The premise is that each person is unique with 'consciousness' and, therefore, needs to be understood with her subjectivity. She should not be reduced to a number or passive respondent who merely reacts to a situation or a trigger from a survey question. Statistical concepts of average sampling are not adequate to give a sense of human beings in their totality. Hence, the inter-subjectivity of the observer and observed is given space in qualitative research. The assumptions and methodology of *PR* are different from that of positivist research and thus need to be recognised squarely at the outset.

(c) The focus on 'person' in phenomenology can be explained in the following way. 'One can explain nature with the logic of rationality and laws of nature, but we have to understand a human, which remains an 'empathic' and imaginative understanding of feelings and not merely a rational understanding of laws of human 'behaviours'. For example, behavioural psychology tries to explain human and animal behaviours as stimulus-response conditioning, but phenomenological insights into human phenomenon radically differ from the explanations of behavioural science in terms of its emphasis on human *intentionality*. The difference is that social science is rather oriented towards controlling human behaviours from the outside, whereas *PR* focuses on liberating a person and developing her human potential. The purpose of qualitative research of PR is to change and transform a person through her intentionality rather than being led by an external agency. A person is helped to take charge of her living by her conscious deployment of intentionality. Researching lived experiences is an essential feature of *PR. W.H. Auden,* reputed poet and thinker, explained the distinction between these two orientations by juxtaposing the difference between two terms: *Individual* and *Person.* 'Individual' is a biological term that classifies a tree, a horse, a man, or a woman, while the term 'person' refers to the uniqueness of each human being. As persons, we are incomparable, unclassifiable, uncountable, and irreplaceable.' Phenomenology is a theory of the 'unique'. Phenomenology studies 'persons' rather than subjects, individuals or respondents, as done in psychology, economics and other social sciences. In this way, Phenomenology is embedded in humanistic values of simultaneous 'concern for self and others' at the human level, and it does not artificially distance the observer from the observed phenomenon in order to maintain conventional 'scientific objectivity' of positivist research.

(d) '*PR* brings to reflective awareness the nature of events experienced in our natural attitude so that we are able to transform or remake ourselves in the true sense of 'education'. Adults educate themselves. 'Phenomenological Research (*PR)* also strives for and encourages a certain attentive awareness to the details and seemingly trivial dimensions of our everyday life experiences'. Therefore, an accurate understanding of phenomenology can only be accomplished by 'actively doing it'; The essential feature of *PR* is the act of systematic writing phenomenological descriptions, because *PR* discipline of writing heightens attentive awareness of the participant-researcher. Documenting and writing of experiential data regularly is an essential part of PR discipline because writing creates a space for individual reflections on the 'lived phenomenon.'

(e) 'PR does not offer us the possibility of effective theory with which we can explain or control the world, but rather it offers us plausible insights that bring us with more direct contact with the world.' *Phenomenological reflection* is not introspective but retrospective. It is re-collective; it is a reflection on an experience that has already passed or lived through. 'The aim of *PR* is to construct an animating, evocative description; it is a text of human actions, behaviours, intentions, and experiences as we meet them in the life world. Thus, *PR* uses the works of poets, authors, artists, and cinematographers since it is in literary works that we find human beings as 'situated persons'. A wide variety and possibilities of human experiences are presented in condensed and transcended forms in literary texts. The author (*Max Van Manen),* cautions us that *PR* should not be confused with poetry, story or art because it aims at making explicit and seeking 'universal meaning' where poetry and literature remain 'implicit and particular'. Phenomenology as a part of human science begins where poetry has reached its endpoint.

(f) 'In *PR,* the terms subjective and objective take special meanings. In

> Positivist research, subjectivity has no place since it aims at objective descriptions based on empirical findings. In contrast, objectivity and subjectivity are not mutually exclusive categories because the researcher, using *PR* methodology, establishes personal relations with the object of her inquiry. Also, the researcher wants to show the object, describe it, interpret it, and be misled, side-tracked or excited by external factors. She is a guardian and defender of the true nature of the object. As a researcher, she is strong in her orientation to the object of the study 'in a unique and personal way' while avoiding the danger of getting arbitrary, self-indulgent or getting captivated and carried away by her un-reflected perceptions.' In this way, PR is closer in orientation to meditative philosophies of Eastern traditions like yoga and zen, which practice non-textual reflective techniques like meditation to develop detached involvement and vigilant attention to the matter at hand simultaneously.'

In this manner, *PR* questions are meaning questions and not problem questions. Problem questions are those that are raised in conventional academic research, which intend to seek solutions and 'correct' knowledge, effective procedures, methods to get results and winning strategies. In contrast, *PR* asks for the meaning and significance of certain phenomena because many questions cannot be solved and done away with, but an deeper understanding of the root of the problem is needed. Meaning questions need to be better or more deeply understood and aptly comprehended so that on the basis of this understanding, one may be able to act more thoughtfully and tactfully in certain situations. In short, *PR* enables us to develop critical 'value-based' competence, distinct from behavioural competence, to deliver 'thoughtful and tactful actions' that are of direct relevance to those studying, teaching, and working in educational and social institutions.

As mentioned above, *PR* asks meaning questions rather than problem questions because meanings are interpreted in a context, and *PR* shows how each phenomenon differs in terms of meaning. As *Max Van Manen* points out in an example of how educators interpret hope. It is interesting to see how '*pedagogic hope*' in the teaching-learning context of schools differs from other types of hope at workplaces.

In an educational context which is influenced by technical rationality, it is commonly observed that educationists, administrators, and subject experts use 'objectives or outcomes' and apply the concept of 'management by objectives' in curriculum design and delivery to measure teaching-learning outcomes. Faculty members are encouraged to see themselves as professionals accountable for outcomes, wherein students hold expectations with a 'hope' of learning and developing competencies for a better future. However, the language used in curriculum and publicity brochures is exclusively a language of 'doing' and shows a total absence of 'being' in it. Neither the faculty nor the students learn to talk in a language where one's being is present with 'hope'. The educational aims, objectives and goals systematically deprive hope of 'being'. In the Essay Eight, Prof *Amartya Sen* also refers to the neglect of 'being' and over emphasis on 'achieving' in the concept of human development.

In this way, aspirations, expectations and anticipations of young faculty and students are reduced to desires, wants, career ambitions, certainties of returns on investment, and market predictions. The myopic vision of higher education deprives future generations of looking at the possibilities that lie beyond the 'mirror images' produced by academic conventions and media messages. The quotation of Mr *S.J Harris* at the beginning of this essay highlights the purpose of education by juxtaposing mirrors and windows; PR opens up widows of meaning and possibility. The analogy of mirror is also used in the case study on '*Nirman*' in Section Two. The case shows how the identity and career of young men and women in India is determined by mirror images without reflecting on personal experiences of day-to-day living.

The real meaning of hope is to 'believe in possibilities', which strengthens and builds confidence in the potential of the self and realising it fully at individual and collective levels. The quotation mentioned at the beginning rightly refers to the purpose of education as 'turning mirrors into windows'; it makes much sense in the backdrop of the contemporary context of higher education in India, influenced by one-dimensional techno-economic rationality.

More specifically, the meanings of educational objectives and aims tend to make us see the past as present and the present as past, more as mirror images. They orient us to view the present as a burden or something to be overcome to hope for the future. The academic climate on campuses is devoid of spaces 'to attend to experiences of here and now living'. Therefore, it is relevant to refer to Case Three on *Nirman* in the book, which describes a temporary learning institution for already educated young men and women in colleges. It offers 'hopeful' opportunities for the young to reflect on their life choices and create self-fulfilling careers through a process of individual and collective 'self-driven learning' by engaging with self-chosen field projects. They learn to take charge of their own learning and future careers.

The curriculum language of 'objectives' in higher education is actually meant for administrative convenience in planning and monitoring the delivery and progress of teaching-learning. In reality, they do not allow any space for 'hope of being' in the early years of adult life of students and on campus. One dimensional focus on 'doing and thought' drives out 'being and feelings' from higher education in India. It damages the healthy or wholesome development of young minds and collectivity on campuses.

Another impact of lopsided emphasis on 'doing' and 'outcomes' is apparent in institutional climate and behaviours on campus, particularly in faculty and classrooms of *HEIs*. It is full of cynical attitudes and uncaring behaviours of faculty towards students on campuses, as illustrated in Essay Five on '*Understanding Behavioural Processes in HEIs*'. It leads to a sense of alienation among important stakeholders like faculty and students, which takes them away from the primary purpose and processes of education. The typical experience of individual faculty and staff, generally called '*burn out*' on higher education campuses, is not always a symptom of excessive workload and output but more often a condition wherein the faculty do not know 'why they are doing what they are doing'. They tend to ask themselves with a hopeless sigh, 'What is the use of doing this?' and it is difficult to give an honest response to the question because the process of capturing hope of 'being' is not alive on educational campuses. In other words, nourishment and periodic replenishment of 'being' at the level of individual and collective are the most neglected aspects of campus life in HEIs. Instead, much of the energy of students and faculty is spent on ritualistic and meaningless routines of curriculum delivery, seminars, and examinations.

It is the responsibility of faculty and institutions to recapture human consciousness and belief in 'living with hope'. It is important to recognise that the negativity in attitudes emerges primarily from the technical-rational perspective that remains unresolved.

Summary

The Phenomenological Reflection *(PR)* methodology discovers the meaning-making process, and Reflective Practice *(RP)* works with professional identities and value-based actions of faculty and staff. Action Research *(AR)* uses experiential learning with data generated on the job and projects in groups to improve organisations. It emphasises collective inquiry and research for problem-solving. Therefore, the above-mentioned qualitative research methods, *PR*, *RP* and *AR*, deserve to be in the mainstream of teaching-learning, managing, and researching professional and institutional processes of higher education in India. They have the potential to strengthen institution building *(IB)* and improve and sustain the quality of higher education as well.

Phenomenology and Development of Consciousness

Consciousness is the only access or gateway that human beings have to the world. By virtue of being conscious, we can relate to the world. Anything that presents it to human consciousness is potentially of interest to phenomenology, whether the object is real or imaginary, empirically measurable or subjectively felt. However, consciousness itself cannot be described directly because the real things in the world are always meaningfully 'constructed' by conscious human beings. Hence, consciousness is expressed with reference to either the world itself or about that experiencing person who attaches meanings to experiences. *PR* is thus based on a constructivist view of cognitive psychology.

Edmund Husserl (1859-1938),[2] a thinker and researcher on phenomenology, said that the fundamental structure of consciousness is intentional. The quality of intentionality means that there is an inseparable connection between human beings and the world. However, it must be recognised that human beings are not just something that 'humans automatically are'; it is something they must 'try to be'. Intentionality, in this sense, is a 'consciously learned and acquired human capability'.

Phenomenology is a perspective and methodology of exploring how we experience the world in order to know the world, which cannot happen without consciously engaging with and being a part of the world through reflection. Intentionality explains the inseparable connection between the person and the world. It is 'to be' in the world, and phenomenology searches for the secrets of the world and human experiences. However, intentionality is only a retrospectively available variable in human consciousness because we cannot experience something while reflecting on it.

Phenomenology research *(PR)*, like Action Research *(AR)*, is discovery-oriented in terms of research and orientation to learning. It wants to find out what a specific phenomenon means and how it is experienced. Human science researcher who uses the *PR* method is expected to be a scholar and also a sensitive observer of the subtleties of everyday life; as a scholar, she is a reader of all relevant texts in humanities, literature, history, philosophy, anthropology and social sciences as her domain of interest. With active engagement with fine or performing arts like poetry, music, dance, and painting, she can further develop her sensibilities.

The primary aim of *PR* is to actively explore the lived experience in all its modalities and aspects. *PR* remains distinct from positivist research in two ways: a) it employs reflection on lived experience in order to reach a thoughtful and reflective grasping of what that experience presents to the consciousness in order to highlight its special significance, and b) *PR* makes a distinction between '*appearance* and *essence*', between the things of our experience and that which 'grounds' the things of our experience, that is its essence.

In other words, the purpose of PR is *'to grasp the nature and significance of the experience in such a way that it is not seen so far'*. It is 'grounded' research in this sense of the term. It gives an original insight into the experience, which reveals the meaning of the specific and also the general in a unique way.

However, as said earlier, a real understanding of phenomenology can only be achieved by actively engaging with it. Phenomenological research gathers a deeper understanding of the nature or meaning of our everyday experiences. It attempts to get insightful descriptions of the way we experience the world without classifying or abstracting it.

It must be emphasised that Phenomenology research is a scientific discipline because it is a systematic, explicit, self-critical, and inter-subjective study of lived experience. Lived experience in everyday context is more complex and elusive than a singular description of experience, and therefore, it is a demanding research discipline. Since it is closely connected with the consciousness of the person experiencing and reflecting, it is of much relevance for all those who are engaged in the process of teaching, learning and managing institutions. Engagement with PR implies writing and reflecting on lived experiences. This is another reason why it is of direct relevance for the development of faculty, staff and students as 'persons' engaged with academic or higher learning in HEIs. It is equally valuable for all others who are constantly engaged in providing human services such as care in the case of administrative staff in education, hospitality, and healthcare.

Writing is an essential part of developing skills in *PR* because it creates an opportunity to be in touch with our 'being' while in the process of experiencing and reflecting. It provides a distinct space for reflecting on lived experiences. 'To write is to measure the depth of things and also to come to a sense of one's own depth.' Writing seeks to make external what somehow remains internal. It creates a distance between us and the world whereby the subjectivities of daily experiences become the object of our reflective awareness. Therefore, writing about our experiences as faculty or as students help us to create a learning space to reflect on our relations with others, that is, students, faculty, colleagues, staff, management and so on and return to them with a deepened understanding of the meanings of the lived experiences and the real life-world on campus.

It is important to remind ourselves that phenomenology, though a human science, is not an empirical science. It does not describe actual states of affairs; it is not a science of empirical facts and scientific generalisations or asking who did what, When? Where? How many? To what extent? Under what conditions? and so on. Instead, *PR* questions, '*What does it mean to be a faculty or parent, by reflecting on self, role, and person situated in context.*' *PR* also asks, '*How come it happened this way?*' so that our attention is drawn retrospectively to the '*process of experiencing and meaning-making*' rather than the factual content of the experience.

Though phenomenology may sometimes appear empirical since it is based on experiences, it is not empirically derived. It goes beyond mere interest in the particularity of a situation. Therefore, it is not appropriate to use survey methods or statistical methods. For *PR*, the primary focus is on the 'uniqueness' of the human experience. Description and narration of lived experiences are the core of *PR*.

PR asks for the meaning and significance of a phenomenon that cannot be solved and done away with. The utility of *PR* is in generating a better or deeper understanding so that our engagement with certain situations can be more thoughtful. It has a potential to create thoughtful and sensitive practitioners in modern professions. Therefore, it deserves to be a part of the curriculum of professional courses in medicine, human resource management, education and law, where human processes constitute a significant part of professional practice.

It would be adequately clear by now, from the above explanation of the discipline of *PR*, that it has the potential to add to the personal and professional development of faculty and students and also to enrich the teaching-learning processes of academic institutions. However, Reflective Practice *(RP)* described in the next section is a specific method of qualitative research designed for the development of professionals in education, which is explained in the next section.

SECTION TWO

Reflective Practice *(RP)* is a method of learning designed for professional development where the knowledge of *PR* is its essential foundation. At the operational level, some principles of *PR* and reflective pedagogy, andragogy and adult learning methods are simimar to that of *RP*. Both *PR* and *RP* rely on the processes of observations, communication, and development of judgement, as well as tact and skills in human interactions and decision-making. However, *RP* is an appropriate method for addressing specific pedagogic, teaching-learning issues of human development in an educational context.

For conducting *PR* as a preparation for *RP*, following guidelines would be useful for students, researchers, and faculty in selecting themes for building an educational ambience on the campus.

PR in *RP* follows a methodical structure of six research activities or procedures that are listed below:

(a) Attending to a phenomenon that seriously interests us and commits us to the world
(b) Investigating experience as we live it rather than as we conceptualise it
(c) Reflecting on the essential themes, for example, hope, tact, care, togetherness, replenishment, relating to others, interest in the subject, interest in students, peer pressure, and safety that characterise the phenomenon
(d) Describing the phenomenon through the art of writing and rewriting
(e) Maintaining a strong pedagogical or learning and educational orientation in relation to the phenomenon
(f) Balancing the research context by considering parts and whole, that is, to step back and link at how the part needs to contribute to the total. It is essential to focus on particular (part) and general (total) also. Writing about a phenomenon of your choice is an effective means to develop critical consciousness for better professional practice because it distances the person from habitual practice in action.

The first case titled 'Self, Career and Institution Development' presented in the Case Study section of this book is a first-person narrative based on the author's own experiences on campus. It documents the emerging tension between the needs of the self and role expectations about new faculty in Indian colleges. It is a kind of experiential (phenomenological) description of the issues and dilemmas in faculty careers confronted by those who opt for a teaching profession. Readers can better appreciate the relevance of *PR* and *RP* in the context of this case written as a first person narration.

Reflective Practice: Issue on Professional Identity of Faculty

Reflective Practice is fundamentally and primarily a pedagogical approach that utilises the research methodology of phenomenology for professional development. Reflective practice as a discipline has been a part of the professional education of teachers and faculty since the 1980s, mainly in Europe, and it focuses on the role of the individual and her personal 'self' and 'identity' as a professional. The challenge for faculty in the teaching profession is that there are many 'images' of the profession that keep floating at the workplace or campus. Initially, there is a gap between the 'self' and the 'professional' identity that faculty would aspire to have. Enthusiasm for imitation of these mirror images of the 'ideal identity' of a professional does not last long, and it takes some time and effort for a newcomer to stabilise oneself in the work role and develop a suitable professional identity.

Reflective Practice and Development of Professionals

RP helps individual faculty and also the postgraduate, doctoral-level students of the discipline of education and other professional disciplines like social work and health care in a) integrating and making sense of their day-to-day experiences with their subjective view of professional learning, along with b) a systematic review process of a mentor or senior faculty at workplaces of *HEI*'s. Thus, reflective practice requires coaching from a senior colleague or a professional coach because it needs initial handholding and guidance from an experienced faculty member who is conversant with the process of 'review-based reflective practices'.

In other words, *RP* is a dynamic, developmental process meant for faculty so that they can become 'reflective practitioners' in the field of education. It is a combination of an attitude, orientation, a state of mind and an educational approach for professionals to orient themselves for 'thoughtful practice'. It is important to recognise that *RP* is a reflection and comprehension of professional actions. It is not a technique but more of an attitude and orientation of a professional's mind that focuses more on processes rather than goals with a specific direction. *RP* creates choices and meanings so that profound change is possible in the mind and practices of the professional because the *RP* approach to practice frees the mind of the professional and enables her to be in touch with the 'being'. In faculty development programmes, *RP* methodology, which is oriented toward a careful examination of both non-critical and critical incidents in professional life on and outside the institutional campus. This can bring significant transformation at individual and collective levels.

In other words, *RP* is a pedagogical approach that helps faculty learn through professional inquiry on personal experiences at the workplace, and it is used as a primary source of learning to work further on improving practices. Such an inquiry is also useful for developing consciousness of pedagogical practice and, more importantly, consciousness of the wider political and social structure of higher education. Thus, *RP* methodology holds the potential for a step towards deeper examination at personal and institutional levels of the values and beliefs that underlie professional practices in teaching and educational administration. It would be apparent from the above description how the engagement of faculty, together with their senior colleagues and mentors in *RP*, holds the potential to contribute significantly to the *IB* process in education. It is a path to build 'robust' institution in true sense of the term.

Donald Schon (1983), a pioneer in the field of *RP*, argued that 'reflection *on* action' is meant to overcome the limitations of 'reflection *in* action' since the latter is relatively common in most professional practices. As practised by professionals,

'*Reflection–in-action*' is the 'almost unconscious, instantaneous reflection' that happens as in the case of a more experienced faculty or other professionals who would solve problems or dilemmas in classroom delivery while engaging with educational and administrative activities on campus. However, '*Reflection-on-action*' takes place after the event, and it includes specific professional actions such as a teaching session in the educational context. Therefore, it is a more deliberate and self-conscious process. Compared to the instantaneous '*Reflection-in-action*' *(RiP)* practices, more attention is given to critical analysis and evaluation of action in *reflection-on-action (RoP)* conducted in *RP* orientation sessions. Moreover, alternative options of actions possible in specific situations are considered retrospectively, either individually or with the help of a coach or facilitator. Both *RiP* and *RoP* approaches are used in *RP* methodology.

It is recognised that while in practice, a professional learns about many hidden aspects and gathers tacit knowledge behind the routine practices through a process of conscious review and reflection post-action. It is different and better than the so-called 'thinking on the feet' approach that most professionals are forced to indulge in due to the work pressure of day-to-day operations. Therefore, a more deliberate review or research on actions taken would benefit and improve professional practice. In other words, Reflective practice is a method for strengthening individual learning. It can also be useful for 'Action Learning' *(AR)* projects in order to facilitate organisational or small group learning to improve institutional systems and practices.

In short, both personal and professional development is facilitated by *Reflective Practice (RP),* which in turn would help faculty and administrators of *HEIs* confront more comprehensive questions of 'institutional identity' along with reflections on the role of 'self' and 'being' in professional practice. It would be a step towards developing an academic climate and culture conducive to building a learning community with professional values and norms, which is considered as an essential part of building world-class, robust educational institutions.

PR as a methodology has the potential to make academic institutions remain vibrant and open to innovations while maintaining continuity and conformity with best practices of the past.

Illustrative examples of Operational Skills and Guidelines for *RP* Writing

Writing and observation skills for *RP*: For faculty and student developmental programmes that are based on the *RP* approach, the following writing activities are usually conducted. *RP* first begins with writing a personal description of the phenomenon that one is interested in exploring, such as: 'How do I see myself in the role of faculty? Or in the role of a research fellow or PG student?' Some specific guidelines are given below for PG students and practising faculty on producing and writing *RP* descriptions:

(a) You need to describe the experience as you lived through it. Avoid causal explanations, generalisations, or abstract interpretations as much as possible. Do not state the causal explanation of why you like something or why you chose a profession.
(b) Instead, describe the experience from the inside, as it were, almost like a state of mind, the feeling, the mood, the emotion.
(c) Focus on a particular example or incident of the object of experience; describe specific events, a happening, and an experience.
(d) Try to focus on examples of the experience that stand out in its vividness, as it were the first time. The clue to identifying such examples is to locate what has touched your heart and soul and troubled you at an 'emotional' rather than 'intellectual' level.
(e) Attend to how the body feels, how things smell, how they sound, and the primary sensations.
(f) Avoid trying to beautify your account with fancy phrases or flowery terminology.
(g) Factual accuracy is not more important than the 'plausibility of the account' that remains true to the 'living sense' in it.

Note: Such narration of personal experience can let the *PR* and *RP* researcher know what a lived experience looks like in his/her interest of study. Then, one can go about obtaining such descriptions from other relevant persons and the published creative literature like novels, poetry, stories, etc., so that the essence of experiences can be synthesised and grounded.

In the academic context of higher education, when young faculty members write about critical incidents in teaching and learning the subject, many record adverse incidents or events. One should not over-focus on negative examples because it may take away the complexity of the teaching-learning process. Other writing pitfalls in faculty narratives worth mentioning are:

(a) A critical incident is summarised in a few generalised words. Here, the problem is that one may lose contact with the incident itself. One should elaborate on it with more details, and one can try to narrate it orally to someone else before writing it.
(b) However, too many details on thoughts, feelings, and actions post-event

may take the description away from the immediate trail of thought that happens as a part of natural thinking or reflective process.

(c) Sometimes, critical incidents are documented as a conversation, which is also a pitfall. Focusing on oral dialogues may take you away from other important details such as gestures, postures, and tone of voice. In *PR*, such details capture the tone and content of the experience.

Phenomenological research methodology blends well with Reflective Practice in its application to pedagogy and andragogy. The focus is to use reflection on practical experiences on campus in the context of teaching, learning, and relating with students and colleagues in order to get valuable insights for improving professional practices. In a manner, PR and RP both aim to improve and change rigid educational routines and practices. Some examples of applications are:

(a) Faculty development programmes in *HEIs* may include 'reflective writing' assignments wherein participants are asked to describe a critical incident that would capture the dilemmas they had experienced in processes of teaching-learning in classrooms and on campus life, in the form of a story or an event. Such cases can be of learning value because they reveal the complexity of real-life problem-solving, decision-making, and collaboration in teaching and learning as a part of their professional roles. The data would help faculty have access to more helpful feedback from colleagues and coaches on perceptions and offer them an analysis and insights on the teaching-learning practices. Such cases can also be shared with others in seminars or case conferences so that it would initiate collaborative analysis and discussions of these cases.

(b) Writing cases based on reflective practices (*RP*) presents multiple perspectives and solutions to address the dilemmas that faculty as an academic community face. Faculty from different institutions would relate easily to such experience-based material, which can be used as a means of professional development. More such creative activities and exercises of reflective writing of real experiences can be designed for students and faculty for mutual benefit.

(c) It is common to find students write about experiences that focus on the content of a specific subject or being in a specific college or university as a problem. However, some students face issues of gender, caste, class, and regionalism of other cultures that is different from the local culture and write about them. In the context of *HEIs* in India, with gender and caste inequalities and regional differences, it would be relevant to counsel students and faculty to write about such experiences on campuses to get authentic, experiential information on critical institutional issues in order to avoid tragic incidents like ragging, leading to suicide. A case study on *Rohit Vemula's letter* in the Second section on cases would illustrate how such writing assignments would help build a conducive climate for developing inclusive university campuses. This case decodes Vemula's letter to get an access to his thinking and feelings in a context.

A note of caution: 'Reflective practice' is now an over-used jargon in academic communities and training colleges for faculty development. RP is more of a *process* of applying critical, self-conscious and creative thinking at the individual or group level rather than a standardised *technique* and *competence*. It begins with a particular focus and purpose in a phenomenon. Reflections are conducted deliberately and consciously so that they lead to actions to improve the situation one intends to change. This process has the potential to make faculty and students aware of the power and authority of the 'self' as implied in the concept of *Agency - Intentionality* and self-directed action through the involvement of self and participation along with others. More importantly, it has the potential to question the instrumental or technical rationality (*TR)* of educational bureaucracy and its rigid power structures. In short, *RP*, as a research tool, necessitates an equal focus on the process and outcomes of practice to remain true to the essentially liberating and empowering process implied in this method.

Critical reflection is an integral part of *PR* and *RP* that can uncover the deeper assumptions and things taken for granted in the academic workplace, curriculum design, pedagogy, classroom behaviours, etc. Also, it facilitates personal interventions like confronting a person at the individual level on her self-image and at the group level about experiences of role-taking. For example, sentences captured in self-talk and conversations in natural settings, such as, *'I am too small a person', 'I am not intelligent', 'we are helpless', 'nothing can be done against those in power'*, and the common-sense wisdom like *'those in power are always right'* can be considered for their implicit meaning and the self-image of the person who has used it so that such utterance and situation can be explored further. They reveal assumptions and self-concept of the members.

With changed or enhanced awareness of prevalent practices, faculty and students can initiate interventions to change undesirable practices, which is the essence of the RP methodology. It thus may lead to *Action Research* projects for planned interventions initiated by top management and supported by faculty, staff and students. It may need the help of external or internal experts and facilitators as it is used in the methodology of *OD*, discussed in the book in the Essay Six.

Professional and Personal Identity of Key Stakeholders of *HEIs*

The theme of individual and professional 'identity' of faculty and administrators needs special attention in the discussion on *RP* because it is a research methodology designed to improve professional identity and practices of faculty on academic campuses. A few concepts developed by three researchers, *Cooley C.H. (1902), Nais J. (1989), and Weik K. (1995),* are relevant to understanding the dynamic and social dimensions of identity formation. They are used as a tool for generating data for research on 'Reflective Practice'. Also, they focus on the evolutionary process of forming individual and professional identities during the careers of teachers and faculty, which is the backbone of educational institutions.

Cooley (1902) describes the 'looking glass' nature of the teaching profession to indicate the reflective nature of identity. A person in the role of faculty finds herself reflected in a variety of mirrors: her colleagues, her students, parents, administrative staff, and neighbours. They send idealised images and role expectations of the faculty's professional identity. The difficult part for the role-holder is that she has to cope with multiple images and the mismatch between her personal identity and professional identity. Such conflicts between personal and professional expectations may distort a person's self-image, which can be restored only with self–reflection and guidance from senior colleagues in the institution or professional coaches.

Karl Weik (1995) has made an important observation that identity at the workplace is not fixed and singular but is multiple, changing and provisional in nature. More importantly, identity involves the continual construction and reconstruction of relationships with others in the workplace. A few examples of the tension between the personal and professional identities of faculty in the initial years of their careers are given below. The author has used them to discuss the issues of personal and professional identities on educational campuses as material on learning resources for faculty development programmes.

Developing Professional Identity

(How faculty 'see' themselves; five examples.)

Early indications of what one enjoys doing are located in childhood experiences or early work experiences. It is a signal to the person to recognise his/ her inner 'need'. It drives the person to do something to satisfy this need. Sometimes, it is a hidden potential that is constrained by the context and culture in which you live. Here are five examples of young faculty and students who talk about themselves in terms of self-images of personal identities and struggle to form appropriate professional identities in the early stages of teaching careers:

A

"*In school days, I enjoyed when I got an opportunity to present myself on stage. I participated and enjoyed playing roles in plays or skits, proposing a vote of thanks, or singing folk songs. I was encouraged by my teachers, though my friends laughed at my performance. Later in life, I realised that I did not have a special talent or patience to develop competence in acting or music, but as a person I felt happy to present and express myself before an audience. This desire or need has remained with me throughout, i.e. to communicate and express myself. In the teaching profession, I could satisfy this need by engaging with students in and outside class and even in writing for newsletters of college and other magazines.*"

B

"*In the classroom, I experience the challenge and feel thrilled when students ask questions or give a contrary opinion to what I had said. I allow all kinds of questions; related or unrelated to the subject that I am teaching. The flip side is that I get carried away by the argument or point under discussion and address only the student who had asked the question, and other students feel sidelined. Therefore, I am very much appreciated by a few students but do not get favorable feedback from many. It is rather demotivating and not good for a career in a competitive climate of the college.*"

C

"*My problem as a faculty is about 'class control'. The last benchers remain disinterested and don't pay attention to what I am saying. If I raise my pitch and voice, I feel exhausted after some time. Perhaps my expectation that all students are interested in the subject that I teach may be wrong, or is there a limitation in my abilities to teach? I should better ask my senior colleague whom I trust. It affects my confidence and teaching.*"

D

"*I came to the teaching profession not by choice but as a compromise. I like performing arts like music, films, dance, and theatre. I like to express myself without inhibition. Being a teacher brings a lot of control over my natural behavior. Since I have to survive in the job, I have to suppress my real talent and desires. However, I like to be in the company of young students and enjoy criticising the school system and authority in informal groups on campus.*"

E

"*I studied in a school from a tribal area and learned to cooperate and help others naturally in school and neighborhoods. When I came to the city for a college education, I learned that one has to compete with others and not share everything with them or not fully trust my classmates. Our coaching class instructor while preparing for admission to professional courses had told us, 'Your classmates are not friends but only competitors on college campuses'. But I am not comfortable with such an attitude. I don't know what is more important, cooperation with others or competing with them. How can we have both? Those who get high marks and ranks are good in individual studies. What is the role of teamwork and helping others on this campus, even when the motto of our college is 'unity is strength'*!"

- How do faculty see their professional role and status in the context of society and college?
- How do students experience culture and values on campuses and its impact on their self-image and relatedness with others?

A rresearch study on the professional identity of school teachers conducted by *J Nias* (1989) shows that the integration of professional identity into an individual's self-image takes longer periods of time. As a part of initial socialisation in career, the personal identity of 'you' is relatively independent of the professional self of a 'teacher' in the school context. 'Being yourself' in the context of educational institutions has less to do with actual teaching-learning processes in the classroom and more to do with generating a sense of community and integrating personal and professional connections between the faculty and students. *Nias's* observation highlights that professional identities are formed in communities of professionals in institutions. Professional identity, however, is distinct from task-related professional practices in teaching-learning-researching.

The larger purpose of *RP* as a research and reflective process is to liberate academics from the influence of educational policies and practices that are based on *technical rationality* with a focus mainly on evidence, efficiency, and external control. This freedom is needed to counterbalance the dominance of bureaucratic culture in higher education and bring in new resources and ideas. Needless to say, it would be resisted by the establishment because it unsettles the rigid hierarchy and bureaucratic procedures. For faculty and students, it offers an opportunity to design a personal and professional agenda (*portfolio*) for continuous learning and self-improvement. It can also be used for self-evaluation of performance along with official evaluations and assessments that often fail to improve performance because it values the education system over faculty as persons.

If *RP* is primarily a methodology of personal and professional improvement and not for assessment of task performance, its focus on reflecting on experiences at the workplace is extended further in the methodology of *'Action Research' (AR)* for institutional building. The phenomenological research and autobiographical approaches of *RP* can encompass personal, institutional and social contexts and develop a sense of personal and collective values of self-belief, autonomy and mutual trust in higher education. This is relevant in the *HEIs* context, which is increasingly influenced by values of competition, ranking, audit, and hard facts rather than experiential data and inclusive culture. However, one must recognise the reality that the prevalent norms and culture of educational institutions are anchored in technical rationality of the bureaucracy and state-controlled regulators. Therefore, one should hold realistic expectations of success and consider *RP* and *AR* mainly as a long-term strategy for building robust institutions.

The last section (Three) of this essay is on methodology of *Action Research (AR)* for institutional change and transformation. It summarises key features *of Action Reseaarch*, which is now widely used as a tool of diagnosis and interventions in organisations the world over, as an integral part of the Organisation Development *(OD)* process. *AR* is a unique methodology that blends action and research or organisational learning that can be used in a variety of contexts—corporate, educational, and voluntary social organisations for initiating change and transformations to build institutional climate and culture.

SECTION THREE

Action research methodology is based on a belief that change in attitude and behaviours is most effectively achieved when opportunities are available for experiential learning at the workplace. Also, it is based on research findings that effective learning essentially occurs at the workplace within a natural workgroup or when the learning context is directly related to the existing conditions of the workplace and its needs. In other words, training sessions in classrooms are not very impactful for initiating organisation-wide change and attitudinal development. *AR* fills this gap between classroom learning and workplace learning or between theory and practice.

Action learning groups (Sets) are often used in *AR* since they are a more effective way to bring behavioural and organisational changes than other methods like conventional training and lectures. These learning groups remain more connected to the ground realities of the workplace, which is not the case even in the context of learning in behavioural training laboratories or Process Labs. *AR* is appropriately suitable for all kinds of organisations in business and non-business sectors, including academic institutions like universities, institutes and colleges because it uniquely combines experiential learning, that is, 'research, reflecting on action taken' leading to further intervention for change, that is, 'revised action, or experimentation'. It integrates reflection and action, leading to improved plan action. It is an iterative process that improves problem-solving that focusses on identifying and resolving the root cause of problems rather than dealing with the symptoms of the problem.

AR recognises that what is taken as a problem statement initially may not remain so after collective inquiry and testing in action. *AR* is a robust methodology that requires new habits of learning or researching on the job.

AR process is built on the seminal academic work of reputed organisational psychologist *David Kolb's (1984)* cycle of learning, and it consists of four stages: *a) Experiencing, b) Observation, c) Reflections, and d) Experimentation.* Action learning is a circular or iterative rather than a linear process of learning wherein one rotation of the cycle naturally leads to the next higher or broader level so that the breadth and depth of collective learning are gradually expanded.

AR is conducted in small and large groups (sets) with the help of a facilitator, which is unlike the conventional individual student as learner and teacher focus of academic learning in formal education. The purpose of *AR* is to develop 'set' members' capability for solving problems, and it is done through '*process learning*' wherein the members acquire '*process awareness*' and problem-solving skills in how to sense, diagnose and intervene at personal, interpersonal, group and institutional levels. Thus, knowledge of the processes in terms of roles, tasks, attitudes, structures and, most importantly, values that influence institutional behaviours are acquired in *AR*. A detailed note on skills in process learning is included in the third section of this book as *Learning Resources.*

Process Learning in *AR*

Process knowledge is applied knowledge learned through experimentation, which is the cycle of action, reflection, and revised action. It requires sensitivity and orientation towards 'learning to learn'. Hence, the focus is not on the so-called rigour of scientific and statistical research but on the applicability of findings to solve practical problems at the workplace through a systematic and iterative cycle of data gathering, analysis and interpretation, action planning and implementation. It is a discipline of sensing, diagnosis, intervention, action, and evaluation through reflections within small groups. It develops a heightened awareness of individual and group learning processes while confronting real-life problems at workplaces.

It is clear that *AR* requires the professional help of an expert or consultant in behavioural processes, qualitative research methods and systems theory. Such a person would be in the best position to guide the members of an organisation in conceptualising the problem, sensing, diagnosing, and refining the problem definition with the help of data on the living system.

The methodology of *AR* does not depend merely on the analysis of the formal system as described in official documents of the organisation, which often gives details on authority structure, role descriptions, and procedures. Instead, *AR* depends on the data and analysis of the '*living system*' rather than the '*formal or technical system*'; the former is made up of perceptions, attitudes and feelings of work groups, departmental members, and at the interpersonal level of superiors, subordinates and peers. Thus, qualitative and phenomenological methods of data generation are more suitable or applicable for the task of diagnosing living systems.

Five Stages of *AR* in Research and Action

1. **Data Gathering:** The task and the related objective is to focus on distinguishing the causes of the problem from its symptoms and anticipating consequences and impact outcomes of the problem. At this stage, the members of the *AR* group explore the implicit and explicit facets of the problem. The process is to help members identify and define the problem with a recognition that the process of learning is not unidirectional but of discovering, in the sense that what is recognised as a problem may not remain as 'the' problem, in the course of inquiry, as the group progresses to the successive five stages of *AR* exploration.
2. **Analysis and interpretation**: This stage focuses on making sense of the gathered data and interpreting what it means. It involves sensing what actions are needed for changing and improving the present state of the workplace. The process is participatory in order to get process insights on the data generated.
3. **Action Planning**: At this stage, alternative courses of action are generated, and their potential impacts are analysed and assessed. Actual steps are charted, and then actions are initiated by the consultant along with the *AR* set members.
4. **Action Taking:** It involves noting and documenting the actual response to problem-intervention, anticipating unforeseen consequences of the action taken and planning for such contingencies; describing the action plan in detail to members and preparing for resistance and non-involvement of members.
5. **Evaluation:** This stage consists of checking the congruence between desired and actual results. In case of unintended consequences, repeat the cycle of the earlier stage of data gathering on the current state of the system.

Relevance of *AR* in *HEIs*

Learning in *AR* projects and groups (sets) is about generating relevant knowledge and discarding outdated knowledge about a living system, which is a dynamic and evolving-unfolding process and may not be congruent with the formal system designed for the workplace. This gives *AR* participants an opportunity to develop a systemic and holistic perspective of the organisation in terms of its formal and emerging systems as well. *AR* connects formal and living systems that provide valid data, which is not possible through surveys and positivist research.

The peculiar strength of *AR* is that it gives access to the experiential but unarticulated data of the living system that participants experience at the day-to-day level. At each step of the learning cycle, *AR* informs the members and the facilitator/consultant suggests new insights into the tasks, systems, processes, people, and values of the workplace. It offers valuable guidance on developing the capabilities of the people and the systems' *robustness* to face challenges in the changing environment. Above all, the experiential learning process of *AR* helps members confront the issue of identity and values of members at individual and institutional levels so that the congruence and incongruence between the two can be identified and explored, reflected upon and resolved for collective benefit.

Impact of Egalitarian and Democratic Values of *AR*: A Perceived Threat to Power Position from Empowerment

On the flip side of it, *AR* methodology has the potential to expose the vulnerability of the top management to the democratic process that values the participation of groups, respect for dignity, freedom to express feelings and fulfilment in the work of each member. Therefore, the application of *AR* may be resisted by those in authority positions because it may be perceived as a threat to the power structure. However, with the development of process sensitivity to power dynamics in groups and organisations, these difficulties can be overcome by building a climate of trust and collaboration among stakeholders.

The participative methodology of *AR* goes beyond the surface-level involvement of people and goes into decision-making processes. Such exposure offers self-direction and self-control to individuals and work groups. It has the potential to offer *HEIs* an opportunity to create parallel but complimentary learning groups in universities, institutes and colleges with a twin focus on research and action for building institutions.

AR is at the core of *OD* and *ID* (Essay Six) because it is based on a genuinely empowered model of change and development that can be applied at individual, organisational, and societal levels. Empowerment is created through process sensitivity among members, which is a 'sensitivity to how the circumstances of their own making are shaping their attitudes and behaviours which are functional and dysfunctional as well'. It enables those who participate in action research projects to take ownership of the conditions in which they find themselves and also initiate actions to improve them for the better.

In summation, empowerment in *AR* implies restoring the natural human capacity for solving problems and self-development that people have lost due to the socialisation process in which they exist and work. Moreover, the systemic perspective and action projects of *AR* enable the participants to come to grips with the realities of the environment, structure, systems and values at an applied level in such a way that they recognise the social conditioning of their attitudes and behaviours. Action research is a methodology of *OD* that uses applied behavioural science and educative approach rather than a coercive and unilateral or bureaucratic top-down view of change and development. Academicians and educationists readily accept it due to its foundation in a democratic, egalitarian value system.

ENDNOTES

1 "There is no objective truth, the observer is part of the observation." In other words, reality cannot be seen in an objective way and is always seen as constructed by the observer. Systemic thinking incorporates elements from the constructivist approach.
Krizanits, J. (2009). Systemic organisation consulting - How it became what it is: An introduction to the professional field. Fcultas Verlag, Vienna: passion& profession

2 Husserl, Edmund (1950), The Idea of Phenomenology. Phenomenology is a philosophy of experience. For phenomenology the ultimate source of all meaning and value is the lived experience of human beings.

REFERENCES

1. Harrison, J. (2010). *Professional Development and the Reflective Practitioner.* Sage Publications India Pvt Ltd.
2. Padaki, V., & Vaz, M. (2005). *Management Development in Non-Profit Organisations: A Program for Governing Boards.* Sage Publications.
3. Ramnarayan, S., & Rao, T.V. (2011). *Organisation Development.* Sage Publications.
4. Rogers, C.R. (1980). *A Way of Being.* Houghton Mifflin.
5. Schon, D.A. (1983). *The Reflective Practitioner: How Professionals Think in Action.* Basic Book.
6. Manen, Max Van. (1990). *Researching Lived Experience: Human Science for Action Sensitive Pedagogy.* Routledge.
7. Pawar Badrinarayan S. (2018). *Theory building for hypothesis specification in organisational studies.* Response Books.

SECTION TWO

CASE STUDIES

Seven case studies in this section illustrate real-life scenarios, issues, and problems in specific historical and socio-economic contexts of HEIs in India. They are illustrative cases pertaining to diverse educational institutions. Each case is followed by an analysis of the issues and problems with the help of relevant concepts and theories from the disciplines of management and social sciences. They provide analysis for a better understanding of institutional problems and processes. The diverse themes covered in the seven cases deal with the professional and team development of faculty, the climate of social discrimination of PG students on campus, the evolution of institutional identity and culture, the induction process of new students, leadership in top positions, innovations in institutional design, growth, development, and degeneration of academic institutions. A case study on the role of students' unions in a reputed central university is also included. Importantly, all cases illustrate the themes and concepts highlighted in the eleven essays of Section One. Two cases are based on the author's personal experiences as faculty and director at a PG institute of management. The sources of information on other cases are duly acknowledged.

Case Study One

First Person: On Self, Career and Institution Building

This case is presented as a first-person narration of the author's personal and professional experiences of three decades at a PG institute of Management in Pune. It is a documentation of his career growth as an academic and process of institutional development. It highlights moments of struggles and self-fulfilment in his engagement with professional growth and institution-building process.

'Education is life itself.' – ***John Dewey***

Early career: This was the time when I approached the college principal to inquire about a lecturer position at a commerce college in Mapusa, Goa, in June 1977. I found him rather positive when he saw my M.A. qualification with a first-class in literature. Also, he remarked that though *UGC* has guidelines of minimum higher second-class postgraduate degree for entry-level posts, it was difficult to get qualified candidates because few seem to be interested in teaching as a career. When I joined the college, he gave me a piece of advice that I remembered for the rest of my academic career. He told me, "This is a good job for those interested in personal development; we have an excellent library that would be adequate for you in the next ten years, but if you compare the pay scale of a young faculty, it is almost the same as that of class III clerk in a government office."

Later, when I came to Pune after marriage, my wife told me that holding a degree from Shivaji University, Kolhapur, would be a barrier to getting a teaching post in a good college because there is an undeclared hierarchy of university status in Pune. A few years later, when I did an administrative job in a library and also taught communication skills at a reputed management institute, the Director told me that my subject was not as important as core management subjects like Production Planning and Quantitative Techniques. In the education system of India, it seems there are layers of hierarchy in terms of subject, college, university, class, caste, community and seniority. During my stay in the city of Pune, I got the impression that one's surname, who you are related to, often becomes a primary source of social and professional identity. It took me seven years and two postgraduate degrees, with first-class, to be promoted to the post of lecturer at the first autonomous B-school in Pune.

A change at the Top: After the retirement of the founder director, who was considered a pioneer of management education in the Pune region, a senior colleague of mine, with whom I worked for seven years, was appointed as the next director of the institute. The founder director had earned ample social recognition and was considered a management guru in the city. I experienced him as a somewhat insecure person who did not allow young faculty to grow and stabilise in the institute. In fact, I sensed that he considered visiting faculty as future competitors for his post. Needless to say, I did not grow professionally and even lost confidence in my teaching competence and career. I had self-doubts and, with family responsibility, felt lonely and anxious in the role of faculty in these initial years and did not know how to deal with these feelings.

Fortunately, all in all, the new Director was my former colleague, who was only thirty-eight years old at the time of the appointment. He felt the immediate need to prove himself in the job. He focused on three things as a part of institutional development: *(a) Admission Process, (b) Curriculum Development*, and *(c) Writing the Vision, Mission and Goals* for the institute in collaboration with full-time and visiting faculty, students and also the alumni of the institute.

Admission of new students is a critical part of educational activity, and the credibility of the institution depends on the impartiality and objectivity of the process. There are chances of nepotism and corruption. Total transparency was consciously maintained in the method of selection for admission, specifically in the appointment of selection of panels, documentation of the database on Behavioural Event Interviews (*BEI)*, and Group Work Observations. The selection panel members made the announcement of the final results with a waiting list without any involvement of the director. No inquiries from parents or outsiders were entertained. It impacted the reputation of the institute positively.

During the induction programme, the new director made a special mention of the fact that each one of the selected students of the *PGDM* programme entered the institute purely on merit and nothing else. However, during the question-answer session, the new students would ask questions on the perceived low profile of the institute in the market and the total absence of visible promotional efforts vis-a-vis the competing institutes. We, as a faculty group, answered such questions with an argument that financial resources are saved to keep the fees of the programme at a moderate level so that middle-class students could get entry on merit, therefore, a promotional advertisement or glossy infrastructure is not prioritised. However, not many students of the professional courses were impressed by the rationale. Nevertheless, most of them recognised the values and practices of the institute in due course, particularly while experiencing the campus culture in and outside the classrooms and with the quality of interactions with faculty and senior students.

Designing and delivering a new curriculum: The process took almost three years and it evolved later into a faculty development programme (*FDP*). The full-time and visiting faculty contributed to the contents of the curriculum collectively. The director, a senior faculty member, and an external expert in the domain of curriculum design anchored the process of structuring the six semesters with vertical and horizontal linkages, with objectives for each subject to be achieved at the end of its delivery in the semester. Subject faculty had to work on the selection of the content and pedagogy. In the process, the diverse faculty group had to study the basic theories of cognitive learning and human devolvement. Most importantly, the faculty 'developed' a sense of ownership in the curriculum design due to their involvement and participation.

The outcome of this detailed exercise in Curriculum Design *(CD)* was a unique curriculum document that was made available to all management students of the institute. It explained the rationale, objectives and outcomes, content and reference of each course and showed its linkages with other modules in the semesters. The students were expected to use it as a tool for self-study and preparation for semester examinations. Students used it to give feedback on the course outcomes. Faculty used it to assess whether their teaching-learning sessions achieved the objectives mentioned in it.

Investing in teaching and learning resources: In order to to deliver the curriculum, faculty and students needed a solid base of teaching-learning resources in terms of lecture notes prepared by the faculty, synthesis and review of best reference materials, case studies and field projects, and above all, a well-developed library with a variety of books and periodicals. As a faculty-in-charge of the library, I took a personal interest in selecting quality reference books on diverse subjects and read and used them in lectures as much as I could. The institute earmarked a separate budget for purchases of reference books and periodicals. Also, substantial initial investment was made in building a computer laboratory and internet connections on the campus. Students had now access to *Vidyaneedhi,* a database of lecture notes, articles, references prepared by the faculty on courses offered in the curriculum.

The application of information technology in classrooms and administration began in the 1990s in the institute, and it made students and staff competent in basic applications of Excel and other IT tools. Since academy-industry contact is critical for a management institute, a project was designed to create a *Dictionary of Jobs* to provide relevant information on the competencies and skills needed for various job profiles in industrial and other organisations. It was based on data generated from the alumni survey and placement interviews on the campus. In short, the educational and professional development of the faculty and the students were integrated with academic and curricular activities on the campus and through teaching and learning resources in a planned way.

Peer culture and group dynamics: The full faculty size was relatively small, and in the initial years, the students often compared us with visiting faculty who were practising managers and consultants from industry in Pune. The visiting faculty had an advantage because they would share their real-life and on-the-job experiences in the application of management concepts in the class. However, there was an institutional investment in full-time faculty in terms of academic and professional development through behavioural process labs and *FDP.* As a consequence, at one point, the full-time faculty were rated better than the visiting professional faculty by students in periodic feedback reviews. Later, more consulting assignments in the industry boosted the confidence and competence of the full-time faculty dramatically.

However, there were personality clashes and differences within the faculty and with the director, but it was always contained within the boundary of the merit of the augment and debate. Importantly, the egalitarian values and democratic tolerance of dissenting opinion were upheld as a norm due to mutual trust among members. As a group, the faculty experienced tensions due to competition for recognition and personal ambitions in a small institute that had limited opportunity for vertical growth. Moreover, in the absence of monetary incentives like those available in the corporate sector, some faculty complained about the inequity between their efforts and the pay scale. Hence, they were allowed to take up consultancy and training assignments outside the institute. However, it was difficult to measure the performance outcomes of faculty and their contribution at individual and institutional levels. In fact, it was challenging to arrive at a common definition of faculty 'performance'. Young faculty members were more inclined towards individual career opportunities and expected monetary benefits at the individual level rather than long-term contributions at the institutional level.

Personally, I learned a lot from the dynamics in the faculty group, particularly in the case of designing and delivery of a unique two-year PG course in Human Resource Management (*PGDHR*). A group of four faculty members were engaged in designing the curriculum and were expected to launch the programme. In fact, the process began with a one-year course to test the pedagogy and content of the course based on behavioural lab and industry projects. This was also the period in which the director, who was involved in and a part of the team, decided to relinquish his post after a long stint in the position. There was no succession plan, and three other faculty members, including myself, were eligible for the post. It was a testing period for the group in terms of commitment to the launch of the course and the uncertainty about the change at the top. There was apparent tension and anxiety in the group. However, the team task demanded cooperation and purposeful action within a time frame. It was no secret that the personal ambition to get the post created a climate of competition, particularly from a faculty who was rather impatient to get the top post in the institute. This led to disruptions in finalising the last details of the programme. I could recognise the undercurrent of personal ambition and the climate of distrust and hostility in the group dynamics and made it a point to drive the attention of the group to the goal of launching a unique programme that would be an asset to the institute and its reputation in the market. I gave signals that my priority was to focus on academic achievement rather than personal ambition, and I was willing to come to terms with the more ambitious faculty. Fortunately, this approach worked, and the group was ready to launch a two-year, full-time programme in the same academic year.

From this experience, I recognised and internalised the importance of handling the emotional knots and tension in the process of working in teams without a formal leader. I also understood the significance and the value of the primary task of the institute over individual ambitions, which are more important for institutional development in the long run. On reflection, I find that the process of collaboration in teams needs the ability to negotiate with oneself and others in handling group dynamics so that emotional issues do not obstruct the delivery of an innovative course and focus on the purpose of an autonomous institution.

Improvement and Decline of Academic Quality and Institutional Norms

As I look back in time, I can distinctly recognise the high and low points in the history and evolution of the institution. The initial period of the founder director was of working with a person who had taken the risk of delinking from Pune

University as an affiliated institute of management and claiming itself as an autonomous management institute without formal recognition from the state or education ministry. It was an unusual and bold initiative in the late seventies when private universities and colleges were non-existent. Nevertheless, that also led to a feeling of insecurity in the promoter about the future of his tenure and of the institute. As a consequence, the climate in internal faculty and staff was marked by mutual suspicion and distrust.

Moreover, the Director considered some of the internal and visiting faculty as competitors for his position. I remember with sadness how I spent seven precious years as a young faculty in a climate of low professional development and personal dis-satisfaction.

A change for the better: As said earlier, I was relieved when my colleague was appointed as the director when the founder director had to retire as he did not get a continuation in the services. The new director and I shared an academic bent of mind and a desire to contribute to the institution. During the next fifteen years, I experienced a vibrant campus culture with many initiates in terms of two innovative, full-time, two-year programmes in International Trade and Human Resource Management, a number of consultancy assignments for faculty and institutional collaboration with the *Indian Society of Individual and Social Development* (*ISISD*), founded by IIM-A's reputed and thoughtful faculty, Prof *Pulin Garg.*

At the professional level, I could complete my *PhD* in *HR* stream, could teach a variety of subjects that I was interested in, such as a one-trimester course titled '*Individual and the Indian Society*' based on creative literature, films and documentaries. This was also a period when the vision, mission and values document of the institute was prepared. It was an outcome of intense and lengthy discussions with faculty, students and other stakeholders. It provided a direction and a set of values such as 'being productive, creative and relatedness with others, simultaneous concern for self and society, being responsible as citizens, working together as a community of learners and for application of knowledge', articulated in Vision-Mission statement.

These values served an essential function of guiding the collectivity of faculty, staff and students in times of crises when the institute faced challenges in terms of decision-making in academic, administrative and strategic areas of development. Most importantly, articulating the vision and mission of the institute gave us a strategic advantage by recognising and sustaining a distinct identity for the institute from other players in the city and at the pan-India level.

The institute is part of a more than a hundred-year-old education society in Pune that was established by freedom fighters during the independence struggle in

India. The first two directors of the affiliated institute from 1975 to 2005 were Life Members of the Society and, therefore, had a say in critical decision-making. However, things changed rapidly when a new group of members were nominated to the Governing Board of the Society. They were not faculty Life Members of the Society but shared a common background in their affiliation to a right-wing political ideology. The group was keen to take control over the colleges and the schools managed by the Society in Pune, particularly after one year of Emergency in India. Moreover, the management institute was considered as cash cow compared to other affiliated colleges and a potential supplier of funds that the board wanted to deploy elsewhere.

It was painful for me to see new practices in governance from the top officials of the Society that violated the tacit norm of non-interference in the autonomy of the institute. Most importantly, the decision-making power of the Director was reduced drastically to the extent that the institute was micromanaged by the Governing Board members. They ensured that even the list of members of the academic council and chief guests for the convocation ceremony were screened to make it consistent with the board's political leanings.

Final years: I was appointed as Director of the institute in April 2010, and it was my second attempt at appearing for an interview before the selection board. I had learned by now that it is the dynamics behind the scenes that determine the selection of top posts, and one of the important criteria is the support one gets from the board members. Personally, I was relieved by my appointment because I had only three years before retirement. Also, I had realised from experiences that more respect and importance is given to the position of power at the top compared to the academic scholarship and teaching competence as faculty. On the flip side, I had an opportunity also to learn about institutional politics and how board members manipulate the director to take decisions so that they could avoid the blame for the consequences of decisions, particularly in areas of selection of students and faculty, which had long-term implication.

In a short period of three years as director of the institute, I had enough exposure to the organisational realities to understand the price one has to pay to hold the top position. My first learning experience was to witness the process of admissions given to new students for management quota seats. I had no say in this decision, though I made a feeble attempt to resist it in the local management committee meeting. I argued that such admissions impact the quality of education and the campus culture, but it had no consequence because the management pushed through economic logic rather than educational logic in order to get more funds.

Unfortunately, I had to be part of and witness to negotiations conducted by the secretary of the society with eager and ignorant parents to arrive at the exact amount of the capitation fee, which depended on the market value or brand status of the two courses and also the paying capacity of the parents. It was a commercial transaction, and they were assured of a stamped receipt on cheque payment to the Society. Though it had a legal basis, it violated educational ethics as every seat on a payment basis meant denial to a meritorious student. I can mention many more instances, but in short, I could sense it as a period of decline in institutional values and its reputation in the public perception, even though the institute continued to survive as an economic and legal entity like many other colleges in India.

Being in the director's seat for three years gave me an opportunity to learn about the decision-making process and the gap between the image and intent of the governing board. Compared to other colleges under the same management, our institute had accumulated a substantial surplus over the years because it ran a full-time and few part time programmes in professional management. The institute was located in the heart of the city and, therefore, convenient for new students and employees of industry and business around the city. These funds were kept in the reserves of the institute's account and sometimes shared with other affiliated colleges and institutes in times of emergency at the directors' discretion in the initial years.

The new management in the Governing Board decided that the funds would go to the common pool of the Society and then be allocated to the affiliated colleges. It was only a technical decision for convenience, I was told. For three decades, the institute could maintain autonomy without any external or government aid. It could invest in learning resources like the library, computer lab, hostel, and process labs for students and faculty because of the surplus it had gained due to the two programmes. However, in the new arrangement, the director of the institute did not have any say or claim in the use of developmental funds.

Another important decision in my tenure was to apply for *AICTE* recognition for PGDM programmes. The rationale was that the *MHRD* ministry treated non-recognised institutes as coaching classes and part of the service industry, and hence, they were liable for a 20% service tax deduction. From the management viewpoint, it meant saving a few lakhs and also gaining recognition for the institute at the all-India level. I managed the project of getting *AICTE* recognition with the cooperation of faculty and staff, and within a year, the *PGDM* course got it.

It was a learning experience as I encountered and was accosted by multifarious experts and panels at central and state levels of bureaucracy. They were primarily interested in infrastructure facilities like the number of toilets, size of the classrooms, and number of books, and they were least interested in softer academic aspects like curriculum or learning climate on campus. They took video shots of the campus but did not show any interest in gathering first-hand experiences of talking to faculty and students on the campus. The official website of *AICTE* announces that panel members are given TA-DA (allowances) and other facilities, and the institute is not expected to provide them. This is to alert institutions of professional courses to guard against such dubious practices. In short, the regulatory process of recognition to institutions has been reduced to filling up the columns and numerical data in the report forms handed over by the committee of hired experts appointed by *AICTE.*

Besides getting the approval, it was also a period, when, our evening diploma programmes for employed personnel from industry were discontinued by the institute. The reason was that management did not find them as lucrative as full-time programmes. Since it demanded classroom teaching for faculty and office work staff in late evenings, both of them readily accepted this decision. Hence, an alternative and additional source of income generation that was possible due to location advantage was lost permanently. There was no new programme offered in its place to date, and the institute had depended on fees from a full-time day course only.

As a consequence, the tuition fees increased by more than 100% for full-time courses. However, the number of students applying for admissions dwindled due to an increase in competition for professional education as well as a decrease in the reputation of the institute due to dilution of admission criteria, management quota seats and lack of innovation in curriculum.

The faculty was given a better salary based on the scales of the new pay commission, but it had no visible impact on improvement in the quality of teaching-learning or the climate of the student community on the campus. In a few years, the campus climate further deteriorated in terms of the quality of teaching and learning and faculty-student relatedness.

Postscript

Remembering thirty-three years of experience in an institution gives me a feeling of pride and also sadness. The post-retirement period reminds me of those painful moments when the new management at the top systemically demolished the invisible foundation of the institutional processes and values at the Governing Board level. It was inadvertently supported by faculty and staff of the institute for short-term personal gains. Personally, I take pride in the fact that I was a part of the institution-building process and contributed my bit to it in the past. However, I am pained to witness the gradual damage to the hard-earned academic stature and culture of an institution of higher learning by those who neither care for it nor believe and value it.

Today, the Institute exists in the same location and holds the same name. It will continue to exist in the future, too. Still, some questions trouble me: Is the institute worthy of being called an institution of higher learning/education? Also, the bigger question is what makes an institute an institution? What are the processes that are critical for building and developing robust institutions of higher learning?

These are pertinent questions that deserve further exploration in the contemporary context of higher education in India. This book attempts to address them to better understand the process of building and developing institutions of higher learning.

I would like to believe that those who care about teaching and learning would be able to relate to the emotional and intellectual struggles of the author as a faculty member in the first-person narration above. Sharing and writing about personal experiences in educational institutions is not an easy task for a variety of reasons. It makes the person vulnerable, but it certainly adds to the knowledge of the self and process of institution building. In short, the development of faculty as a person (self), as a professional (role), and institution building (system) are three processes that operate simultaneously and are mutually reinforcing.

Case Study Two

Leadership and Institution Building

This case describes the contribution of Prof Ravi J Mathai, who was the first full-time director of the Indian Institute of Management, Ahmedabad (IIM-A). He is still remembered for his out-of-the-box style of leadership that laid the foundation of an educational institution that has remained the most reputed institute in the field of professional management in India. In 1965, Vikram Sarabhai, a well-known scientist and founder of ISRO, invited Mr Ravi Mathai to take charge of the IIM-A. His extraordinary work as full-time director of IIM-A is a lesson in institutional leadership for professional education of 21st-century India.

Mr Ravi Mathai was a practising executive in industry and a professor of Marketing. He intuitively recognised the difference between leading a business organisation and building an educational institution. He brought together the innovative spirit of corporate management and the institutional orientation of the university system. It is remarkable that he had only two years of academic experience as faculty at IIM-Calcutta and was only thirty-eight years old when he took charge of IIM-Ahmedabad as director.

In an interview taken by his colleague Prof Udai Pareek, he had commented that 'my ignorance was strength' as a director. This was not merely a polite expression but a fact since he had no baggage of the bureaucratic mind-set that cripples innovation and reforms in the Indian education system, which the Ministry of Education centrally controls. The objective of this illustrative case study is to highlight the distinguishing features of Mr Mathai's leadership style demonstrated at IIM-A and its relevance to contemporary higher education institutions in India.

First thing first, defining the purpose: As an initial step, he zeroed in upon the primary purpose of the institute, which was conceived as 'teaching-learning, consulting and research in applied knowledge of management'. Accordingly, the curriculum, pedagogy of its delivery, research and consulting projects were designed. He was convinced that the impact and quality of teaching-learning in professional programmes is sustained only when its faculty gives equal importance to and is engaged simultaneously in teaching, consulting and research activities. Moreover, he thought that the application of knowledge of management was not restricted to business and industry only. Therefore, he initiated research and developmental projects on undermanaged sectors like agriculture and the empowerment of village communities.

Mr. Mathai had a talent for mentoring faculty and students. He recognised early that at the centre of a higher education institution are faculty, students, and their interactions on the campus. The quality of education depends on the quality of relatedness and involvement between the two. Moreover, he went a step further to underline the connection between higher education institutions and Indian society. This is an important insight that has the potential to create a lasting impact on the development of the Indian economy and society with the help of higher education. This broader perspective of professional education is a feature that makes Mr Mathai's leadership relevant in the contemporary context, particularly when higher education is facing many challenges and is disconnected from the socio-economic problems of India.

After relinquishing his post as director of IIM-A, Mr Mathai took up a project on the development and empowerment of village communities in Rajasthan. He had mentioned that self-reliance and taking initiative were two virtues he had learned early in life from his father, *John Mathai.*

Value of Autonomy: Autonomy of institutions of higher learning is a most talked about idea today, but the term 'institutional autonomy' was practised in letter and spirit by Mr Mathai in his tenure of six years at IIM-A and more importantly, it continued later as a central value of the institute. This autonomy was not merely for management but also for faculty and students of the institute. He knew that creativity and innovation would not be nurtured in a climate of bureaucratic controls and a top-down style of management. Instead, mutual trust, freedom, and collaboration are required in decision-making processes. Institutional autonomy as a value enables faculty and students to realise their potential and learn to take responsibility. It also implies tolerance for learning from mistakes and mutual respect. However, the most challenging part of the application of the autonomy principle at the workplace is the inability of those in authority positions to let go of their control and power. *Ravi Mathai* had the courage and conviction to share power so that the institutional purpose and mission were achieved. Though he was not an academic in terms of scholarship, he had the intuition and understanding to build an academic institution that would have a lasting impact for decades ahead.

Once, while interacting with students in the classroom on reading habits, he is reported to have told them, "I keep only two books in my bedroom; one is the Oxford Dictionary of the English language, and another is the Bible." Needless to say, the dictionary is known as a treasure of thoughts and experiences of human history represented as words, and the Bible is about the application of ethical principles in day-to-day life.

At the workplace, *Mr Mathai* kept himself away from the selection process for appointment of faculty and admission of students. He knew that the involvement of the director could be an obstacle in an objective and impartial selection process, and it would negatively impact the academic climate on the campus later.

Leader and Leadership: While discussing the concept of leadership, we often fail to distinguish the 'leader' from 'leadership'. Though the leader is essential for giving direction to academic pursuits and governance, the institutes also require leadership at all levels of faculty and administration. If the formal leader does not consciously promote institutional leadership at all levels within the institute, then it would stunt its development in the long run. In other words, strong, centralised, and charismatic leadership would restrict growth of leadership qualities in others. Remarkably, Mr Mathai had the right attitude to nurture the process of leadership development. He, therefore, encouraged his faculty colleagues to work in a structure of self-managing teams. This team had multilateral structures suitable for facilitative leadership in the areas of full-time programmes, admissions, research, and consultancy so that they could learn to take ownership of the projects and develop a commitment to the institutional purpose.

Though team structures are followed in many work organisations, it is often observed that the leader is too eager to intervene when problems or disagreements arise. Mr Mathai did not succumb to the temptation of such interference that would reinforce dependence on the leader's power and thus deprive others of learning and practising the value of autonomy. In challenging problem situations, the faculty group was frustrated by the director's non-response to their struggle, which created internal tensions caused by their inability to resolve conflict and make decisions together as a faculty group without a formal leader. However, they eventually learned the process of working together and developed norms to deal with such difficulties, which arose mainly due to a lack of confidence in their own abilities.

Later, they understood that the director intended to make them self-reliant and less dependent on the authority at the top, which is not a common feature of the work culture in India. It was a process of nurturing faculty leadership that would sustain the institutional responsibility in future. It is said that the best leader is one who makes himself redundant. However, it requires an unusual level of self-belief and confidence in one's life mission.

Climate and Culture: Autonomous institutions need collaborative behaviours across structures so that initiative to take risks in decision-making and implementation of decisions occur at the collective level. It is based on behavioural competencies like self and interpersonal awareness, tolerance of dissent and differences, learning to learn and unlearning as well. Such things are best learned from experiences and reflecting on them when members are engaged in group and team tasks. At the workplace, one can get the experience of working in groups. However, no space is provided for reflection in and on action. Mr Mathai deliberately created such spaces during faculty meetings for reflexive activity, similar to the *Reflective Practice* method, which gave equal importance to the behavioural process used in meetings along with the content of the discussion. This kind of 'process awareness' was an essential part of how faculty gained a significant level of emotional and interpersonal maturity, which is a critical part of building a climate of collective consciousness for collaboration. Important lessons such as discerning freedom from licentiousness, candidness from arrogance, and humility from dependence are learned mainly through reflexivity and process awareness as a human skill. Here lies a rare managerial insight and contribution of Mr Mathai on building institutional processes.

After laying a solid institutional foundation of IIM-A in a short span of six years, Mr Mathai decided to relinquish the post of director and recommended one of his senior colleagues in the position. It was an unusual decision because he was considered as very successful as a director. But he had shown a kind of unusual sense of detachment even while he was working. He said that the most important qualification needed for the top post in an educational institution of higher learning is that the person holding it should have no need for it. In fact, he made the decision to relinquish the post consciously because he honestly believed that a person holding a position in an educational institution should not remain in it for more than five years. He believed that in doing so, the person might not use it for the development and excellence of the institute but for personal gains, which would be detrimental to institutional building. In a way, he had literally kept a resignation letter in his pocket while working. Perhaps that is the secret of his innovative approach to managing even in the context of state-funded institutions marked by bureaucracy and red tape.

The significant legacy of *Ravi Mathai's* leadership is the fact that IIM-A has always remained an institution of eminence since its inception. The foundation he laid in building the institution helped to sustain its capacity for self-renewal and maintain a value-based culture. His leadership did not make the institution dependent on him, nor did he use it for personal advantage. His example is worth emulating by those in leadership positions in institutions of higher education in India for years to come.

The interview with *Prof. Mathai*, conducted by his colleague at IIM-A, Prof Udai Pareek, gives more details of the thought processes that governed his leadership role. The following observations are based on this interview and offer valuable insights into institutional leadership. Ravi J Mathai, who was the first full-time director of the institute from 1965 to 1971, laid the foundation of the institutional processes on the principle of a self-regulatory system.

Since it was the early period of post-graduate education in professional management, the development of an institution meant the development of people working in it.

The key feature of institution building, according to *Mr Mathai*, is the principle of self-regulation at the individual faculty, groups, and institution levels. As a first step, efforts were made to develop attitudes and norms that were conducive to self-regulated behaviours. Attitude influences behaviours, and, in turn, it is influenced by processes and procedures. Therefore, faculty worked in matrix-type autonomous work groups on different projects and tasks, such as PGP and EDP programmes, research, and consultancy. The director, as the institutional leader, adhered to the principle of autonomy and self-discipline while dealing with the group heads and faculty. It meant that he avoided direct intervention in the operations and decision-making processes because attitudes are formed on the basis of day-to-day work experiences with peers and the authority. Such a decentralised structure makes people uncomfortable in the Indian context because it requires the willingness to take initiative and responsibility without commensurate authority. Public institutions in education hold a bureaucratic mind set wherein innovation and allied risks are avoided at the workplace.

Institutions distinguish themselves from other work organisations by the normative values they hold and practice at the behavioural level. Generally, they are anchored in the vision of the founder or the top leader. Ravi Mathai believed that creativity and innovation are intrinsically good. Individuals need the freedom to hold views and express them within a space created for this purpose. However, it requires self-discipline, which can only emerge from the self-esteem of the individual and mutual respect among peers.

For Institution building, it is not enough to have a vision about what an educational institution 'should be'; it also needs knowledge about the processes that would develop and sustain its institutional strengths without overdependence on either its leader or on external patronage, government, or philanthropic agency.

The role of the leader is critical to developing a self-confident team of faculty, and Mr Mathai had an intuitive understanding of the connection between the use of power and its effectiveness. He described it in the following words, "the more power, implicitly or explicitly, I kept to myself, the more faculty members would be dependent on me, the more aspects of the institute I would get involved with greater detail. I would, therefore, have that much less time to spend on major development on which I thought a director should spend his time, like initiating new activities or building external links for support and resources, searching for new faculty and spending time with them to develop a culture in the institution without getting bogged down to operational details."

The essence of *IB* is people development in terms of capability, and it can be achieved not by a top-down direction or rules but through shared norms of behaviours at individual and group levels. It includes goal setting, collaboration, interpersonal relations, use of authority and discretion, role taking and role making, acceptance of responsibility, and exercising freedom wisely. Such behaviours can only be developed while working in groups with guidance from a leader as a mentor.

Ravi Mathai guided the faculty by creating work structures that gave them exposure to institutional perspectives beyond their functional or academic view. Each faculty member was involved in teaching and administrative tasks carried out in a work culture that was not hierarchical and egalitarian, without differentiation based on designation or status.

Mr Mathai believed that autonomy or freedom to self-manage has to be earned and that it is not a thing to be bestowed upon as patronage. When the chairman of a large PGP committee tried to push the difficult decisions upward and expected the director to intervene, he refused to intervene, though the faculty was unhappy and frustrated with his inaction. In due course, the committee members realised that they had to solve their problems and formed a sub-committee with decision-making power, which in turn gave more power to the chairman of the committee.

This is an illustrative case that highlights the contribution of Mr Mathai to building an institution of excellence in the field of management education in India.

It is an insightful case study on what contains the essence of institution building and the role of the leader. In terms of systems thinking theory (*Mills Theodore M, 1988)*, it is captured in the following words. It not only summarises the qualities of a leader but also the essence of the institution-building process.

> "Leader's responsibility is not for the parts, sectors, functions of subsystems or selected levels, but for the total dynamic configuration of the whole system or group, within a changing environment. ... responsibility to the meta system as parents in a family, head of the government in a nation. Leader's consciousness includes all important experiences of the system like routine interactions, pervasive feeling of the collective such as trust or mistrust, confidence or lack of it, anxiety, elation, sadness. A set of written and unwritten, conscious, and unconscious rules, implicit and explicit beliefs and values. The leader's concern pervades through this differentiated and interdependent configuration."

Institutional leadership requires a pervasive consciousness of *drashta* that goes beyond the conventional administrative or managerial roles of a leader in the workplace. Visionary leadership in educational institutions is the most precious asset that sustains them for generations.

REFERENCES

1. Mills, Theodore M. (1988). *The Sociology of Small Groups*. Prentice-Hall of India, New Delhi.
2. Pareek, Udai (1980). *Beyond Management*. Oxford University Press.

Case Study Three

Innovative Models in Higher Education

Three relatively contemporary cases (1990-2020) on innovative designs in Institution Building, are presented below. When educational organisations perform a larger role and take wider responsibility through change and innovation, they are considered institutions. The three cases given below illustrate these processes.

(A) IMDR – In search of an institutional identity: The first self-regulated, autonomous management institute (B-School) in Pune

(B) A Collaborative Design of higher education to facilitate employment opportunities and Skill learning (MKCL)

(C) Nirman: A Gandhian model of purposeful education

Together, these cases share a similarity as they offer alternative models of institution building (IB). Each one has a distinct vision, mission, and strategy for bringing change and innovation.

The first case concerns ***IMDR,*** which narrates the evolution of the first autonomous B-School in Pune. The second case is on ***MKCL,*** which is about a collaborative model of institution building based on public-private partnership in higher education; the third case is on ***'Nirman'****, a unique institution* promoted by social activists Mr *Abhay Bang* and Mrs *Rani Bang*. It is a purposeful learning institution based on Mahatma Gandhi's philosophy of education, which is explained in his book '*Nayi Talim*'.

(A) *IMDR*: In Search of an Institutional Identity

***Context*:** This case describes the history and evolution of the first autonomous B-School (Management Institute) not affiliated with a state university in Pune, a city considered the hub of higher and professional education in India. The narration focuses mainly on how the first two directors struggled to define a unique identity for the institute in a highly competitive market of management education. Also, it is a case that highlights the vital role of vision and distinct identity in the process of institution building. Existing over a period of four decades, the narrative of the case, delineates and tracks the high and low points in the history of an institution while discussing its success and setbacks in its mission to build a unique identity and institutional culture. The case is based partly on a first-person account on 'Institution Building' taken from an unpublished note written by *Dr AP Bhupatkar* (2005), who was the director of the institute for a decade and a half.

This is an illustrative and illuminative case of how the first autonomous B-School, a management institute in Pune city had evolved a distinct institutional identity in a span of thirty years. It is an unusual story against the backdrop of hundreds of management institutes/colleges in Maharashtra, a two fifty in Pune city alone. They invariably follow either a corporate model of higher education in terms of market-oriented values and strategy or remain affiliated as a department in management for PG courses of state universities.

History: The *Institute of Management Development and Research (IMDR)* started as a Pune-based management institute catering to the needs of management training for local students and local industry in and around Pune. It was an affiliated institute of the *Deccan Education Society*, which runs reputed colleges like *Fergusson College, Wellington College, and B M College of Commerce* in cities of western Maharashtra. For a decade, IMDR remained a local, simple, down-to-earth, not-ostentatious college that could sustain on the yearly surplus it could generate due to low fees and more number of students for part-time diploma courses in management in the absence of competition in the Pune University area in the 1970s. The founder director initiated an unusual decision to go for self-chosen autonomy and delinked itself from Pune University in 1979. Neither the board of management of DES nor the stakeholders were convinced of the rationale behind this decision. However, the curriculum and the behaviours of the faculty and students did not change significantly despite the self-selected 'autonomy' of the institute.

The change happened during the decade of 1980s when students from all over India started applying for admission to full-time courses. They expected placements at a pan-India level. The institution faced the challenge of transforming itself from a local institution to a regional-national level one. So far, it was an academic institution of the old-world type, revolving around the high-profile leadership of an academician, the director of the institute. However, he was reluctant to recruit full-time faculty and depended mainly on practising managers and consultants for teaching work. He hired one full-time faculty member to help him upgrade the academic standards of the flagship full-time course.

The Institute could gain credibility, and more recruiters participated in the placement of students due to consistent efforts to upgrade the quality of teaching-learning. Students recognised the difference in the academic flavour of the institute, which was distinct from other institutes in Pune, which had a distinct and well delineated corporate style and appearance. There was pressure on the Director to go the corporate way, but by now, the institute had evolved an identity of its own due to its autonomous status.

After the retirement of the founder Director, the only full-time faculty member who was inducted as a Life Member of the *DE Society*, was, appointed as the next director at the age of 38 years. Now, there was a significant change in the leadership style. The charismatic personality of the founder director, who managed many things with personal discretion, was replaced by systems and processes. For example, the method of selection of students was now based on a rating scheme that was strictly adhered to without any use of discretion of the director. Over the years, word spread about the imperviousness of the admission process at the institute. The watchful stakeholders like parents, students, trustees, and life members of the D E Society recognised the difference between the earlier process of admissions based on arbitrary, vulnerable to pressures of vested interests and the new process that was just and fair. For all high-stakes, high-visibility decisions like examination or recruitment of faculty, the same principle was followed. Most significantly, there were no management quota seats, and this was mentioned upfront in the prospectus of the institute. Admissions for a coveted PG course in management was based entirely on merit, devoid of any malpractices, and it helped build the reputation of the institution. It sent a strong signal to the students that one's merit is the first and foremost on campus.

In the same manner, the operational system of examination and assessment was streamlined so that discretion was used very rarely. Since the institute was autonomous and offered its own certification, it was critical that the assessment process was above doubts and suspicions. When loopholes were found, systemic corrections were made immediately to prevent such occurrences. Such actions of the management created an academic ambience where merit was valued.

Three Challenges that shaped the Identity of the Institute

(a) **Recruiting Faculty:** Since the primary focus of the institute was on teaching and learning, the first challenge was recruiting a core, full-time faculty to be complemented by visiting faculty of managers and professionals. It started with the recruitment of two faculty members and was raised to five later. The prevalent model of management institutes in Pune was not in favour of full-time faculty since management discipline was more about practice and less about theoretical foundations. The director and the faculty group believed that such a dichotomy between theoretical and practical was harming the learning process on the campus and resulted in a lack of depth in both theoretical and applied knowledge. Later, the faculty underwent an in-house faculty development programme based on self-study, applied work and presentation cum discussion sessions with the help of an educational consultant.

(b) **Selection Process:** The second challenge lay in the area of selecting the right students for the two-year programme. Admission to *MBA* and *PGDM* courses in India is based on group discussions and personal interviews, and there are plenty of coaching classes in the cities that cater to the needs of the students. Thus, candidates had prior training in a packaged approach of coaching institutes so that they could make the right noises with jargon to impress the selection panel members. It was difficult to get through to the real person behind the mask. Based on consultation with industry HR experts, the faculty adopted the Competency-based approach to select students. It was an experiment that faced much resistance and led to heated debates on the theory and application of the method used in industry to an educational context. Issues were discussed at length to build a consensus on its relative merit. It was thus an experiment in faculty participation in joint decision-making and innovation in the selection method. Well-wishers and alumni of the institute were roped in as associates in the selection process. The 'competency-based selection' methodology had become an important contribution to management education, which was also used later by the faculty for industrial consultancy projects.

(c) **Designing a New Curriculum**: The third challenge was designing a curriculum for the PG course in management. There was dissatisfaction with incremental, arbitrary and ad hoc changes in the curriculum by borrowing designs and suggestions from external faculty and practitioners. New subjects like Services marketing, Indigenous management, and Individual and Indian Society were introduced due to their relevance and topicality. However, they failed to stimulate the interest of the students while also remaining disconnected from other subjects. A consultant was invited to work as a guide to expose the faculty to the principles of curriculum design, and he conducted workshops on applied assignments. Since the design path was uncharted and involved participation, cynicism prevailed among the faculty group that had to create and implement the

> design of the new curriculum. In the face of resistance, the director had to use his formal authority to navigate and push through the programme on curriculum development. After consistent work for one year, similar design principles were used for another course on the PG Diploma course in International Trade. There was welcome feedback from the industry and the alumni as well. Gradually, other part-time courses were reviewed and re-designed.

One of the most significant principles used for curriculum design was the unity of theory and practice in the minds of both students and faculty engaged with teaching and learning processes. It was found that such unity results in productive learning and gives immense satisfaction to students and teachers as well.

New initiatives were introduced in the areas of (a) self-study methodology for students, (b) process-behavioural labs for students and faculty, and (c) Application of computer technology for administrative work.

The most difficult challenge the institute faced was in the area of attracting, retaining and developing faculty. Finding faculty with an academic bent of mind was a challenging task for many reasons. One is that students and practitioners regard management as a 'practical' subject. It is observed that less than 20% of faculty members have an academic mind-set and are interested in developing themselves conceptually and with a genuine interest in theory. The small size and budget of the institution also limited its capacity to attract faculty with better remuneration. In academically oriented institutions in India and abroad, senior faculty members mentor the junior members to do the academic work of review, critique, editing, and research. The institute tried several methods to encourage such work through weekly presentations on a topic of self-interest, field projects, real-life case studies, and consulting work. It had limited success and did not take root for continuity and consistency. Intrinsic motivation was absent, and the pay scales were also less attractive. With more institutes of the 'corporate model' in Pune, faculty was more attracted towards them.

Impact of Neoliberalism on Higher Education

The future of Institutions such as *IMDR,* which is built on the foundation of 'identity' and values and considered a 'unique place', faces uncertainty about its future strategy in the twenty-first century in India. A process work professional, who, participated in the process lab programmes of the institute described the institute as a *'delightfully original and frightfully innovative'* place. Can it sustain itself and grow with its unique identity and values in the changed scenario of higher education in India? The answer lies in the leadership capability of the institution and the Governing Board of DES.

The question of whether such a spirit of innovation can be institutionalised for later generations remains unanswered. The top management of DE Society has chosen a different path of getting the institute into the mainstream by getting it recognised by *AICTE* and compromising the curriculum of its acclaimed courses in Human Resources and International Trade by conforming to the standardised template of the apex body of higher education. Though the recognition from AICTE has given legitimacy to the certification and assured the students and parents to some extent, it has weakened the 'conscientiously nurtured identity' and academic values that made it a unique institution in management. *IMDR* as an institute is on its way to become one like the many other institutes in India that tend to invest in marketing and brand building in order to project its identity artificially. To complicate matters, the top management of the Deccan Education Society in recent years seems more committed to the right-wing ideology than to the vision, mission and academic identity of *IMDR*.

After the voluntary retirement of the second director, who contributed much to the institution-building process for sixteen years, five directors were appointed in a short span of twelve years. The institution continues to conduct the same course with more batches, and minor charges in curriculum. It continues to perform routine cycle of tasks of admission, examination, placements and convocation every year. However, the focus on institutional purpose and identity remains unattended by the top management of the institute. The fact is that centralised decision-making process of the present board of the *DE Society* and the earlier participative and democratic processes of identity formation used in the past at *IMDR* remain disconnected. Organic model of institutional identity is embedded in the values and processes, and therefore, it cannot be replicated or sustained when appropriate values and behaviours do not exist.

(Partly based on an unpublished note written by Dr. A.P. Bhupatkar, 2005)

(B) Collaborative Design of Institution of Higher Education

This is an unusual case of an experiment in a collaborative, institutional model for bridging the academia-industry gap in higher education in India. This innovation in design has developed a curriculum that synergistically combines the domain strengths of a public Open University, a private technology institute and a few reputed manufacturing companies from Pune. It offers a 'learn and earn model' (not earn and learn) for students of lower-middle-class families from drought-prone districts in Maharashtra. The course has empowered them in terms of career prospects and personal growth, and they could financially support their families during their education.

The main challenge in designing an educational programme at the college level is to integrate the interests and expectations of different stakeholders such as a) Young men and women from different socio-economic backgrounds, b) Industry with specific needs of human resources, c) The mission of a college and university, d) Parents and society and e) Government regulatory agency. It is a challenge to coordinate all divergent expectations and stakeholders in an educational programme.

The experiment in higher education institutions (*HEI),* which is described here, is an outcome of the collaboration of three different institutions from Maharashtra with a common aim to make higher education meaningful and relevant to the young and the society at large. The institutions that came together are 1) *Yashwantrao Chavan Open University, Nasik*, 2) *Maharashtra Knowledge Corporation Ltd (MKCL),* and 3) a few large size companies in the manufacturing sector from Pune, who participated in a unique design that synergises the strengths of university and industry in a collaborative effort.

Interestingly, akin to the next case of *Nirman,* initiated by *Dr Bang*, the guiding principle in the design of this programme is the *Gandhian* principle of engaging the students with socially valuable and productive work, which also becomes a medium for receiving and generating knowledge. The *Gandhian* idea is strikingly different from the commonly understood notion of social work done as a voluntary activity. Here, work is used as a means of knowledge creation, which differs from the passive reception of information and knowledge that students receive from the conventional courses in higher education at universities.

However, the idea of '*learn and work*' in this experiment is different from the work in industrial settings and manufacturing companies, wherein the worker tends to experience alienation or psychological separation from the product, self, and fellow workers. Hence, it is not merely an 'on-the-job learning' because it is designed in such a way that it tries to integrate individual students with social or community needs. It is an attempt to combine the elements of learning, knowledge and socially productive work as espoused in his remarkable book *Nayi Talim* by *Mahatma Gandhi.*

In this programme, knowledge is constructed by the student as he encounters problems and difficulties and searches for solutions through the application of his/ her intellect individually and with others in groups. Thus, it is a development of intellect rather than merely learning a set of skills. Intellect is multi-faceted and broad in its potential for application rather than a narrow job-specific skill. As an instance, in behavioural sciences, social etiquette or office skills are context-relevant, however, working to build capabilities of 'attention, awareness and perception' have the potential to develop lifelong learning for the student. Self-study skills regulated by the student himself have a lasting impact on his capacity as a learner in the future.

A major bottleneck of the contemporary higher education system is that it is inadequate to give direction to the career of students. Even highly educated students are unclear about their life goals and remain anchorless for a long period. Education is delinked from the processes of living and has lost its utility. This often misleads the young, making them join the reactionary forces since they are unable to get gainful employment even after acquiring a university degree. They feel dejected and cynical about the system of education and experience themselves as a burden to their families. This is a very depressing experience for many young boys and girls in India.

The perspective of *Nayi Talim* offers a nonviolent, productive, constructive, and revolutionary alternative to the modern education system. It proposes a simultaneous development of the person and the society. Unlike technological rationality, it does not separate an individual from the community for the sake of efficiency. Instead, it is based on the premise that only when society's needs for functional and productive work are satisfied, the individual would receive the means of livelihood and gain wholesome knowledge that would develop her intellect.

It is not a person-centric, subject-centric, or system-centric education. It is based on cooperation rather than competition and social harmony than social inequity. It is based on the belief that work, even though small, can be elevated to a high level by personal involvement. Therefore, the status of work depends on its relevance to society and the knowledge it produces. At the workplace, one learns to face problems and challenges while working with others. It does not encourage blind imitation but nurtures independent thinking in problem-solving. It builds self-reliance and self-direction, along with creating a space for imagination and creativity.

In short, the perspective of *Nayi Talim* integrates processes of living, working and knowledge creation. It legitimises autonomy in education by emphasising productive and socially needed work rather than a job for survival. It is a meaningful engagement because it connects the self and society.

The Design of an Undergraduate Programme: The above description of integrated learning may appear to be a theoretical idea, but it is made practical by the curriculum design and its implementation, in this experiment, which is described below.

Fifty students were selected from drought-prone rural regions of Maharashtra, like *Vidharba* and *Marathwada.* They belonged to deprived sections of the society. Companies from the Pune region assured them a monthly stipend for three years.

It was outside the tag of *CSR* or philanthropy but based on a need-based contract for mutual benefit wherein students offered to do productive work that would add value to the company business. Before entering the industry premises, *MKCL*, a digital training and consultancy company, conducted a training programme in digital technology, English language on spoken English for conversations, soft skills, personality development for services, skills in problem-solving, teamwork, interpersonal skills with practice sessions.

Counselling and Applications: After daily work hours, students were given e-learning modules that would last for 2-3 hours. Smartphones and laptops were provided along with booklets as learning resources. The assessment was based on open-ended questions to measure independent, reflective thinking regarding work experiences. A well-designed, open-ended question would fetch multiple answers, and the class, as a collective of fifty students, had an opportunity to present and listen to a diverse pool of talents with multiple viewpoints. It was an 'experiential learning' in groups after work hours. Students learned democratic values of tolerance, diversity of ideas, and collaboration. Faculty from *YC Open University and MKCL* provided guidance and counselling, which provided a family-like support and nurturance for these students with rural background. They were exposed to industrial work-life and had this kind of learning for the first time. The *YC University* recognised the programme with a *BBA* certification.

The assessment was based on credit points for on the job work given by supervisors from the company side and knowledge credit points given by *MKCL*. In this way, students received certification from private industry and a degree from a public Open University. The families of the students received much-needed economic support as stipend during the internship period of three years. Post training, these students could easily gain entry into Indian and *MNC* companies based on their educational qualifications and work experience. More importantly, students could discover their talents from real work experience that conventional educational programmes of universities do not provide. This boosted the self-confidence and self-esteem of the students and they could inspire other young boys and girls from their villages. Feedback from the industry on the performance and motivation of the students was very positive.

For the next six years, the programme offered a unique opportunity to three hundred students. Other Open Universities in India followed this model at the *BBA* and *MBA* levels. Large-size *NGOs* showed interest in using the model for diploma certification. *Neeti Aayog* appealed to Open Universities to initiate such programmes.

Summary and Review: The case of a successful experiment in an innovative design of applied education described above highlights the need for an inter-institutional collaboration in higher education in India. The most crucial factor that contributed to the success is the synergic pooling of strengths of three stakeholders, that is, an Open university with strength in academic education at the undergraduate level, a training and consultancy company with expertise and resources in digital technology, and large size manufacturing companies that offered long term internship for three years with a stipend Also, the design of the programme was partly based on the Gandhian principles of *Nayi Talim*. It promotes the idea that education should be connected to the needs of society and should provide work experience that is useful for knowledge-building and developing self-esteem through collaborative work with fellow students. Hence, the programme is not merely an 'earn and learn' opportunity for needy students but offers a more holistic purpose of simultaneous individual and social development. Therefore, the role of the faculty and supervisors remains very critical to achieve the mission of their programmes. Supervisors offered practical training on the job, and this fact helped students conceptualise what they had learned with guidance from faculty and the sharing of relevant learning resources to supplement practical training. Also, the financial support of stipends and the promise of future employment motivated the students to take the programme seriously which added value to the workplace and learning process. The long-term external benefits of such programmes are evident as the students of this programme continue to be considered as role models in the deprived sections of society.

A note of caution: When an educational programme is successful, many established players in professional education tend to copy the design and initiate more 'me too' type courses. The intent of these operators from both private universities and the training industry side would determine the credibility of such initiatives. If it is conducted without sincerity of purpose that combines gainful employment and skill development, it would quickly degenerate into a business opportunity for private players to get cheap labour for companies in order to provide a market for training companies at the cost of unemployed youth. Importantly key stakeholders of the above experiments, i.e., three collaborators, an Open University, a training company and manufacturing companies, had already acquired a reputation in their fields of operations. They had a pool of subject experts with credibility to ensure quality practices in learning and development. Ultimately, the quality of people who lead the institutions of higher education and industrial organisations determines the outcome of such holistic programmes in applied education based on the vision of *Nayi Talim*.

Source: The case is based on an article written by Mr. Vivek Sawant, (former MD, MKCL) in Sadhana Weekly (2015), Pune.

(C) *NIRMAN*: A CASE OF TEMPORARY ACTION-LEARNING GROUPS TO CONNECT HIGHER EDUCATION WITH SOCIETY

Abstract: *This case is about building temporary Action-Learning groups for students who have completed graduation and higher studies but wish to explore options for making meaningful and fulfilling careers and jobs. Mr Abhay and Mrs Rani Bang have been engaged in social and developmental work in Maharashtra for decades. They started a novel educational programme, 'Nirman', in Maharashtra. It is for the youth who have already taken college education, and they undergo a sequence of three modules conducted in workshop mode, designed by Mr and Mrs Bang. The case highlights the importance of initiatives to bridge the gaps between higher education and its application in terms of careers and jobs. Temporary learning groups with the right strategy can make conventional higher education impactful in terms of guiding educated, unemployed young men and women in India. More such innovative models are needed to compensate for weaknesses in the university education system in India.*

About Nirman: Since 2006, more than 1,200 young adult boys and girls have completed this uniquely designed programme with a mission. It aims to connect the much-needed link between a) the aspiration of the young to lead a meaningful life after higher education studies and b) addressing the 'critical' problems faced by the society they live in. Integrating personal and professional growth with social and developmental issues is *Nirman*'s focus.

Process: The first step in the discovery mode of learning is a workshop called 'Search', which focuses on self-exploration for knowing oneself. The design takes the participants through a series of activities and self-reflection on topics like i) the community in which we live, ii) nature and physical environment, iii) different modes of intervention to solve social issues and problems, and iv) active engagement and interaction with those who are working in the field of their choice at a day-to-day level. The students learn from active and simultaneous engagement with the self as learners, as well as with the people and the problems they face. The theoretical basis of the programme lies in *Mahatma Gandhi's* ideas in his book and his experiments mentioned in *Nayi Talim.*

Dr Bang has designed the programme on the premise that we do not get knowledge of self by sitting in a cave or isolating ourselves from the world around us. The process of knowing 'self' is similar to seeing the light. One never sees the light in pure form, but only when it reflects from the object it illuminates. We see light when the object is visible. Similarly, the self is seen or understood only when we are confronted with a problem or predicament. By engaging oneself with challenges, one discovers oneself and not by avoiding them. When we engage with people around us, we learn what society is and also who we are! It is an important insight that connects the self with other persons in society.

The point is that only from live contact with the location of action, where the problem and the bottleneck exists, does a student learn better and more fruitfully or meaningfully. Problems and the related bottlenecks of the public health system, can, be better understood only when a student undergoes an internship in a primary health centre. Similarly, she also learns the complexity of the problem of waste management when she visits and 'shadows' or follows the daily operations of the waste pickers or when she visits a huge dumping ground in a growing city and town. When a student visits and attends the hearings in the labour court, she gets first-hand knowledge of the complexity of industrial relations issues. Thus, personal engagement with the situation is an opportunity for constructive learning.

Dr Bang observed that today's youth of India is eager to get answers to fundamental questions such as whether the higher education that she has acquired would benefit anyone else, whether her knowledge and skills would help in solving community problems or the larger issues in society. They are restless about knowing the purpose of their existence and whether higher education is only a means to survive and earn money or if there is anything more to it. These are practical and philosophical questions at the same time.

Dr. Bang took inspiration from *Mahatma Gandhi* in his quest to find indigenous solutions to make education relevant even at a global level. This is a unique perspective in present times when our models of higher education are imitating models from Western universities. It is essential to recognise that the most critical part of the Gandhian model of *Nayi Talim* is to make the 'self' a centre of experiments and rely on experiential learning. Interestingly, his autobiography is titled '*My Experiments with Truth*'. An essential aspect of the Gandhian perspective on Indian society was that it uses a diagnostic approach to solve social problems. He was a keen observer of people's problems, and he believed that radical change in society is possible by persuading them to think and behave differently.

As of now, nine batches of students from thirty-six districts of Maharashtra and sixteen states of India have participated in *Nirman*. They emanate from a diverse educational backgrounds, medicine, engineering, law, teaching, agriculture, science, arts, commerce, filmmaking, and journalism. What binds them together is their quest for meaningful learning that would enable them to deploy their talents to benefit society and also receive personal self-fulfilment.

The structure of this experiment in action learning (Action Research) groups resembles an institution with a specific purpose and loosely structured 'organisation of organisations'. *Nirman* is based on an informal network of eighty governmental organisations and NGOs, wherein 'Action Learning' opportunities are provided to young men and women under the guidance of more than one hundred advisors and professionals working in different fields.

Interestingly, most of the participants in these action learning groups are young adults who have already completed their graduation courses from reputed educational institutions in India, the USA, and Europe. The common link that binds them together is the urge to find a path that would offer them career experiences that are meaningful to them and also productive to society. This does not mean that they tend to neglect financial responsibilities towards their families. In the course based on workshops, they learn individual level financial planning, goal setting and learning relevant skills and developing competencies while working on projects and internships that offer active engagement with jobs related to a) public health, pollution, b) transportation, c) waste disposal, d) water supply and other fields related to their interest and educational background. These projects are in those areas that are relevant to the needs of the society and require local solutions.

This is a model of informal but purposeful education that is complementary to the conventional education in science, commerce and humanities or professional disciplines provided by the university system. The deficiencies of the formal system are compensated by the loosely structured network of experts who have designed a curriculum that is based on a robust methodology and values. Needless to say, both students and facilitators hold a high level of commitment to learning and development.

Nirman is a unique institutional model of higher learning that would be relevant for 21st-century India, when many routine jobs based on information processing would be taken over by machines and artificial intelligence (AI). Innovative designs of higher education oriented towards problem-solving and self-fulfillment are possible in such out-of-the-box models of institutional designs. *Dr Bang's* experiment is a thoughful attempt to create an alternative model of higher learning which proposes a constructive alternative to the gaps in formal higher education. However, it operates outside the mainstream model of the University system. It, therefore, has limitations in challenging the status quo of the higher education system in India, but offers an option for complimentary and meaningful education designed for educated adults.

(Source: Gokhale, Charutta; Savwad, Nirman, A community of youth in search of direction, Sunday Supplement, 19 December, 2020, Maharashtra Times)

CASE STUDY FOUR

DECODING ROHIT VEMULA'S LETTER

Social Discrimination, Alienation, and Liberation

Rohit Vemula was a research scholar at the Central University at Hyderabad. Before he committed suicide on 17 January 2016, he wrote a letter that remains the only explanation of his intent behind the tragic action. The text of the letter gives us an idea about his inner aspirations and reflections on life experiences. It poignantly captures his struggle to come to a sense of his identity in an unequal society, which requires a closer reading to decode its meaning. The full text is available in the public domain (*The Wire, 2019)*

This case study is presented in two parts; the first part focuses on the textual analysis of the letter and decodes its underlying meanings. The second part analyses the larger problem to address the issue of caste-based discrimination and suicides of Dalit students on *HEI* campuses in India.

Part One: Textual analysis of Rohit Vemula's letter

Rohit Vemula's suicide note in a letter form is a sad and significant event in the recent history of university education in India in many ways. Vemula wanted to be a writer of science fiction but mentions that this letter was the only piece of writing he could write to date. Some excerpts from his letter are given below.

> *Good morning,*
>
> *I would not be around when you read this letter. ... I have no complaints about anyone. It was always with myself I had problems. I feel a growing gap between my soul and my body. And I have become a monster. I always wanted to be a writer. A writer of science, like Carl Sagan. At last, this is the only letter I am going to write.*

> *My birth is a fatal accident. I can never recover from my childhood loneliness. The unappreciated child from my past. Maybe I am wrong, all the while in understanding the world... There was no urgency. But I was always rushing. Desperate to start a life.*
>
> *I am not hurt at this moment. I am not sad. I am just empty. Unconcerned about myself. That's pathetic. And that is why I am doing it. ... I believe that I can travel to the stars. And know about the other worlds...*
>
> *Let my funeral be silent and smooth. ... Know that I am happy dead than being alive.*
>
> *"From shadows to the stars".*

The letter begins with 'Good Morning', a familiar salutation used by faculty and students on educational campuses. However, the next sentence reminds the readers that he would not be alive when his letter is read by 'you', the reader. It establishes a direct but uneasy connection with those who wish to read further. Gruesome incidents of the order of ghastly suicides on campuses of Indian universities are not unusual, but this case is rather exceptional because it is a self-conscious decision and not a reactive one. The letter is addressed to all those he knew, that is, friends from the *Ambedkar Students' Association*, faculty and staff of the *Central University, Hyderabad,* his close relatives, and family members. However, it was also read and responded to by many more whom he did not know, and it made *Rohit*'s case rather extraordinary at the national and international levels.

The epistle has become a document that is primarily addressed to the Indian society at large, written by a person, who was born and brought up in a free and democratic country. Since Rohit belonged to the lower caste strata of society, readers are likely to presume, from the writer's social background and context in which he wrote the letter, that it would be primarily about the issues of caste prejudices and discrimination. However, a careful reading reveals that the letter is not merely about caste discrimination on the university campus. It also draws our attention to and reflects on the larger existential question of alienation of an individual from others, community, and even one's 'self'. It is a cryptic comment on the dehumanised climate in which the young, irrespective of caste class they belong, are exposed in social institutions that have lost human sensitivity. With few words, the letter reminds the readers of the social, political and cultural realities of contemporary India.

Rohit comes out in the letter as a disillusioned young man who had aspirations to live in a better world where each person is "*treated as a mind... a glorious thing made up of stardust*". The question arises: What is a person if he is treated as if he is without a mind? Is he a body, an object, a slave, a robot? Therefore, *Rohit* is not merely complaining about social discrimination per se but laments the loss of dignity and respect for a person's intrinsic human value. A person hold only an instrumental value meant for use by vested interests.

The letter is unusual in the sense that, unlike many other suicide notes, it does not accuse anyone or make the accusation on the basis of caste discrimination on the university campus. Instead, he chooses to describe his existential and mental state of mind just before making a self-conscious decision to commit suicide. The explanation is neither a justification nor a defence but only a detached observation of his thinking, feelings, and reflections on his experiences from his childhood days, his neighbourhood and his experiences as a research scholar in a reputed university, where he was admitted on merit. The quality of the language used in the letter is a testimony of his potential for and desire to become a science fiction writer. His ability and writing skill to describe his life situation vividly with exceptional self-control is apparent in each sentence of the letter.

Rohit captures his personal suffering vividly in a few lines: *"My birth is a fatal accident... I would never recover from the loneliness of childhood."*

The past and present in his life have continuity and commonality in terms of persistent feelings of neglect and loneliness. It underlines the basic condition and urge of human existence where a person's self is mirrored in others. Mutual care and concern for others are essential to maintaining one's identity and mental health. It is important to explore how *Rohit* was fully convinced that his situation would not change in future and that death was the only way to escape into his ideal world of being. He would instead prefer to enter into his world created by his imagination, wherein he is a part of the cosmos and the luminous stars. The imagery and description show he loved reading the science fiction of *Carl Sagan.* He would rather live in an imaginary world to liberate himself rather than live in a climate of unjust discrimination and manipulation designed by cultural, social and political systems.

Rohit's intense sensitivity to his innermost feelings and thoughts is evident in the description based on images and metaphors.

"*I am experiencing an ever-widening gap between my body and soul, and now it has taken a monstrous form*".

The metaphoric expression suggests how he is gradually losing the quality that is essential to remain 'human' in the real sense of the term. He exists in a dehumanised state, a huge, deformed monster, and he is unable to keep his body and soul together. It may remind the readers of *Frank Kafka's* description of a salesman who finds himself being transformed into an insect in the story '*Metamorphosis*'. At the practical level, *Rohit* may be hinting at the depravation of the scholarship for months, his struggle for survival, and the difficulties caused by the university administration. Mental health and well-being depend on a balance between the physical needs of the body and the desires of the soul as well. A person does not live for bread alone, but he also needs bread! The impact of depriving *Rohit* of his legitimate scholarship is a comment on the insensitivity and communal politics on the campuses of *HEIs* in India.

Apart from a reference to 'last, one more time, *Jai Bhim*' at the end, the aforesaid epistle does not particularly refer to the problems of Dalit students on the university campus. *Jai Bhim* is the assertive Dalit voice of all those deprived of their legitimate right to human dignity. Some sentences refer to his mental state of being, and they describe his inner struggles to liberate himself from suffering as a human being. In a way, *Rohit's* letter transcends the stereotype of Dalit identity and draws our attention to the universal feeling of meaninglessness and emptiness of one's existence as a human being. It implies that social discrimination and inequity on campus are not issues restricted only to the reservation of seats in universities but are also a part of the human experience in society, irrespective of caste, class, gender, time and place.

Considering the impact of *Rohit's* letter at the national level, the issue is more about a climate of inclusiveness jointly generated by those who are benefitted from positive discrimination, as well as those from the upper castes. Therefore, the vital question is, 'Why does the reservation policy fail to do justice and how come?' The answer lies in the systems' failure to recognise, identify and articulate the underlying values associated with the policy and its implementation both at the level of the Central University and at the level of the Ministry of Education. The core values implied in the constitutionally guaranteed policy of reservation are: a) unconditional respect for all human beings at the core, and b) ensuring the associated facets of equal opportunity, participation, and commitment to empowerment. Above all, the value requires a basic humility to recognise that all humans are equals and deserved to be treated as equals as a universal value of being human.

With a closer and a much more intimate delving inside in the epistle, one can recognise the importance of articulating the value set embedded in the purpose of public institutions for higher education in the Indian context. Making structural and policy changes is one thing and implementing the attitudinal and behavioural changes implied in the reservation policy is another thing. Important policy decisions would fail if they do not reduce the social-psychological suffering and improve conditions of those who deserve to benefit from them, which is evident in the case of *Rohit Vemula.*

At the existential level, a sensitive research scholar with a desire to be a writer of science fiction finds himself estranged from his 'self'. 'I feel empty'—This is an experience of an extreme form of alienation and meaninglessness of a person who feels separated from his own 'self'.

Rohit also refers to other aspects of a larger societal alienation that readers would relate to easily, such as election-oriented democracy in India with its vote bank politics. A person is reduced to an *Aadhar* number. In the context of interpersonal relations, there are chances of being hurt in an intimate relationship of love and difficulty in relating to the other without caste considerations in the Indian society. The most significant observation in the letter throws light on the essence of Rohit's life experiences. He writes,

> *"The value of a man is reduced to his immediate identity and nearest responsibility. To a vote, To a number, To a thing. Never was a man treated as a mind, as a glorious thing made up of stardust. In every field, in studies, in streets, in politics, in dying and living."*

The observation is not posed as a problem but is a pointer to the meaning society has given to every field of human endeavour: relationships, identity, education, politics, existence and death. The real meaning of being human, as Rohit expected, is realised only when a person is recognised "*as a mind and as a glorious thing made of stardust*", an acceptance of the limitless potential of being human. In essence, it is about having freedom and confidence to give meaning to life that helps a person transcend those social, cultural, political and power conflicts and unites everyone with the sole criteria of humanness. This is the vision that Rohit aspired for and wanted to liberate himself to actualise through death.

In other words, the letter is about a philosophical and fundamental issue, and it is not a problem; it is about living a meaningful existence that goes beyond a constitutional guarantee of reservation of seats for scheduled castes and tribes. In the context of *HEIs* in India, it is the responsibility of social, political, religious and other institutions to actively promote a climate that offers a free and egalitarian environment for young men and women, in and outside the campus of *HEIs*. Indian Education system deserves fraternity and equality in schools, colleges and universities.

Campus politics and consequences: At the factual level, the letter avoids mentioning anything about campus politics, but it was widely reported in the media later, particularly the fact about the withdrawal of *Rohit's* research scholarship for seven months by the university administration and also the reversal of his admission to the hostel due to complaints by *ABVP* against *Ambedkar Student Union.*

Rohit had to borrow eighty thousand rupees from a relative to sustain his mother and himself. The metaphor of a 'demon-like and ever-growing monster' points to the violent and uncontrolled feeling that he would have experienced then. As part of the student union, Rohit and his friends staged a protest for the unfair treatment given by the university administration. He mentions in his letter how disappointed his friends in the union would be by his decision to quit the struggle tragically halfway. But he had consciously decided to choose another path of protest against the injustice.

Rohit's academic performance in the realm of higher education was quite good and he was admitted to the fellowship programme on sheer academic merit. In the letter, there is no direct mention of the rivalry between the student union or prejudice of the administration against Dalit students and the union. This omission is understandable because it is difficult to prove how such prejudices operate and influence the administrative systems of the University. It is a matter of climate and ambience wherein things happen through informal networks. Caste affiliations work tacitly in Indian society and remain covert but always alive.

In order to overcome his failure to come to grips concretely with the myriad ways in which the caste system works in social and educational systems, Rohit, in the letter, refers to an existential level alienation of his self from nature and from building meaningful relatedness with others on the basis of love and trust. Fake emotions, art, and beliefs around him disturb him for this reason. Human identity is reduced to a vote and number to be manipulated by the political system in the name of democracy.

Against the backdrop of such disillusionment with the world, he decides to liberate himself with a mythical fantasy of a self-created world after death, where a utopia of equal and free society exists. For a Dalit student, it is a radical solution to liberate himself from the slavery of the caste-based society. As an anti-climax, the letter ends on a pragmatic note of request to his friends to return the loan taken and owning the responsibility for his decision to commit suicide. Strangely, it echoes Socrates's instruction to his disciples to return a cock he had taken from his friend just before he was poisoned to death in prison as a punishment.

Part Two: Caste discrimination

This segment of the case study focuses on the problem of caste discrimination on campuses of *HEIs* at the national level and provides an analysis of suicides of Dalit students admitted to professional courses and proposals for solutions to the problem.

Years after Rohit Vemula's suicide on the Hyderabad Central University campus, important questions about caste-based discrimination on the University campuses remain unanswered. Is there any change in the Central University of Hyderabad in order to avoid discrimination against Dalit students on the campus? Also, who is responsible and accountable for these problems? How can an inclusive campus climate be created to prevent the recurrence of such suicides? What needs to be done to improve campus climate so that it becomes inclusive, plural and equal?

So far, the answer to the first question is in the negative for the simple reason that neither the political nor educational system have tried to understand the problem at the level of institutional values and purpose. The university system and colleges still believe that giving access and admission to Dalit students is the only way to impart social justice. They fail to recognise that though the education system can make it mandatory by law to provide access, but it would not automatically make them 'acceptable' to those who run the system. In other words, 'access' does not necessarily mean 'inclusion'. The issue of inclusive climate is intimately connected with the purpose and values of the institution, which is not considered with the kind of seriousness that it deserves in *HEIs*.

The objectives of universities in India focus on knowledge creation and economic development. However, they are not integrated with constitutional values of inclusiveness, equality and brotherhood. There is less evidence that central ministers or vice chancellors of universities have done anything to intervene in institutional structures and values in this regard. The recent evidence reported in national media only shows that those university administration, who were responsible are actually rewarded for not doing anything in this direction and for maintaining the status quo in favour of those in power positions in society and *HEIs*.

Rohit Vemula's hopelessness and despair emerge from his experiences in the struggle for inclusion and acceptance. He repeats the phrase twice, 'fatal accident of my birth', and his image as a lonely child haunts him even when in adulthood. Institutions of higher education, like universities, have not made any serious attempt to include and accept Dalits as a part of the learning community on campus. Neither the university administration and faculty nor the student community have made any social investment in this direction. Therefore, the problem has remained unresolved for decades due to deep rooted prejudices of caste based social culture.

What can be done to improve these institutions of higher learning and promote inclusiveness? What kind of inclusiveness and for what purpose? What is the role of students, faculty and the administration in the process?

The possible answers based on the theoretical framework of institution building *(IB)* and organisation development *(OD)* are: a) As the problem occurs on the educational campus, the solution needs to be located in the structure and processes of education, that is, its academic programmes, research and students extension service, b) From *Rohit's* case, it is evident that the problem of recognition and acceptance by others has to be resolved at individual and collective levels. It requires a methodology and resources to address the issue of institutional climate and norms. It would need personal and social developmental work, which can be in the form of an Action Research project, experiential learning and pedagogy that brings empathy and sensitivity to the collective on campuses.

A few learning resources, as mentioned in Essay Eleven of this book, for this kind of work can be considered, such as Phenomenological Research, Process and Behavioural Labs, and Reflective Practice for students and faculty, which would focus on systematic documentation of and reflections on day-to-day experiences and conversations to discover the meaning-making processes that influence human intentions and behaviours. The author remember a discussion on a TV channel when the incident of *Rohit's* suicide took place. A spokesperson of the establishment commented that he failed to understand how such an intelligent student, which is so evident from the quality of thoughts expressed in the letter, could decide to commit suicide, and it not justifiable. He evaluated intelligence in terms of a person's competence in thinking and analysis but completely failed to recognise the intensity of *Rohit's* feelings and the predicament he was in. This kind of insensitivity is relatively common in the so-called educated elite in India. The point is that the perspective of Phenomenology and its 'process learning' methodology is an antidote to the so-called 'rational thinking' overemphasised in higher education institutions. The act of suicide would also be interpreted as an act of revolt against an oppressive system and in order to make people realise the chasm between the appearance and reality of the education system. The spontaneous responses that *Rohit's* letter received from many in India and also other countries vindicate that his fantasy to liberate himself and enter a world of his imagination that could empower him to be his true self, is actualised strangely and radically in the act of suicide.

It is a positive fact that access to higher education in India has increased substantially in recent years. Many students belonging to scheduled castes, scheduled tribes and OBC categories, whose parents are uneducated or half-educated, enrol for higher education in universities and colleges. They certainly benefit from the constitutional provision of reservation in education and employment. However, legitimising access by law does not imply social inclusion of these students in educational institutions and workplaces. Rohit Vemula's suicide highlights this limitation of legal protection and underlines the need for social support required for deprived young men and women.

Perceived from a sociological research point of view, it is also important to diagnose the processes that led up to this predicament of many Dalit students and to understand how the social systems in *HEIs* and other social institutions operate. American researcher *Isabel Wilkerson* mentions it in her book, 'Caste as a Pathology,' and explains the genesis of the caste system. It has been defined as "any action or structure that seeks to limit, hold back or put someone in a defined ranking, seeks to keep someone in their place by elevating or denigrating that person on the basis of their perceived category can be seen as *casteism*." She further adds, "Many people, good and kind, can be casteist, interested in keeping the hierarchy as it is or content to do nothing to change, nor active or openly hateful of this or that group". The observation is true in the hierarchical social structure based on caste and class in India and beyond.

It is also significant that caste conflict on educational campuses got a political legitimacy post-2015 period, with clashes between Dalit associations of students and *ABVP*, a wing of *RSS* at *JNU-Delhi,* and *IIT-Chennai*, *Fergusson College, Pune,* to name some of them. Though the invisible social divide and cultural differences between lower and upper castes on campuses prevailed for long, there were no direct confrontations and violence between them on campus. Now, it is blatantly apparent and institutionally supported. It is widely reported in the media, on the floor of the parliament and discussed on campuses, but it does not create an impact or change the system and therefore the hidden and potent reasons need to be identified and addressed.

It is important to note that most of the suicides of Dalit students have taken place in educational institutions that offer professional courses in Engineering, Medicine, Management, etc. The common cause is located in the insults and demeaning behaviours by faculty and peers towards them. Also, they are perceived as less intelligent and of low merit because of the special concessions they get. Moreover, they are poor, and their parents are uneducated to defend socially since they are not articulate. There is another hidden reason for the resentment of upper castes towards Dalit students; it is the promise of a better social status they would be entitled to after receiving a professional degree. In addition, almost all faculty members belong to upper castes; for example, IIM-A management believes that faculty recruitment on the basis of caste reservation would dilute the merit and lower the quality of the institute. The point is that the problem is at a higher societal level, and it is an issue of social structures and cultural prejudices. It would require inter-institutional collaboration among educational and other socioeconomic institutions, which is a domain of institutional development *(ID)*. Developing inclusive campus culture is imperative for building robust educational institutions.

Case Study Five

JNU: The Rise and Decline of an Academic Institution

The case is presented in two parts: The first part describes the history and gradual evolution of Jawaharlal Nehru University (JNU) as a premier central university. The second part narrates the rapid decline of the institution in a series of events like students' agitations and the response of the administration under a new Vice-Chancellor. It ends with an analysis of the unfolding of violence on the campus and applies theoretical frameworks of Neoliberalism, Agency theory and Psychoanalysis to draw insights into institutional dynamics and its negative impact on academic climate, leadership, with its use of violence that had damaged the fabric of other higher educational institutions for political gains.

PART 1

'Education is for improving the lives of others and for improving your community and make the world better than you found.' – ***Marian Wright Edelman***

In 2019, Jawaharlal Nehru University (JNU) completed its fifty years of existence, and ironically, it was the most turbulent and violent year for its faculty and students. In order to understand the present of JNU, it is essential to revisit its past. The official website describes and proudly declares it as a 'premier university with a unique model of interdisciplinary teaching and research'. Institutions are built and sustained on the foundation of shared values. However, they are often vulnerable to the risk of an attack on those values that bind this collective of a living system called a university. With the exposure to 24by7 media channels and their narratives, people in India and the world over have witnessed an unusual confrontation between those who are committed to defending the legacy of liberal and critical thought, social commitment, the institutional culture of equality, and academic excellence and those who are determined to demolish and destroy these values with a vengeance.

JNU's story appears unique in the context of the history of the Indian university system. When the former cabinet minister, Shri *M.C. Chagla*, presented the bill in the Indian parliament to form a public university, he proposed that this would be *"an entirely different and new type in terms of a free atmosphere where students can enquire and investigate, challenge every dogma and every doctrine and start a voyage of discovery... a university should provide an experience of living as well as an opportunity of living."*

It was indeed an adventurous experiment in the university system of the 1960s that was replete with hierarchies and structures. *JNU* was, avowedly, an Institution of excellence and, at the same time, provided equity in access, a fact that 21st-century India has yet to reconcile and extend. Educationists and ministers have reasoned that quality and quantity (access) in higher education cannot coexist. However, the fact is that *JNU* has challenged this untested assumption by integrating so-called paradoxical values in practices. This can be considered an example of building relevant and value-based institutions of higher learning. Instead of taking it as evidence of best practices in the university system, the central government has been actively engaged in painting it as a campus of anti-nationalists.

The truth is that the alumni of *JNU* are both establishment intellectuals and anti-establishment intellectuals. It has produced bureaucrats, civil servants, and politicians of opposing ideologies, activists, critical scholars and commentators.

The real strength and the unique attribute of *JNU* as an institution is its capacity to balance commitment to the maintenance of an established social structure and to work on alternatives through innovative ideas. It is a unique combination of conformity and innovation, which is the secret to its success and development. By holding these opposing but internally consistent impulses of the human mind, conformity and innovation, *JNU* has discovered its purpose, mission, and direction. It is consistently ranked as one of the top universities by Indian and global standards, a logical consequence of its remarkable capability to sustain diversity, intellectual fervour, ability to question the status quo and provide alternatives that are consistent with the vision of the founders of independent India and its constitution.

However, it must be noted that these achievements have emerged from the active struggles of students and faculty of JNU. In 1974, the admission policy gave weightage to regional, class, and caste deprivations and assured a fair and transparent admission process. Such access to higher education for the underprivileged is reinforced by access to these students to the residential campus of the university, as it gives an opportunity to.deprived students of being exposed to a cross section of Indian society on a common platform. This unique benefit to the students is not available to them in the community they come from. *JNU* has also nurtured this facility by offering students opportunities to participate in all administrative and intellectual activities on campus.

Student elections are conducted in a phenomenally fair and constitutional manner every year, so the usual use of money and violence visible during elections in other colleges of Delhi University are absent on the *JNU* campus. Also, it offers a less expensive and more educative process for young adults. The Election Commission of the university is composed of students themselves who permit representatives from all ideologies to contest and present their viewpoints, which provides healthy training for democratic processes in the future.

Dr *V Deepa*, an alumnus of *JNU* and a faculty member at the University of Delhi, describes the unique culture on the campus in the following words:

> *"JNU is a place that nurtures differences but still makes one feel like one belongs there; it doesn't come with a burden of linguistic hegemony. The teacher-student equation is built on mutual trust and cordiality. It enhances creative and critical thinking, with deep sensitivity towards social practices. During special lectures, classrooms are filled with students for the sheer joy of learning. The hostel messes after dinner are used as platforms for dialogues or invited talks, with discussions on every debatable issue in society, like oppression, inequalities, and resistance. It makes students sensitive and aware of different inequities in society and encourages them to stand and fight against them".*

JNU imparts complete freedom and autonomy to govern themselves and instilling self-reliance. However, the short-sighted administrative reforms of the new Vice-chancellor after 2018 ignored the institutional culture and values nurtured for decades. The introduction of a new rule on compulsory class attendance exposes the assumption that in higher education, students only study when the teacher enters the class. In contrast, the collective wisdom of *JNU* faculty is that higher learning is a continuous process without limits of time and space. The library is accessible 24 hours a day, and the faculty is available on the residential campus for consultation and guidance. The role of faculty is that of a resource person and not merely of an instructor in the classroom.

Another so-called reform happened to be that of an exorbitant fee hike, which was opposed by students' unions. As a public university, *JNU* fees are kept at a low level, and the fact is that historically, education at this university is seen as a source of empowerment for those from deprived sections of society, like women, people with disabilities, and the poor.

An alumnus of *JNU* from Pune, *Madhura Joshi,* who joined the M.Phil. programme in Sociology, mentions the campus culture very vividly to highlight its open and caring culture, particularly in the backdrop of many recent attempts to demonise students of *JNU* as anti-nationals.

She writes,

> *"While seeking admission, I felt secure and reassured when the seniors on campus helped me in completing the procedures, and later, my classmates accommodated me in their rooms as I got a hostel room after six months due to procedural problems. It was an important initial experience of the JNU community. At that time, most of us did not have much knowledge of party politics and ideologies, nor did we know the full form of AISA, SFI, and other student unions.*
>
> *However, there were regular discussions on social and political topics in hostels and Dhabbas on campus. There were talks by eminent social workers and students after 9.30 p.m. when the mess was closed. It was not compulsory for us, but there was a climate of vibrant intellectual life that rubbed on us. Without any use of force or brainwashing, students of JNU are more informed and mature in terms of awareness of socio-political conditions from distant countries to small villages in India.*
>
> *The creativity and self-expression of students find a space on campus through graffiti, posters, poetry and street plays. I would return to hostels late at night from the department when we were working on project completion. JNU is a very safe place for ladies. The campus has an open and democratic climate that is conducive to critical and rational thinking. Most importantly, we got exposure to students from different economic classes and communities. I learned much more from the campus life of JNU, which is very inclusive and tolerant of economic and cultural differences.*
>
> *Those of us who had studied in colleges of Pune, we were scared to speak in the class; some of us did not speak because of our inability to use the English language correctly. In contrast, I saw that students of JNU were confident in self-expression in class and other platforms. They were articulate without any inhibitions and spoke in broken Hindi or English, and they were readily accepted by other students and faculty. JNU does not evaluate students on the basis of language, and it is an encouraging climate to develop self-confidence and self-respect, which is so critical for the development of university students. Such an academic and social climate is more important than posh campuses with slick buildings and internationally qualified faculty. It is these institutional processes of JNU that make it distinct from other universities in India.*

> *As I look back, I believe that I had learned something more valuable than subject knowledge; I learnt the rare quality of 'humanness' on this campus."*

The most insightful observations on faculty behaviours are made by Prof *Rajén Harshe*, an alumnus and faculty of JNU who has been associated with this institution for fifty years, from 1973 to 2023. He is of the opinion that media, backed by political patronage, had spread misinformation and damaged the image of a reputed Institution, avowedly. It was maligned as a *Tukade-Tukade Gang* and anti-national university. As he looks back on his experiences with faculty on campus, he finds that so-called progressive and liberal-minded faculty remained feudal in values. Unfortunately, they were unaware of the impact of their actual behaviours. Another weakness of *JNU* is its tendency to recruit new faculty internally, which leads to 'inbreeding'. Often, PhD students are appointed as faculty after completion, even though they may lack competencies for this position. *JNU* has rather failed to attract talented faculty from India and other countries. Inbreeding has created *client-patron* relationships between senior and junior faculty, resulting in *guru-chela* relations that are not conducive to free thinking. Sycophancy and hero-worship are dysfunctional attitudes in academic institutions. Mediocre faculty get an advantage in employment at *JNU* largely due to the reputation of other excellent faculty. According to Prof *Harshe*, the over-politicisation on campus has done more harm than benefit from the process of democratisation. In spite of better infrastructure and internet facilities, the faculty has not contributed to subject knowledge.

Despite these weaknesses, Prof *Harshe* finds that *JNU* remains a rare institution that has benefitted students from deprived and poor sections of Indian society. They receive quality education, sometimes with scholarship, which expands their perspective and worldview drastically. *JNU* remains a top-ranking university in India, and this needs to be supported and improved further for academic excellence.

PART 2

The second part of the JNU story is a striking contrast to the first. It describes the ingenious and devious ways in which the egalitarian and democratic culture that the institution sustained for fifty years through the struggles and efforts of its faculty and students is dismantled systematically by the new VC, appointed by the Ministry of *HRD* in 2016. There was an incessant onslaught for four years through revision of rules, procedures, and show cause notices to faculty and students, followed by violent attacks on them on campus. The misdeeds totally demoralised the faculty and students of *JNU* and were vividly and widely presented on national print and TV media. However, one can detect a method and hidden agenda of the establishment to systematically demolish the edifice of an exceptional institution of higher learning.

The strategy and game plan behind the policy of neoliberalism in education can be deconstructed at the micro level from the *JNU* case in the unfolding of the following a sequence or chronology of steps taken by the university authorities after 2017.

First step: Students resist steep hikes in the entrance test and hostel fees because 50 per cent of the student population comes from families from different states in India whose average monthly income is only five to eight thousand rupees. In other words, the new fee structure would make access to higher education for aspiring students of low-income families more difficult and almost impossible.

Second step: Self-financing initiatives such as technology-related and marketable courses are floated to reduce dependence on state funding. It indicates the reduction of state funding to higher education.

Third step: Compulsory class attendance is used to monitor the performance of students and faculty.

Fourth step: Change is introduced in the structure of student participation in campus elections.

Fifth step: Some faculty members who had participated in the protest against the fee hike by the university authority were selectively reprimanded so that the community of faculty would remain divided rather than united.

Sixth step: Academic and administrative decisions are made by the VC without taking faculty and students into confidence or engaging with them; in fact, the VC consistently refused to interact with students on their problems under some pretext.

Interestingly, most of the action steps of the authorities mentioned above are consistent with the neoliberal economic policy and the ideological bias of the state as explained below.

Theoretically, neoliberalism shares some of the premises with classical liberalism, such as:

> *(a) An individual is a self-interest seeker, (b) The market is the best institution to allocate resources, (c) commitment to the principle of laissez-faire and minimum intervention of the state, (d) invisible hand of market competition, (e) competition would bring efficiency and quality, (f) positives of self-interest, together with market competition, would be beneficial for society.*

However, neoliberalism differs from classical economic liberalism in one aspect: it expects an active role of the state in the positive construction of a market and in controlling the market from a distance. It implies that the state would fulfil the role of Principal and monitor the implementation of its policies through Agents as envisaged in the *Principal-Agent Theory (PAT).* An important assumption of *PAT* is that those making the decisions on behalf of the Principal, the *MoE* in this case, and those affected, that is stakeholders like students, parents, faculty, and staff, can be manipulated and would be responsive without resistance to the execution of changes in policy initiated by the Agent, which in this case is the VC of *JNU.* In a sense, Agents are also the state's regulatory organs, such as the *UGC, AICTE,* and universities. They are driven by an education policy to build a competitive economy for nation-building. It shows how assumptions of a neoliberal policy and Principal-Agent relations fit into the narrative of *JNU* and explains its rationale. The economic and political agenda of the state is strategically pushed and executed in the context of reputed public universities in India, who resist the assumptions and logic of the market of higher education.

In the present context of *JNU,* the decisions of Agents like the VC to hike admission and hostel fees, are, presumed to be in the interest of the larger objective of the state, which is to build a competitive economy and nation. Resistance to such decisions is not expected as it is legitimate to allocate financial resources efficiently, which are drawn from taxpayers' money. Also, another assumption is that *JNU* is a university with a high reputation and hence is expected to generate its own resources from the market and should not depend on state resources to subsidise the fees of the students. Thus, the reputation of *JNU* would be dependent on its competitiveness in the education market, which has nothing to do with the needs of society and of the student community on the campus.

One would recollect that it is the same logic and related rationale that was used when the students of the *Film and Television Institute of India (FTII),* Pune, protested against excessive fee hikes (2013). It is important to note that both institutes are funded by the government and they are autonomous, like IIMs and IITs. Each institution is designed to be unique and different in terms of curriculum and those who apply for their programmes. However they commonly consider higher education as a part of 'public goods' and not 'private goods' or meant only for those who can afford it. In the case of *JNU,* half the students come from low-income families who live in less prosperous states and take courses in social sciences. However, such social and cultural features of the institutions have no place when the State as Principal, with an economic agenda, is relentless and intolerant in its pursuit of constructing a competitive market of higher education in India. Universities, as Agents of the state, have no other option but to accept it and be in the good books of the Principal. Thus, the autonomy of institutions is systematically curtailed.

In context of the *Agency theory*, one can appreciate and deliberate upon the notion that why the new VC behaves more like an Agent appointed by the Principal, which is the State, and who is expected to manage JNU on its behalf and is totally unconcerned about the impact of his decisions on faculty and students. The unfortunate part of the JNU story is that students' resistances to the decisions of the VC (Agent) were ruthlessly suppressed through police interventions directed by the Ministry of Home Affairs on behalf of the State (Principal), monitoring covertly from a distance. The unrest on the JNU campus was debated and reported with videos and photographs in the biased national print and electronic media. These narratives and propaganda on TV and social media are a telling commentary on how universities are projected to be perceived in a particular way by common citizens to propagate a dominant political ideology of the state. One of the narratives in the media compared the contribution of *Jawans* on the borders with that of *JNU* faculty and students. It painted them as anti-national activists who are fed on taxpayers' money. The ministers of the government advised students to focus on studies given in the syllabus rather than indulge in protests and urged them to be productive for nation-building. Protest, criticism and dissent are considered as vices of students, according to the political ideology of the ruling government that claims to represent the state. These protests are considered a threat to State power and underline the fact that higher education is embedded in a socio-political context in a democratic country and is not limited to the ivory tower, examination-oriented studies.

Though the primary goal of the university as *HEI* remains academic pursuits and the development of capability for critical thinking, it is suppressed under the one-dimensional political propaganda of the State. Instead, the resistance of JNU students and faculty was polarised into debates on anti-national vs '*deshbhakta*' and side-tracked the focus on undesirable and blatant state interventions in the autonomy of the central universities and institutes.

The story of *JNU* has been repeated on the campuses of other public universities in recent years whenever assumptions and policies of the neoliberal approach of the state towards higher education are challenged or resisted by the students and faculty. From a political perspective, JNU is a positive story for Indian democracy. It signifies the intellectual and moral strength of the new generation of student leaders in India, who, are not passive, unthinking, recipients of educational policies and actions of the political bosses. Union ministers' advice to university students to focus on studies rather than waste their energies on protests exposes their premise that education is not an integral part of social and political processes but only a means to supply an unquestioning workforce for economic growth. However, what makes the present situation complex and worrisome for *HEIs* in India is that it shows similarity with the international trend of weakening of the public and state-aided institutions of higher education and its singular focus on market orientation and commodification of education to serve the interests of the elite sections of the society.

Some of the inevitable academic consequences of the neoliberal approach of institutions of higher education are: a) the values of the market would determine the decisions and behaviours on the campus, b) new pragmatic values anchored in self-interest would replace collective idealism of the idea of a university, for instance, faculty would be compelled to design only those courses that are saleable in market, c) the teaching and research would be judged in terms of their saleability rather than its social and ethical relevance. Such changes would be more harmful in the case of universities like *JNU* that has offered excellent courses and conducted path breaking research in social sciences and humanities.

One of the positive qualities of *JNU* mentioned by students is reflected in terms of campus values, climate and community behaviours, which had reset the traditional gender hierarchies of Indian society marked by violence against women and their harassment in social spaces. The most remarkable achievement of *JNU is* that it has enabled female students to feel relatively free in their daily lives and academic interactions on and outside campus. Also, a subsidised residential campus has helped students immensely since they could determine the parameters of institutional life in terms of defining the use of library and hostel facilities and electing their representatives.

Application of Agency Theory (PAT): Impact on Institutional Behaviours and Governance

Agency Theory is developed by economists in 1970s to explain the problems arising from the separation of ownership of the asset and its control. It describes the pitfalls that often arise when one person, the 'agent' is representing another person, known as 'principal', owner of the asset who has delegated the power to control and decision making, to the agent. The separation of power from the owner is done because Agent is expected to work on behalf of the owner and protect the interest of the Principal.

However, the priorities and the goals of the owner and agent differ. In corporate context, the owner wants stock prices to increase for better dividends, Agent (Executive) would prefer to pay more incentives to managers. In university setting, the challenge for the administrator like VC or HOD would be how to prevent faculty who are subject expert and in direct contact with students from taking advantage of their privileged and non-programmable positions, by way of putting minimal efforts into teaching, or research. There is an information asymmetry between faculty and the HOD/VC since the latter is not directly involved with academic processes. For good governance, it is important to maintain the balance between goals of the administrator and faculty which do not converge or diverge completely in education institutions. The solution is to work on building commitment to institutional purpose and its values.

It would be revealing to understand the behaviors of new VC of JNU in the context of his role as Principal and role of JNU faculty as Agent. It is pertinent to mention a reported experience Prof. *Rajen Harshe*,(2023) when he was a part of the committee to select assistant professors at JNU in 2017. The professor was appointed on the selection committee as an external expert; however, he learned that the VC had directly appointed two other experts to the panel without following the rules of appointment given by the academic council. He was rather shocked to see that the VC and the panel had already made the choice of the new faculty before the start of the selection process. He also witnessed that even after two days of interviewing, the committee did not conduct a review of the performance of those candidate who had appeared for the interview. The external expert insisted on the review process by the committee in the meeting because the candidate selected was of dismal academic quality and Prof Harshe, as external expert was very upset with the decision. He tried to explain to the VC about the harmful consequences of the appointment of a wrong person on the reputation of the university for the next three decades. Sadly, this persuasion had no impact on the VC and Prof *Harshe* had to leave the meeting in despair. However, he declined to sign on the minutes of the meeting. The candidate was selected by a majority vote by the panel!

The experience mentioned above explains how appointment to faculty is based on political affiliation rather than on academic performance. In the context Principal – Agent theory on the conflict of interest and the role of Principal to protect the interests of stakeholders like community of faculty and students, the VC has acted less as Principal but clearly as an Agent of the MoE to protect the political interests of those in power. Such behaviors of VC would raise serious issues of governance and commitment to the institutional and academic values of JNU. It is an example of how hard earned reputation of an institution degenerates when the person in the position of VC (Principal) gives preference to narrow self-interest and violates institutional integrity. The travesty of Agency Theory is that those who are in the position of Principal, as an institutional head (VC in this case) are acting more like an agent of those who are owner/principal. Conflict of interest in Agency theory impact negatively good governance practices. The attempt to resolve the conflict by external expert, failed as there was no possibility of collaboration on the part of the VC to focus in the larger goal of protecting the interest of students and reputation of *JNU.*

The episode is a symptom of systemic failure in governance practices by blatant violation of established procedures on selection of faculty positions in a university. Such practices are neither professional nor ethical.

Campus Violence at JNU: Psychoanalytic Analysis of the Unconscious

A psycho-analytical study of the community dynamics on the *JNU* campus would help in having a better understanding of the criminal aggression and violence on the *JNU* campus (2019).

It is useful to refer to the analysis of Prof *Gauranga Chattopadhyay* (2004), a former faculty in Organisational Behaviour at IIM-Calcutta, who has conceptualised the destructive unconscious processes that affect role behaviours in various work organisations and societies. He has described these processes as '*invaders in the mind*', a notion that exists primarily in the unconscious of the Indian psyche, which is further supported and nurtured by the Indian caste system. The '*invader in the unconscious mind*' and the caste system legitimise aggression into boundaries of space and the human existence of others whose ideas and perspectives may differ from their own. It emerges from an intolerant and unitary view of singular Truth. In the context of the *JNU* case, it matches with the political ideology of the aggressor.

Prof Chattopadhyay contends that knowledge and awareness of dealing with unconscious fears need to be an integral part of higher education to avoid the destructive tendencies that emerge from ignorance of these forces and their impact on managing institutions of higher learning. The core of the theory of the unconscious is its potential to unleash aggression and violate boundaries of thinking, feeling and actions. It is an anti-learning and anti-democratic force that does not allow the management of resources, physical and human, in rational terms.

Historically, due to litany of aggressions, particularly in northern states, Indians carry unconscious pictures or images of both in terms of 'invading others' and 'being invaded' by them. The collective behaviour of *JNU* authorities, the VC, and the registrar, backed by the power of the ruling party in government and its students' wing, towards *JNU* faculty and students on campus is the most telling example of the unfolding reality of the unconscious forces in the collective mind.

The factual details on the causes of the invasion, that is, continuing rivalry between student unions belonging to left and right-wing politics or whether the 'invaders' were outsiders or within JNU, who enacted the psychodrama to unleash violence on campus, is best left to official legal inquiry. However, the fact is that the moral and official authority of the VC and the administrator was missing in critical times on the campus. It is a deep-rooted, irrational fear projected on others as being invaded by those who do not share their beliefs turns out to be a reality. It was a real, physical invasion against the imagined enemy that was unleashed on the campuses of JNU, Jamia-Millia University, and Aligarh Muslim University, with communal and caste overtones.

The ability and the related capacity to think and act rationally is hijacked by irrational and unconscious fears because they are neither confronted and processed emotionally nor intellectually on educational campuses by those in authority positions, the administrator, the faculty, and students. It is a comment on the lack of a robust intellectual climate in *HEIs* of India. Also, it is a blatant use of collective irrationality in society for political gains by those in power.

Such actions are also an indication of guilt of those in charge of academic governance as they fail to connect with the students and faculty at an equal level and confront their conscious and unconscious issues in a climate of trust and safety. This unconscious guilt is projected on the students as 'evil' forces. Thus, it leads to the abdication of moral and academic authority and invites the intervention of security guards on educational campuses. The process of violent invasion and aggression is very similar to the experiences of the lower castes in rural India in caste-related violence and communal violence in cities.

Prof *Chattopadhyaya* delineates that India has a long history of invasion, either as invaders or victims of invasion. The political system has also sustained the myth of the superiority of the conquerors and the upper castes and the inferiority of the conquered and the lower castes. Moreover, there is a religious notion of purity and pollution that dehumanises those at the lower level of the social hierarchy. Those qualities and characteristics that are unacceptable in one group were projected onto the next lower group. *Brahmins* would see *Kshatriyas* as inferior, and the first three castes would find *Shudra* or *Dalit* lowest in the *Varna* hierarchy as untouchables, not worthy of even a touch. Even the state fails to see citizens as participants in a democratic process that had elected the representatives for governance. Instead, the citizens are seen as 'subjects', and elected ministers see themselves as 'feudal lords or kings' who rule them.

The behaviour is an antithesis of democratic values, and it prevails in all kinds of social institutions in India. As a consequence, neither the ministers nor the agency of the police are able to take their legitimate role and work for the purpose of the system. In the case of a university, one can imagine the damaging impact of those in an authority position, who hold in disdain and distrust those with less authority because of the unconscious myth of the superiority of those who have the power. Therefore, they believe they have the right to invade and attack those who would resist their actions in order to force their ideas and beliefs on them. For an institution of higher learning, such an acceptance of unconscious "invaders" in the mind is an antithesis of higher learning and rational thinking.

In the present situation, the *JNU* faculty appears completely tired and demoralised, fighting the ideas of those in power, who have been relentlessly attacked for their convictions and academic values.

The story of the downfall and subsequent decline in governance at *JNU* is a sad story of an extraordinary institution of academic excellence that has achieved excellence over five decades. The case study of *JNU* is about the rise of a liberal university in a democratic country and its subsequent decline in a non-liberal state. It is pertinent to end the story with a comment by Prof *R. Harshe,* an alumnus of *JNU.* "It is sad to see the rapid decline and destruction of *JNU.* It is tragic but not impossible that an excellent institution built upon day and night hard work and collective efforts of faculty and students can be destroyed in such a short time!"

REFERENCES

1. Chattopadhaya, G.P. (2004). *Effectiveness of manager depends on managing self in role.* Convocation address, Institute of Management Development and Research, Pune.
2. Deepa, V. (2018). *Higher education in India is at risk.* The Indian Writers' Forum Newsletter.
3. Harshe, R. (2023). *Pakshi Unhacha: On campuses of seven universities.* Sadhana Prakashan.
4. Janaki, N. (2019). *Jasn-e-JNU: What lies behind the call to dismantle public university education?* The Wire. Retrieved from https://thewire.in/author/janaki-nair
5. Jensen M.C, Mackling W.H, (1976); *Theory of the Firm*
6. Joshi, M. (2020). *'JNU': A place to dream!* Savwad, Maharashtra Times.
7. Pathak, A. (2019). *JNU: The story of the fall of a great university.* The Wire. Retrieved from https://thewire.in/education/jnu-the-story-of-the-fall-of-a-great-university

ILLUSTRATIVE CASE STUDY SIX

DESIGNING INDUCTION PROGRAMME FOR PG STUDENT

This case is a first-person narration of a faculty member based on his experiences during the designing of an Induction programme. It describes the process of how the design evolved, which was revised while implementing it. It illustrates formal and informal collaboration among the participants: the director, faculty, staff, and students as a community of learners on the campus.

Till a few years ago, the induction of new students was limited to an inaugural speech by the director of the institute. The first induction function of *MDBA,* a two-year management course that I attended at IMDR, was in June 1982 in a large classroom since the auditorium was not built on the premises of the institute then. I vividly remember that it was primarily an emphatic speech delivered by the founder Director. He described and elaborated upon the history and evolution of IMDR, the first B-School in Pune. He talked about his career and exposure to a seminar on management education where stalwarts like Prof *Kamla Chaudhari*, the then faculty at *IIM-A*, and *Prakash Tandon*, Chairman of HLL, participated. He also recounted the challenges the institute faced during the initial years in getting accepted as the first non-aided PG course. He also introduced visiting faculty members and others who were present in the audience.

The speech culminated with an emotional statement that the students had demonstrated faith in the persona of the director by way of taking admission to an institute that was autonomous and de-linked from Pune University. The director expressed satisfaction with the personal trust of newly admitted students and their parents and his assurance of being responsible for their career in management.

The speech lasted for about 90 minutes, and it was an impressive attempt to project the efforts of the founder director to start the first B-school in Pune. It highlighted the resources of experienced visiting faculty from the industry who would teach these students.

In those days, students at *IMDR* were primarily from Pune and Maharashtra. The institute was associated in the public mind with its director, and generally, it was identified by the personality of the founder director.

Seven years later, my senior colleague was appointed as the second Director of the Institute. Subsequently, I was promoted as a lecturer at the institute. The institute had two full-time faculty members who were in their thirties and about 10 to 15 visiting faculty who were practising managers. From then on, I would participate in many important academic decisions like admissions, curriculum design and conduct of a unique induction programme. I shall describe how this programme evolved over the years.

Within a year or two, we realised the significance, pertinent requirement and the need for an improved induction programme since it was the first experience for students after an elaborate admission process through written tests, group discussions and personal interviews. The process of how they interacted initially with their new classmates, faculty, and staff impacted their behaviours later during the two years of their stay on campus. The conventional method of selection and then the 'inaugural address by the director' mode of induction was not an organic experience of being introduced to an institution. Moreover, the personality and temperament of the new director were different from that of the founder director, who was a senior and established faculty member in the academic and industry circles of Pune.

The primary concern of the faculty was that newly inducted students' behaviours remained hooked to their undergraduate days. This affected classroom teaching and learning processes, as well as interaction with faculty and the staff on campus. It goes without saying that our undergraduate colleges are managed by unilateral, bureaucratic controls of the university and colleges, which alienates the students from the faculty and the institution. The only learning goal placed before students is to clear a series of examinations. Our own experience as students in our colleges was no different.

The faculty group of five was in their thirties, and they did not wish to create such a system-dependent and anti-learning climate on the campus. We had experienced the consequences of such a personal and authority-dependent relationship that deprives students of learning how to manage themselves in the situation and develop themselves as self-reliant and concerned professionals. The mission statement of the institute officially articulated it as 'developing strong professional values and sensitive, concerned citizens.'

Indeed, we needed a new induction design that would address the needs of the students, faculty, staff, and external stakeholders. For the first time, we paid careful attention to the design and also the process of implementing the induction programme.

The design process considered the following areas to structure a two-day induction programme; for specific details, a copy of the two-day programme schedule is given at the end of this case.

Students' profile: The students were young adults in the age group of 20-24 years hailing from different states of India; the proportion of male and female students was almost equal. This was an outcome of the institute's admissions through the Common Admission Test *(CAT)* conducted by IIMs and also due to the fact that students came from different disciplines and courses at the undergraduate level. Due to this variety in class composition, new entrants were eager but anxious to know about their peers in the class and seniors on the campus.

At the same time, they wished to meet and interact with their prospective faculty. Therefore, we thought of using the *Micro lab* format of self-introduction to address these concerns and anxieties of new students. Hence, students and faculty participated together in the induction programme.

The *Micro Lab* was designed in such a way that the new entrants would share their ideas and experiences on a variety of questions in pairs, triads and small and large groups so that they were exposed to almost everyone in the class at a rapid pace of 60 minutes in a Micro Lab session. It was an informal socialisation to peers and faculty. The director was regarded as one of the members of the faculty group, though with a distinct role and responsibility, as a 'first among equals' of the peer group of faculty, as it is in a collegiate structure of teams.

Some of the items on the information-sharing activities in the *Micro lab* called as 'Breaking the Ice' are mentioned below:

(a) Share in small groups the prominent features of the place you belong to and the people there
(b) Share the prominent features of your family and your positive qualities
(c) Share the things you value and qualities you would like to develop in yourself on campus.

Knowing the role of office staff on the campus: From day one, students come in contact with office staff, the accountant, the librarian and later with computer lab staff and the rector of the hostel. An early introduction to the dos and don'ts and norms of behaviours in these places on the campus certainly helps students know the role expectations of the staff and vice versa. A visit to the library, computer lab and office, playground, and canteen on campus to actually meet the staff who are role-holders in small groups for interactions is an essential part of the design of the programme.

Senior students: The faculty experience on campus is that new entrants rely more on the information given by the seniors than that given officially by the institute. Also, there is some anxiety and curiosity about the so-called informal interaction or ragging that they had earlier experienced in their undergraduate days. We thought that creating a formal space where new entrants meet their seniors is a good idea to legitimatise the informal interaction of senior and junior students.

Influencing attitudes and norms: Historically, the institute's campus is known for its informal and student-friendly ambience. This is because their interaction with the director, faculty, and staff is based on mutual respect and warmth rather than on authority and impersonal or bureaucratic rules.

As an autonomous institute, IMDR has developed an independent curriculum and extensively used experiential learning methods of field assignments, role-plays/behavioural simulation, process labs and case studies in small groups. The induction programme needed activities that would give a direct or vicarious experience of some of these methods. This was introduced in the form of role-play, quick survey and skit during the induction.

Admission and selection: The new entrant had undergone a radically different methodology of group work and interviews at IMDR. The conventional group discussion is replaced by group work and Behavioural Event Interview (*BEI)*, which asks a common trigger question to invite narration of an event experienced by the student in the recent past rather than the conventional questions like 'tell us about yourself' or 'how you see yourself after five years'. *BEI* is now widely practised in the corporate world for competency-based selection. Students selected were eager to know the rationale and explanation of such a methodology. A theoretical explanation and logic of the selection methodology was expected from the students. This lecturette was included in the induction, where the faculty in charge of selection briefed new entrants. In other words, the induction design focussed on addressing the expectations of students and their information needs.

Process of Designing

Reflections and learnings from past experiences in the delivery of the induction programme: The exercise on the need-identification of students was revisited by the faculty group every year when they met ahead of induction to fine-tune the design based on previous years' experience. It was used as a benchmark of reflective practice or learning from experience. It is somewhat similar to the action learning cycle of plan-action-reflection-revised plan methodology. Also, the process of experience-sharing, brainstorming, experimenting, and debating is used to develop revised objectives and the content of the induction.

When the faculty reviewed the process immediately after the end of the induction programme, they realised that a ritualistic or mechanical approach to conducting it as an activity did not create the desired impact. The genuineness and authenticity of the individual faculty and the understanding within the peer group are critical factors in the delivery.

Unlike a classroom session, the faculty engaged in induction at the beginning of the course every year was perceived as a team and collective rather than as individuals while engaging with the students.

Some of the faculty members had prior experience with *Process Work Labs,* and their insights were used for the group-building process. One of the guidelines given to the faculty was that they were to remain in touch with their emotive self while sharing information and experiences with the students. Roles and masks are subordinated to the genuineness of self and the person. The faculty is expected to be in touch with 'where they are' and maintain a process awareness of how they feel and think at that moment. This is radically different from the conventional 'know all' stance of faculty as subject experts in the classroom. This is an area that needed more attention and practice to develop interpersonal sensitivity.

Contents of Programme

Curriculum Design: IMDR has used the methodology of an instructional design system (IDS) that integrates all the courses in six trimesters or four semesters. The structure of the curriculum is logically linked with the vision, mission, and curriculum goals down to the course objectives. The horizontal and vertical linkages within the subjects and other courses of the trimester and preceding and next trimesters are explained in the curriculum document (CD). The approach to teaching-learning each semester was also explained, and this remains an academic/cognitive part of the induction programme. For many students, it was a new knowledge to recognise that there is a basic difference between the so-called syllabus and a scientifically designed curriculum.

Vision and Mission of the Institute: With the Vision-Mission statement in place (1992) and the word-of-mouth publicity based on the direct experiences of alumni, the institute was now identified as a special institute that distinguished itself from other institutes. The number of institutes in Pune increases every year. The difference was in terms of its democratic and progressive values, simplicity, moderate fees, and academic quality. Articulating these values based on personal experience is the central part of the directorial address in the new design of induction. The focus has been on projecting the distinct identity of the institute in terms of vision and values rather than a person or brand-driven institute. More importantly, institutional identity was presented in terms of actual experiences and practices rather than a set of prescriptions or moralising that are easier said than done.

The Closing session: The last activity of the induction of new entrants encouraged an intense sharing among the batch mates and also creative self-expression of young boys and girls selected for the PG course. From now on, they will be perceived as adults and called ladies and gentlemen in the process of two years on campus! The students in the closing session were asked to prepare in small groups and present a Skit or group role-play on a topic that would help them project their immediate thinking and feeling, for example, *A Day in the Life of a Young Executive.*

Skit or theatre play is a medium that encourages group action and imagination. It directs the physical and mental energy of the young men and women in a focused manner. Also, it gives an opportunity for the faculty to briefly reflect on the '*Here and Now*' concerns of the students depicted in the script and enactment of the skit. Faculty would offer their feedback immediately after the presentation by highlighting the process and meanings that they decoded from group performance in skit presentations. With experience, they gradually became self-conscious and avoided unnecessary cynical or over-critical remarks and judgmental or evaluative comments in the context of an induction meant to introduce them to the institutional process rather than an assessment of students. The occasion and the purpose were to listen and attend to the aspirations of the young entrants and not to evaluate them as a task performance.

Later in the evening of day two, the senior and second-year students were invited as an audience for the presentation of the skit, and they shared their comments. The induction process was then formally closed. However, informally it was taken over by senior students. It was an activity in which faculty had no direct involvement and was an entirely student-driven, fraternal community activity. The norm of the senior student as mentor and newcomer as mentee was established in such informal interactions. It was an essential part of the campus climate, which was conducive to academic and co-curricular activities in the next two years of the batch.

Institutional and Collective Learning

It is important to mention in this narrative that while conducting the induction process in a planned way, faculty learned later that senior students who were exposed to it in the previous year designed a similar plan of informal induction. For the next two weeks, with permission from the director and faculty, they conducted a similar induction process after lecture hours in the evening that included items like debate competitions, case analysis, extempore speeches, songs, dances, and sports. It was a mix of academic and recreational activities. The best items were presented at the Alumni Meet of that year, and the cycle of induction was then completed, which vindicated the vision statement:

> *The institute is a community of students, faculty and staff striving to be vibrant with learning processes in which individuals discover themselves while being productive with their capabilities and creative with their energy.*

The values of self-driven learning and development in the community are seen to be practised and demonstrated on campus. This is a testimony to the success of the 'evolving' design of the induction programme.

The process of conducting induction was exhausting for the organisers, particularly for senior students and the full-time faculty. However, it had a very positive impact on students' behaviours on campus throughout the academic year. There was a climate of trust and rapport among the crucial stakeholders on and off the campus, as well as students, faculty, and staff of the institute. It did set the right tone and attitude for interaction with peers, faculty, and staff. The anxiety level of being exposed to a new place and people was greatly reduced. The students learned to take the first step toward the recognition and acceptance of their personal identity and that of the institute. They developed positive and humanistic attitudes towards others based on mutual respect and personal growth.

Physical spaces on the campus

The students were asked to search the location of faculty and staff through clues like those given in a treasure hunt game. They moved around the buildings and open spaces of the campus and met people at their desks, cabins and other places. The tea breaks between sessions were arranged in the open space of the quadrangle, which is the most favoured space for students. It presented a wall painting of a collage symbolically presenting an unstructured collectivity of different shapes and bright colours. It is called 'United Colours of IMDR.'

The Library

Every year, the library staff conducted quizzes for locating books in the open-access cabinets, and it tested their familiarity with using the software meant for accessing books and journals. Similarly, students visited the computer lab and interacted with its staff.

Institutional Processes and Values

It needs to be mentioned that, and it may not be evident from the above description, the design of induction emerged gradually in the initial three to four years and was stabilised in the later years.

It needs to be noted that the process awareness of the faculty remained rather uneven depending on the reflective personal work done by each faculty member. As Carl Rogers's law of interpersonal congruence states, personal authenticity is directly proportionate to the level of self-awareness, openness in the climate, and trust levels within the group members. Sometimes, faculty continued to indulge in self-exhibition and cynical side remarks in order to play to the gallery. Such behaviour was mistaken for individual freedom and honesty. However, it was inconsistent with the collectivity model of learning and the spirit of collaboration necessary for institutional development.

Similarly, new faculty showed eagerness to conform to the norms of the institute. However, they remained cautious and guarded as they were not entirely convinced of unconventional and egalitarian norms of the collective model of institution. Hence, they were not able to express their self and their 'here and now consciousness of feelings' adequately. However, gradually, the overall attempt to remain integrated with the self and the ethos of the institute has emerged, and it communicated the distinct identity of the institute as a place that students, faculty and staff would admire and like to relate to.

Appendix: A sample copy of the PGDM-1 induction programme of 2011

INDUCTION PROGRAMME PGDM-1

Venue: Auditorium

CONTEXT: The Induction Programme aims at introducing new students to the Institute, faculty and staff. Students come from different places and have diverse educational and cultural backgrounds. They therefore experience some anxiety about joining the course and being accepted by others. They join the course with preconceived notions and expectations.

PURPOSE: The Induction Programme gives basic and essential information mentioned in the handbook in a rather personalised way. Students experience the people and their locations on campus. Intangible aspects like values and culture of IMDR are shared with them.

Objectives:

1. To clarify institute's approach and philosophy of education
2. To share mutual expectations
3. To facilitate class cohesiveness and learning

Programme:

Thursday, 12th June

Venue: Auditorium

10.10 a.m. to 11.10 a.m.: Breaking the Ice

11.10 a.m. to 11.25 a.m.: Tea in the Quadrangle

11.30 to 12.10: About Deccan Education Society and the institute

12.10 to 12.30

Other Educational Programmes & Facilities at the institute

12.30 to 2.00 p.m.

Lunch: 2.00 to 4.00

Small groups meet faculty and staff

At 4 p.m.

Groups reassemble in Auditorium to share experiences of the day.

Curriculum document and timetable to be collected from the office

Friday 13th June

Venue: Auditorium

10.10 to 10.25 Tea

10.30 to 11.00

Curriculum objectives and structure of the curriculum

11.00 to 11.30

Criterion for selection and selection process

11.30 to 12.00

Vision and Mission of IMDR

12.00 to 1.00

Quiz in the Library

1.00-2.00 p.m.

Lunch: 2.00 p.m.

Announcement of skit and guidelines

2.10 to 3.10

Preparation of skit

3.15 to 4.15 p.m.

Skit presentations and reflections (Auditorium)

(The article was first published in The Linkpin (2010), a newsletter of IMDR)

Case Study Seven

The Role of Students' Union in a Central University

This is a real-life story of how the vice-chancellor of the University of Allahabad (UoA) confronted rowdy leaders of its students' union (AUSU). Prof Rajén Harshe was appointed as VC when the university was given the status of a central university in 2005. The newly appointed VC faced numerous obstacles during his five-year tenure, particularly aggressive student leaders of AUSU and scheming faculty members of various departments, in his endeavour to bring back the lost reputation of the university. It is a fascinating real-life story of determination, courage, and conviction that involved the newly appointed VC and his team of faculty and UoA officials. The story is followed by an analysis of the purpose of student unions and the competencies needed in the leadership role of the Vice-chancellor of public universities in India.

In the initial days of VC in office, Prof *Rajén Harshe* had all kinds of visitors, well-known professors of the university, and student leaders. He found it rather strange that high officials of the students' union, like the president and vice president, would come in two large cars along with security guards. They were in their late thirties and would touch the feet of VC to show respect in obeisance; however, they spoke in an overbearing, haughty tone. The VC could sense that they were least interested in studies, and *'netagiri'* or so-called leadership, was their primary interest. They carried visiting cards and were proficient in delivering speeches in Hindi.

Uttar Pradesh is not a developed state, and due to the '*Angreji Hatao*' policy of leaders since the late 1960s, most students did not know any other language except

Hindi. Also, there is an absence of large and medium size private industries, which has resulted in very low-level of employment opportunities. Like Bihar, young adults have to work hard to get into government jobs at the state and national levels, which was not easy for many. In the meantime, they were continuously engaged in taking admission to available courses in affiliated colleges and universities. They had only two options to face the severe problem of unemployment in the state: wait for a government job or indulge in *netagiri* to create a leadership role for themselves as a career.

Historically, Allahabad University has a glorious legacy from the pre and post-independence period, with many educated Indians becoming national leaders. However, in the contemporary context of the weakening of educational institutions along with low levels of academic standards, the quality of leadership in students' unions has also rapidly declined and is in a state of decadence. The incumbent VC, who was appointed immediately after central university status to UoA, noticed that many so-called student leaders had a criminal background with a proven record as mafias, known for *'goondagiri' or* hooliganism, to gather hoodlums to threaten those who opposed them. They were feared even by security guards of the university, and the secretary in VC's office would give them early entry. Sometimes, they would demand immediate sacking of a faculty member and point out loopholes in administration to pressurise those in authority positions and other stakeholders.

The most persistent demand was to hold an election of office bearers of the university students' union. Considering chaotic conditions on campus, laxity in administration, and students' indiscipline, the VC was reluctant to hold an election initially but agreed to it.

Immediately after the announcement of the election, there was chaos and vandalism all over the city. Posters of candidates contesting were displayed on and outside the campus. Innocent citizens were harassed. Students' leaders collected donations to fight elections from shopkeepers, coaching centres, hotel owners, and professionals like doctors and lawyers. Canvassing on loudspeakers occurred in lanes of crowded areas, intrusion in the classroom, and sloganeering on campus was rampant; it was done with a plan and executed systematically. To his surprise and dismay, the VC found that the candidate contesting for president's post was a 45-year young student! His son was a second-year student taking a degree course and participated intensely in canvassing for his father.

Immediately after conducting the election on campus, a tragic incident happened in November 2005. A candidate who contested was allegedly murdered by another candidate. Police arrested the suspected student who stood for the post of president's post in the election. The registrar informed the VC that the caste of the candidate who was murdered was similar to that of the Chief Minister of UP, which led to further escalation of the tensions on campus and in the city. A mob indulged in rioting in the city; police tried to control the situation but could not succeed. The mob attacked the police with stone pelting and chased those who fled, trying to save themselves from attack. The matter went to the court, which ordered not to announce results of the elections till the posters and banners were cleared from the city lanes.

These seven to eight initial months in office were a tough period for the new VC, both emotionally and as a leader in the top position of an institution. Every day, around 11.30 am, a group of students would gather near his office and indulge in anti-VC sloganeering, sometimes burning his effigy and conducting a mock funeral procession on campus. When VC came outside the cabin to meet the group of students, TV channels and press reporters would take photos in order to publicise how they could pressurise VC to go on the back foot so that so-called leaders of students would keep themselves in the limelight in the media every day.

In June 2006, the VC had an opportunity to represent the university along with a committee of faculty representatives to the *J.M. Lingadoh* Commission in Lucknow. The government of India had appointed the commission to inquire into the role of student unions in institutions of higher education. The VC informed them about the indiscipline and criminal activities on the campus. In September 2006, the committee submitted its recommendations, which the Supreme Court accepted. The report specified the maximum limit on the amount spent on election expenses, the age limit of the candidates, and compulsory attendance in classrooms and labs as criteria to qualify as a legitimate candidate for election. It also recommended that students' unions/leaders should stay away from political party affiliation.

In the process, the VC observed that the university campus was a hub of people with a criminal mind-set who were indulging in all kinds of illegal activities like acting as commission agents to get or change mark sheets and pressurising the controller of examinations to postpone exams. There was rampant corruption as they would get administrative work done through informal links with university employees for a commission, to get contracts for construction work or security staffing for cycle stand for income. As a consequence, many students were unable to complete their courses in the scheduled period since some exams were postponed for two to three years. No wonder, the premises of the university near the entrance gate almost resembled the Road Transport Authority (*RTA*) office of the city.

Dire conditions of university hostels: Some students continued their stay on campus for 15 to 20 years. One was married and had combined two rooms to accommodate his family members in the hostel. One was a wrestler who assured the VC that he would protect him like his *hanuman*, the monkey god of *Ramayana.* Many students illegally used electric appliances, and it was a serious issue to pay heavy electricity bills. These irregularities in hostel administration made it difficult for legitimate students to get hostel admission every year. Criminal-minded hostel occupants used the premises to consume alcohol, collect ransom and indulge in drug trafficking. In short, some of the Allahabad university hostels looked like an underworld occupied by goons.

These were serious challenges before the incumbent VC, and he reflected day and night on how to transform the university to regain its lost reputation. He recognised that it would take tremendous effort to bring discipline, and a strong intent was required to face the so-called student leaders on campus. He was reflecting deeply day and night on how to transform the university campus. However, he did not want to use force and violence to bring the turnaround he wanted.

In the past, the VC was impacted greatly by Gandhian thought and his life. This time, too, he reread the autobiography of *Gandhiji: 'My Experiment with Truth,'* which he had last read in his forties. At the time, the book influenced him so much that he quit smoking as a mark of respect and gratitude towards *Gandhiji.* In the second reading, at the age of 56, he could grasp and understand it better. Gandhi put great faith in the idea of Truth and was equally convinced that he would use non-violent methods to realise it. Only a person with internal strength can hold a firm belief in this premise. A deep contemplation of Gandhian values of truth and non-violence provided essential internal moral support to the VC in this period of crisis. It prepared him emotionally and intellectually to face the challenge.

This time, the VC was mentally prepared to work on a two-pronged strategy to confront rowdy students on the university campus. One part of the plan was to face squarely and courageously criminal-minded student leaders and their protests. The second part was to simultaneously and consistently work to bring positive change to the university at a tangible level. Some of the steps he took to transform campus life are given below.

Confronting politics of vested interests: Some faculty members of the university were plotting to destabilise the position of the person working as proctor and controller of examination with the intention of getting this coveted role for personal gains. They used student leaders to achieve the hidden agenda, and they encouraged them with the distribution of sim cards to organise protests against the VC. In June 2006, the VC learned from intelligence bureau officials that during the entrance test of the university, some of the faculty members, student leaders and police officers had conspired to destabilise the examination process by accusing the university administration of a paper leak; it was followed by protests from students. A police officer had even advised the VC to cancel entrance test examinations. It was planned in such a way that it would coerce the VC to resign from the post on moral grounds. Students also created a nuisance and on one occasion insulted external experts when the architect for the university was being selected in the VC's chamber on July 3, 2006. This kind of serious misbehaviour in front of external experts hurt the VC the most and created a deep sense of dejection and anger in him.

All these events led to severe stress on the VC, which made him come up with a strong resolve to fight against these forces. In July 2006, he came to a conclusion after prolonged meditation on Gandhian values and invited the police and the press to his residence to announce his decision. He told them he would embark on a peace march, *Shanti Morcha (Peace March),* the next day, and it would be the responsibility of the state police to give him security. The next day, he went to the office at noon, where a gathering of about a thousand students, university staff, and faculty had come to welcome him on campus. Students' leaders had vanished from the scene at the sight of this crowd. The VC spoke with deep passion and emotion and informed the gathering specifically, "I am going to fight against the *goons* non-violently and am ready to make all efforts to bring back the past glory of the University of Allahabad." The procession walked from the senate hall of the university to Gandhi Bhavan. The media gave national coverage to the event. In the press conference, the VC told the reporters how he was fighting against rowdy students and also explained why he was doing it.

The VC and his team, which included the proctor, dean of students' welfare, registrar, and the finance officer of the university, worked hard together as a team in the subsequent months. The local police helped the staff remove the so-called students who stayed in the hostel illegally so that legitimate and deserving students could get admission to the hostel. Some of the outcomes of these collective efforts during the remaining four-year period of the VC's tenure are given below.

Positive Steps to improve and transform the university

1. The VC continued to deliver fortnightly lectures in the Department of Political Science. They were attended by a large number of students since the topics he covered were relevant to those preparing for competitive examinations. He spoke on subjects like challenges of globalisation, terrorism, imperialism, and foreign policy of the Indian government in South Asia. These lectures expanded his connection with the campus students, and he could hold frank discussions with them on matters of their concern and problems.

2. The faculty and administration developed contacts with industry and activated its 'placement cell'. The director of the cell tirelessly worked to ensure the best employment opportunities for 4,000 young boys and girls through campus placements over four years. The cell carried out a survey and field study to learn more about the needs of the industry and recommended suitable changes in the curriculum. Students got access to e-learning facilities and coaching in the English language. The Law Department of the university introduced a five-year integrated course and organised a guest lecture series by reputed lawyers of the High Court and Supreme Court. This soon became one of the most popular courses in the student community.
3. New programmes like 'Earn and Learn' were launched, which provided work on campus in the library and other ad-hoc work assignments that earned them compensation to support their education. The university funded a campus magazine initiated by faculty and students.
4. The VC brought funds from the Indian Council of Cultural Relations to produce an international play called *Mistaken Annie Besant in India.* The university organised *Kala Mela* (art festival) every year. Considering the exceptional talent of most students of *Allahabad* and *UP* in dramatics and cinema, the university started an institute of film and theatre with a mini-theatre to perform. The Music department invited reputed singers and musicians. A new centre for differently abled students was created for visually challenged students.
5. It was significant that the VC consciously avoided using severe punishment for indiscipline since he believed that positive punishment is more impactful in such situations. For example, eight students were found guilty of participating in a ragging incident on campus. The parents of the victim who suffered from ragging wanted severe punishment for the leader of the group. The father of the leader came from Chennai to pay the fine imposed. The boy was a student in the fourth year of the degree course, and it would have destroyed his career if he had been rusticated from the university. The case was handled differently; eight students were given books and asked to present a 1000-word review. Interestingly, the most mischievous student wrote the best review and repented about his behaviour. All students were forgiven and the best reviewer is a reputed lawyer in the Supreme Court of India today.

Analysis and conclusions: The Vice-Chancellor of the University of Allahabad (UoA) finds himself in an unenviable position wherein he has to manage two institutions simultaneously: the university and the students' union. In the early stage of his five-year tenure, he recognised that it is wiser to focus on improving the university as a system and postpone holding elections for the students' union. When universities are considered as an institution, they assume more significant roles and broader responsibilities. One of the definitions of institution is, 'An institution is an innovative organisation that brings about and protects change' (*Esman et al., 1974*). Therefore, institutional leadership requires a sense of psychological ownership or commitment with an inner drive to govern them. Fortunately, the UoA had a newly appointed competent person with these qualities.

However, the students' union had leadership that followed the model of political leadership in the state of UP. The fact that officials of the university had to call the police to control indiscipline on campus speaks a lot about the weak governance practices on the campus. Though *UoA* had a glorious past record of excellent faculty and student community, in the post-1960 period, greater access to university education impacted the academic climate on campus. Most students were first-generation young adults in their families who had the opportunity to pursue higher education. Greater access to higher education had a direct impact on wider democratic processes in social-political institutions.

The main challenge was that the intellectual and cultural development of the society was at a nascent, feudal stage. In fact, a highly caste-based, politicised climate in UoA had impacted not only the students' union but also the faculty and administrative staff of the university. Historically in the developed countries,, institutions of University and student Union are the creation of modernity and liberalism of Western European countries, which values cultural and intellectual diversity of ideas so that creative expression, dialogue, debates, equality, and tolerance become a part of academic ethos on the campus.

It is intriguing for the VC to understand the dynamics of how faction-ridden teachers of the university would use unruly students as a weapon to attack and score points against each other's group; in addition, the local politicians of political parties viewed such student leaders as a resource to tap for their political activities. Hence, the VC's office was a site of contending factions of faculty based on caste, who were keen to gain power for a factional agenda. In other words, the intertwined nature of teacher and students' politics was very active on the university campus. It became a major obstacle in the path of institutional change in university that the VC intended to bring to regain UoA's past glory. However, it was challenging to fight battles on two fronts. Therefore, real change and improvement in the institution of students' union could not take place. However, it does not mean that it is a less important task because the students' right to organise a legitimate representative body in a democratic country like India is always desirable. It is also a part of higher learning in the role and responsibility of citizenship. It is interesting to see how the story unfolds where the VC gets a grip over the tricky situation of campus politics.

Though the VC had to confront a variety of problems in the initial period, it boiled down to only one problem, that is 'how to manage boundary conditions of a university system so that its stakeholders can engage with its primary task of delivery of quality education. The system's boundaries were invaded almost daily, for example, the intrusion of students in the VC's office during a visit of invited guests, repeated cancellation of the examination schedule, conspiracy by faculty to grab the proctor post, and similar instances. The main cause of such invasions on boundary conditions of the system was rooted in the intent and behaviours of those who managed the system. Their (staff, faculty and student leaders) basic assumption was that the university system is created not for the primary task of knowledge generation and delivery but for the secondary task of getting positions and work for vested interest. Hence, the secondary tasks were driven by a personal agenda that neglected engagement with the primary task, which is the vision and mission of *UoA*.

It was a formidable challenge to change this tacit premise, and the VC had to make valiant efforts to present himself as a role model who could focus on the primary task and did not tolerate vested interests. To a large extent, he succeeded, but it did not ensure that *UoA*, as an institution, would not go back to dysfunctional behaviours and disrupt the system. In other words, there was no immediate evidence in the initial years, that a significant change has occured in personal and institutional values and behaviours of the faculty, staff, and student leaders of UoA.

Similarly, the role of the students' union narrated in the story needs to be understood in the context of the VC's intent of strengthening the university as an educational institution because its students are major stakeholders. In fact, the most harmful impact of the indiscipline and instability in the administrative system was on the academic career of the student community and the expectations of their parents. In theory, the existence of a students' union balances the power equations between the authority of faculty and administration on the one hand and the student community on the other.

Moreover, in an educational context, it is the responsibility of those in authority to ensure that students internalise the democratic principle of balancing rights and responsibilities. In the process, students learn how to focus on legitimate demands in terms of facilities and do not intrude on the legitimate rights of the VC and faculty in terms of imparting knowledge and maintaining governance of the system. For that to happen, a real-life, experiential opportunity for the application of self-regulation is provided by the institution of the students' union on campus via conducting activities like standing for election, campaigning, canvassing, holding discussions, debates with students and faculty, negotiating and collaborating with officials, which are essential for the development of abilities and skills to become concerned and sensitive citizens in society. In other words, the postponement of holding the election for four years by the VC gave only a temporary solution for the pragmatic reason of attending to the more urgent tasks. The larger role of the students' union remains an integral part of the university as a liberal democratic system in India wherein freedom of expression is a fundamental right

Leadership

It is an insightful real-life story documented by the VC himself as it illustrates the role and competencies needed in the top position of any university. The foremost role in the VC position is to manage boundaries of tasks, emotions, thoughts, relatedness with staff and students, time, and space so that the system's human resources can engage with the primary purpose of the university. In order to do that, the VC is expected to possess facilitative and leadership qualities that go beyond conventional expertise and specialisation in a knowledge area. Along with the ability to lead a team, the VC in the case also demonstrated his competence in 'Independent thinking', as he resisted the pressures from student leaders, local politicians, and the *HRD* ministry to hold union elections early. He postponed it for good reasons and remained firm with his judgment and convictions. This behavioural competence is about an 'ability to hold to own convictions in the face of resistance, anticipated or actual'. It involves 'standing up for one's ideas and not being afraid to express them to colleagues, bosses, or other more important people. It means not giving in unduly to group pressures in the desire to please or to avoid confrontation and conflict.' (*Boyatziz, 2006*). Such a person takes a stand on critical issues, follows judgment in the face of opposition or threat, takes a stand on a potentially unpopular issue and is prepared to question established systems, organisational norms and values.

The most significant incident in the story is about the moment the VC deeply contemplates what he would do to handle the stressful predicament of confronting unruly student leaders, scheming faculty members, and pressures from the police and *HRD* minister, all complications at the same time. As a seasoned academician and scholar, he preferred to go back to basics, his innermost intent and values. He referred to Gandhi's autobiography so that he would be in touch with the internal process of handling deep emotions of conscience, the so-called 'inner voice'. This is an excellent example of managing boundaries between his innermost feelings and external pressures from other role-holders. With deep reflection, he arrived at a two-pronged plan to face the situation by addressing the most crucial stakeholder of the university, that is, the community of Allahabad city. He held a public rally, press conference and delivered a speech on the public platform on the same day. He achieved many goals simultaneously, such as building credibility for his actions, defeating the vested interests of union leaders and faculty, and getting a direction for his main task for the next four years of his tenure. Perhaps it is one of the rare real-life stories that happened on an educational campus. It offers a positive message for those who care for improving institutional processes in higher education. The VC and his team members engaged with the mission without succumbing to the pressures of the vested interests. The case also highlights the conflict between democratic, progressive institutions and feudal regressive forces. Leadership with vision and character plays an important role in building robust institutions.

REFERENCES

Harshe, R. (2023). *Inside seven university campuses. Pakshi Unhacha.* Sadhana Prakashan. Pune

Harshe, R. (2012) Handling student indiscipline. *Seminar*, 638.

SECTION THREE

LEARNING RESOURCES

The purpose of this section on Learning Resources (LR) is to provide instruments and concepts for building personal ability and skill to pursue lifelong learning that goes beyond formal education. LR can be used productively by students, faculty and institution builders. Process skills are essential for personal and institutional growth; soft and life skills are helpful for academic processes of teaching, learning, and strengthening interpersonal, group processes to improve institutional climate.

Specifically,, the section covers notes on Mentoring and Coaching, Soft skills in mindful attention and empathic listening, Self-study techniques to improve the academic performance for PG students and Guidelines on giving and receiving feedback. The material can be used as a learning resource by faculty, academic administrators, and students. It would also facilitate a better understanding of the practical application of concepts and methodology for self and group development. The last note explains the role and the competencies needed for faculty, HOD, and VC of universities. In short, Section 3 provides practical guidelines for building reflective, interpersonal, and self-managing skills for improving performance in academic and institutional roles.

Four notes are:

(a) Process and Life Skills for Students and Professionals

(b) Self-driven Learning System for College and PG Students

(c) The Art of Mentoring and Coaching for Institution Building

(d) Role and Competencies of Faculty, HOD and VC in Universities

A: Process and Life Skills for Students and Professionals

This note explains the most important human and communication skills: a) Attention, b) Empathic and active listening, and c) Giving and receiving feedback. The purpose and relevance of three process skills is to enhance interpersonal and group competencies are discussed below with examples, which can be used for developing human resources in all types of organisations.

Skills are learned and developed on the basis of acquired knowledge and an opportunity for their application and practice. Along with an understanding of theoretical perspectives and methodology of organisational development *(OD)*, those who are engaged with the task of institutional building *(IB)* need process skills because educational institutions are socio-technical systems wherein both formal-technical and living-human systems coexist. Therefore, skills that facilitate the development of individual consciousness and interactions among people, play a critical role in sustaining effectiveness of institutions.

These skills are more relevant in *HEIs* because their value premises include academic autonomy, freedom of expression, independent thinking, development of persons at the individual level, collaborating with others, interdependence, and an attitude of having a simultaneous concern for self and others. Process skills are anchored in the perspective of *IB* in the sense that relationship between the individual and the collectivity or community depends on a climate of inclusiveness and interdependency.

Conversely, the perspective of *IB* expects each individual to see her connectedness with others in order to achieve a common purpose. Process skills need to be understood with a systemic perspective since they rely on a combination of tangible aspects, that is, structural and technical aspects in man-made living systems like institutions, with the soft aspects, such as feelings, beliefs and values, which are an integral part of humans. It implies a simultaneous balancing of concern for the self and concern for others at the collective level. It also balances complementary forces of competition and collaboration, as well as autonomy and interdependence at institutional levels, which is imperative for building robust institutions.

The facilitative role of leadership in *HEIs* is to maintain this balance by deploying a variety of process skills like reverse attention, empathic listening, facilitating, confronting, dialogue, discussion, giving and receiving feedback, conflict management, and decision-making by consensus. These are intrapersonal and interpersonal skills demanding openness to feedback and self-awareness.

Let us consider three process skills in more depth. They are: a) Reverse Attention, b) Empathic listening, and c) Giving and Receiving Feedback

(A) Types of Human Attention

The note addresses three questions: 'What is the role of attention as a process skill in academic and experiential learning?' 'How does it contribute to the institutional development of *HEIs*?' and 'How would the knowledge and practice of skill in attention benefit citizens who are engaged with human communication in society?'

The answers to these questions would require knowledge of invisible cognitive processes on how humans understand the world around them with the use of sensory abilities. It also requires knowledge about the human ability of 'apperception'. It is a conscious perception of sensory impression. Importantly, attention as 'apperception' does not happen naturally and has to be learned consciously. Also, it cannot be learned as a skill with forced practice because the purpose of being attentive in daily life is to keep oneself in charge of the situation that one encounters and thus not be a passive recipient to the external influences, including the 'forced practice to learn apperception'. Hence, 'attention' is always anchored in one's own self-consciousness along with the ever-evolving identity of the person. It is also dependent on one's ability to reflect on day-to-day behaviours and actions in practical life. Therefore, the ability to hold or pay attention is not merely a thinking ability but is connected with how one handles feelings and gives direction to one's actions. In other words, the human capacity for 'attention' improves with a simultaneous increase in self-awareness and reflection.

The fact is that human faculties of attention, self-awareness and reflection are not developed through formal learning or training, even though it is expected to be deployed in institutions of higher learning. However, the reality is that many educated people are ignorant of cognitive and human *process skills*. As a consequence, individually and collectively, society is susceptible to and consumes all kinds of noises and muddles received from electronic media, TV, the internet, and WhatsApp messages. Also, in day-to-day human interactions, one has to engage with people who bring in their moods, temperaments, negativity, and reactive dispositions that emerge primarily from an underdeveloped consciousness. There is a need for *directed attention and reverse attention* because it is rather challenging to cope with reactivity in others and maintain one's individual sanity and composure. An orientation and conscious practice of remaining located in a '*directed attention*' (*DA*) is helpful. Skill in 'directed attention' is essential for all in contemporary society so that we are not sucked into the hypnosis created by other individuals or by an ideology of the system or media that we are exposed to. The way to maintain a capacity for '*directed attention*' is to remain anchored in one's self or internal registers so that external propaganda does not distract one's attention.

'Reverse attention' (*RA*), on the other hand, is about being self-critical, which also does not happen naturally because it requires a '*reference of self*' against which you compare all the messages that you receive day in and out. Without this attitude or mind-set to discern outside stimuli with self-reference, one cannot evaluate them objectively. The ability to remain self-critical is the most valued quality in today's times because it protects us from self-created illusions.

Human attention is deeply connected with the simultaneous evaluation of self and outside stimuli, since we are bombarded with them in the contemporary world of information technology. Therefore, the human ability of 'attention' has a crucial role in how one perceives and responds to external stimuli, which one cannot control. Since this process happens at the day-to-day level and continuously, it demands careful examination of how we attend to the stimulus and how the received data is processed in the mind. In the contemporary context, wherein our minds are greatly influenced by media and its racial, communal, and ideological propaganda, every citizen needs to strengthen the process of attention and counter these influences rationally so that she is not misguided or carried away by them.

There are five types of attention, according to *Silo* (*http://Silo.net*), an Argentinian philosopher, activist, and founder of the Humanist Movement, an international organisation committed to the goal of simultaneous development of individuals as persons and society.

1. *Conditioned or dog's attention*: The first type of attention concerns our daily attention, which goes in the direction of the stimuli from the external environment. The famous experiment of *Ivan Pavlov*, a Russian behavioural psychologist, demonstrated the experiment wherein when a bell rings, the dog learns to reach for food. Here, the attention is drawn by sensory stimulus. It is a mechanical conditioning of the mind.

2. *Self-driven attention:* The second kind of attention is equally mechanical in terms of being attracted by selecting a stimulus that is consistent with one's own interests. The first type is dog-like attention, where the stimulus controls our attention entirely; the second is a little more conscious, as we are moving in the direction of our interests and yet it is not fully conscious attention. Attention in this case is drawn by our interests and aspirations, which we have not fully reviewed or reflected upon. One does not know where our needs are coming from. It is a kind of conditioning of the mind that we are not fully aware of. Though it is not dog-level conditioning, one cannot claim it to be entirely human in the sense that our actions are not truly in our control or we do not fully know what we are doing or why we are doing so. In other words, human consciousness and intentionality are missing in this type of attention.
3. *Divided attention*: The third kind of attention is 'divided attention', wherein one can attend to two or three things at a time with practice, such as driving and talking on a cell phone at the same time. Sometimes, even three activities are done by a person in some professions, such as a circus clown who cycles and plays with many balls and plays a tune on the mouth organ.
4. *Directed attention*: The fourth type of attention is called '*directed attention*' that can only be achieved by deliberate practice, which demonstrates the fact that human capacity for attention is very elastic in the sense that one can learn to attend to many stimuli with training and exercises such as those in gymnastics and team sports. But one gets bored and fatigued by such exercise beyond a point as they become mechanical, lose human interest and hence consistency as well. However, such practices of 'directed attention' are helpful as they indicate that the human capacity for developing self-conscious attention is flexible, therefore, even when we are simultaneously engaged in actions like conversing, walking, and listening, we do not lose our centre of self-awareness. We are not taken in easily by the mass communication and systematic hypnosis created by media, TV or political and religious leaders. This happens because directed attention enables us to develop a capacity to make comparisons, which is possible for only those who can maintain their self-reference to maintain contact with internal register to process cognitively received information. This is also a kind of '*reverse attention*' that helps us to remain open for self-criticism and for a comparison of self with data received from others' feedback. The person is ready to reconsider her opinions with new data that would invalidate the deeply held prejudices.

5. *Attention with consciousness and self-knowledge*: Importantly, one cannot develop the capacity for self-criticism internally and therefore requires an objective reference of 'self-knowledge'. Self-criticism without self-knowledge would not be authentic because when a person accepts criticism offered by others readily or conveniently, it is not a well-thought-out response. There is no conscious attempt to come out of external influences and think independently about self. With self-knowledge and process awareness, one can be conscious of the self without forcing oneself towards it and still attend to what we are doing with a feeling of internal assurance or strength. This kind of attention is self-conscious and non-compulsive. It is neither mechanical nor compulsive. It leads to effortless actions that are centred on self and not driven externally.

Importantly, perception, apperception and attention are not separate skills to be learned mechanically. It is more of an attitude or a mind-set to be developed consciously without forcing ourselves on it. It requires practice of dynamic meditation (*Silo*) It is an art, and therefore, a sense of humility, openness, reflection and attentive care is needed. Skill in attention is based on the cognitive processes of the brain. However, it is a human or soft skill that operates both at conscious and subconscious levels.

Attention and Listening

Self-critical attitude is an essential attribute for better listening. It is necessary to recognise that a disposition towards self-criticism is possible when a person is ready to question her beliefs and values in the context of the here-and-now situation. Also, it implies an attitude of not accepting anything at face value, the things offered by people in power and authority positions. Attending to external messages critically allows a person to maintain her right to form an independent opinion. This kind of mental disposition is crucial while working for *IB* processes, where it is important to avoid the tendency for conformity and subservience in taking up institutional roles, which is detrimental to the growth and development of self and others as well.

Difficulty with the development of an attitude towards directed and self-critical attention in an individual is that there cannot be a training programme in developing skills in 'attention' because it has to be internalised as an attitude and mind-set so that one naturally carries it while experiencing day-to-day living. It is not a fully conscious state of mind because one unconsciously accepts many untested, not validated ideas and assumptions with reference to the things around us. Directed attention is a discipline that is developed through reflection of our behaviours while living and experiencing. It cannot happen in a training-hall context. However, it can be learned in *Action Research* projects or in *Reflective Practice*, where reflections on actions taken during the projects in small groups or on how human interactions are carried out at workplaces in natural settings. In *AR* projects, individual and collective attitudes and mind-sets are recalibrated with the reality faced during actual experiences of engaging with task and group behaviours. The point is that distinct spaces and methods for learning the five kinds of attention mentioned above are needed in formal and informal work groups in oganisations. (refer to *Essay Eleven on 'Qualitative research methods for personal and institutional change and transformation.')*

Let us now consider another important process skill, 'Listening', in more depth because we spend a significant part of our institutional and social lives applying it.

(B) Listening Skills

In the context of education, the ability to communicate is an essential skill for classroom teaching-learning but ironically, listening is not considered an essential quality for effective interactions with students in the class. Formal education that transfers subject-specific information from the teacher to the student is equated with learning. The conventional pedagogy accepts this kind of teacher-centred, one-directional learning in schools and colleges. At the workplace, on the other hand, people complain, "No one listens to you in the department", in fact listening is a scarce but most appreciated and productive skill in work and social organisations.

Why are listening skills a scarce resource in organisations?

It is rather unusual to have a listener who is non-evaluative without approving or disapproving of what you are saying. There are many training courses on communication and public speaking, but the topic of listening is rarely given the attention that it deserves, and there are deep-rooted reasons for this in our social power structures. The common idea of communication is that it is a one-way proficiency in the delivery of information, and it is a blunder reinforced by those in power positions. Though listening is a familiar activity, it is often taken for granted, and its quality or effectiveness is never tested. The leading cause of poor listening seems to be its total absence from the formal system of school and college education.

Even in teaching language courses, it is found that more importance is given to skills in writing and reading, less to speaking and the least to listening. Ironically, in real-life situations, the order is reversed. When using language as a medium of social and human communication, it is listening that takes maximum time, followed by speaking in day-to-day living and writing for tasks or work-related matters.

Empathic and attentive listening: Listening as a skill needs to be differentiated from 'hearing'; listening as a skill includes empathic and attentive or active listening. It also constitutes listening with a non-judgemental attitude. The good news is that listening skills, unlike attention, can be developed with systematic practice, and such opportunities for practising are plentiful in daily social interactions with family, friends and colleagues at workplaces.

However, the ability to pay attention is necessary not only for accurate or attentive listening for the listener in terms of reducing loss of facts, information and connotations or implied meanings of words used but also for registering the impact of the person who is interacting with the listener. Attention strengthens listening capacity and also builds trust and better mutual understanding.

Attending to the speaker, physically and psychologically, is an essential part of listening because it signifies the involvement of the listener in the process of two-way communication. Here, the listener is personally present, receptive, and grounded in the situation without being listless. Quality of attention and listening determines the receptiveness of verbal and nonverbal communication, and both are equally important to the listener in decoding messages received while communicating. For example, the body postures and mental orientation of the listener influence the quality of reception. Maintaining eye contact and being physically relaxed communicates a sense of authenticity to the speaker. However, it should happen naturally without any manipulation for a desired impact; otherwise, it would be as distracting as aggressive gestures, unnecessary staring, or being preoccupied with objects and pets while listening.

Attention to nonverbal messages: About 90 per cent of human communication is transmitted by non-verbal and voice modulations in tone, pitch, volume or grunts (*Argyle, 1975*). However, reading and interpretation of nonverbal cues should not be done in isolation because attentive listening implies understanding of the overall meaning that the speaker is trying to convey. Specific non-verbal data should not be mistaken for the totality of the intended message.

Beware of empathy: Empathy is the ability to imagine how another person is feeling and thinking so as to understand his/her mood. While listening, empathy can also be a trap in 'not listening' because, in this case, a listener may get involved in her own reflective thinking, feeling about her own parallel experiences rather than attending to those of the speaker. It is advisable to put our empathic listening ability or compassion aside, suspend judgment and listen from the viewpoint of the speaker in terms of where she is coming from. This is a mind-set and attitude that allows acceptance of messages without necessarily agreeing with them; it is a mental stance that helps one to go beyond approval or disapproval or indulging in past memories in order to listen with mindfulness.

Non-empathic, non-judgmental, conscious listening helps the listener understand the person objectively and sensitively as well. Moreover, listening is always done in a cultural context, and socio-cultural factors provide important clues for active or attentive listening. Notions and values of caring, face-saving, and concern for self and others are embedded in the speakers' socio-cultural context, and sensitivity to these factors enhances attentive listening.

Active Listening: Active and careful listening is needed for those who offer help and coaching, personal guidance, or counselling, which often occurs in the context of student-faculty or senior-junior faculty relationships. Needless to say, attentive listening is a great asset in maintaining social relations as well. In human communication, the common problem is interpersonal incompetence or inability to communicate with congruence and with internal coherence. In this case, if what is being said is not supported through nonverbal body language such as voice tone, postures, and choice of words, then a deep listener can easily notice these inconsistencies and use this data later to convey the decoded message on incongruence to the speaker as a feedback later. The point is that one's lack of listening does not go unnoticed by others.

The ultimate test of active listening is measured by its impact on the speaker, who ultimately recognises whether he/she is really listened to. It is a very demanding cognitive process because it requires additional energy in the listener to register her *impact* on the speaker. The confirmation of listening has to come from the speaker, who may express that the listener is connected in the process through verbal or nonverbal responses.

Listening to the whole person is more important than listening only cognitively or intellectually. Intellectual listening limits itself to what is being said, though culturally or legally, it is an acceptable practice wherein data is received and stored in the memory. However, the vocal channels or tonality of the human voice and body postures also convey related messages along with the verbal part. Important content on feelings, level of trust, and confidence is conveyed nonverbally. Therefore, listening to the person, both intellectually and emotionally, is very important to understand the complexity and nuances of human communication.

Blocks to effective listening

Evaluative listening: This is about a common tendency to impose one's own values upon the speaker's message and judge what she is hearing and not listening while the message is being transmitted. What is actually required is to put one's thoughts aside to hear what is being conveyed. Though it is rather difficult to set one's thinking aside, as the first step, it is helpful for the listener to recognise where the evaluation is coming from, as well as the norms and values that govern it.

Filtering: This is listening to what one wants to hear and omitting what does not fit into one's worldview as a listener.

Distracted listening: Attention to the subject or content is a critical quality of good listening. Distraction or diversion takes one away from it. Many people find listening an exhausting activity because they have to struggle with distraction from internal and external causes like tiredness, emotional reactions, or listlessness. In the context of classroom learning, the shortening of the attention span of youngsters, who are overexposed to visual media, is the main cause of poor listening to the verbal messages delivered by the teacher or faculty in formal education. Electronic media use visual, audio and other human communication devices to capture the attention. However, only self-discipline and interest in the subject can enable a student to listen with full attention.

Listening with sympathy rather than empathy: It is important to recognise that listening with sympathy may reduce the quality of listening. This happens because, in the context of formal learning and at the workplace, such sympathy may influence the speaker in a way that would block her from getting impartial feedback from the listener. Sympathetic listening hinders the listener's ability to receive the messages—verbal, tactile, and nonverbal—in an objective and unbiased way.

On Empathy: The ultimate purpose of listening is to make a ground for connected dialogue and discussion rather than one-way communication. In other words, listening is a skill and an attitude as well; it includes care and respect for the speaker. For a connected or engaged dialogue, the listener is open to accepting the subjective and emotional reality of the speaker. Engagement with dialogue demands self-control in the listener to empathise with the speaker.

Empathy is defined as 'Projection of self into the feelings of others. It implies psychological involvement.' Also, it is defined as the 'ability of one person to come to know first-hand the experience of another'. This includes thoughts as well as feelings.

For a connected dialogue and better understanding, thinking and feelings cannot be separated but go together. The problem lies with conventional ideas of modern living and progress, wherein thinking or cognitive ability is considered superior to feeling. People are more comfortable with the cognitive content of the message rather than the content of the feeling. In fact, incompetence in dealing with feelings and emotions is relatively common in so-called advanced societies.

Carl Rogers (1951), an American psychologist, aptly describes 'empathy' with its complexity in the following words, 'Being empathic involves a choice on the part of the speaker and listener as to what they will pay attention to, ... such as 'the world of the speaker as that person perceives it' – in such a way that it assists her to gain a clearer understanding of, and hence a greater control over her own world and her own behaviour.'

In other words, empathy includes an understanding of the world from the other's point of view, her feelings, experience, and behaviour, and also communication of that understanding to the other person entirely. The real test of the application of empathy is the skill to express and communicate what one understands as a listener to the speaker. Needless to say, a complete understanding of another's worldview does not mean agreeing with it.

The benefit of such an empathic understanding and communication is that the speaker, in interpersonal and group settings in family or workplace, can make progress towards discovering one's own solutions and strategy to solve problems at hand. It strengthens one's ability to learn and reflect, which is necessary for personal and professional development.

However, it must be noted that the deployment of the skill of empathy is a rare experience in social and work-related interactions mainly because it is based on the belief that the speaker is valuable and worthy of respect and trust. In the absence of these values, it is challenging to get empathic listening in a society. However, when such social conditions exist or are created, the interactions become conducive for engagement in reflective dialogue and discussions. For productive and creative interaction in social and educational institutions, such a climate of empathic listening is valuable to build climate conducive for learning and development.

Limitations and risks in empathic listening for professional practice: Here, it is important to recognise that empathic listening needs to be balanced by self-conscious 'distancing' to come to a better grasp of the complex social reality that professionals like teachers, administrators, and social researchers usually encounter in practice. It is observed that those who happen to work in their own culture do not have enough 'critical distance' from what they study or the people they work with. They are guided by untested assumptions on roles and practices. Overfamiliarity with the cultural context blinds them to their biases, which is harmful to essential critical awareness about how they perceive and interpret social reality. Hence, they need to learn this skill on how to 'manufacture critical distance' from 'taken–for–granted beliefs and assumptions. This would enable them to observe and participate in social interactions with detached objectivity without losing human feelings. Acts of psychological distancing help in coming closer to the hidden and subtle rules that govern social and cultural life. One can see the familiar reality in an unfamiliar sense and can free oneself from the traps of cultural expectations and frames of thinking. Teacher–student and researcher-respondent interactions give ample opportunities to practice the skill of distancing that can enrich one's understanding of the multiple layers of social and institutional reality.

(C) Giving and Receiving Impactful Feedback

Role of effective feedback in the work context: A climate of mutual respect, trust, openness and a shared value of personal and professional growth is an essential backdrop for developing interpersonal skills in how to give and receive feedback effectively so that personal development and task performance are achieved simultaneously.

Critical factors that determine the effectiveness of interpersonal feedback are primarily sensitivity to the emotional or affective dimensions of communicating feedback. Awareness of emotions in both the giver and receiver of the feedback is the starting point in learning the behavioural skill of communicating feedback. The giver learns to recognise the kind of emotions triggered in her while preparing and delivering such feedback. It is not a routine communication or information sharing. It requires self-awareness and conscious planning since it has a rational and emotional impact.

Positive feedback and self-awareness: Individuals develop awareness of self mainly from positive and negative feedback received from others. Interestingly, our positive qualities are not fully known to us. Therefore, positive feedback is valuable because a person never knows herself unless she is informed about it with evidence from others. Also, the fear of giving negative feedback is based on the anticipated impact on the receiver, real or unreal. However, the fact is that when negative feedback is postponed for a long time, it leads to pent-up emotions that explode unproductively, only to harm relatedness with others.

Some practical tips for giving and receiving feedback effectively:

The effectiveness of feedback is determined by its impact on the giver and receiver. Generally, when feedback leads to personal growth and productive outcomes, it is considered effective and/or impactful.

1. *Own the feedback*: Effective feedback is 'owned' in the sense that it is stated

in first person by the sender, beginning with 'I 'or 'to my mind, 'in my view', rather than a generalised opinion of a person as 'you are'. Ownership suggests that the giver is ready to take responsibility for stating it.

2. *Specific rather than general:* General feedback is not helpful in commenting on a person's behaviour. Feedback like 'You are cynical, you are creative' does not help a person learn what made the giver comment like that and act on it. Specific instances of observed behaviour need to be accompanied with such comments.
3. *Focus on behaviour rather than the person*: Reporting on what was seen and heard is more valuable than general comments on a person. For example, ' you did not reply to my email twice' is better than 'you don't bother about others' as feedback because it is concrete and specific rather than general and evaluative.
4. *Refer to behaviours that can be changed*: This is a matter of interpersonal sensitivity. It is not enough to point out the mistakes or weaknesses of a person in a general way because some of them may be beyond the capacity of a person, such as 'deficiency in foreign language, accent, etc. Speaking about behaviours gives concrete evidence of what can be controlled and changed by a person.
5. *Describe and do not evaluate*: The efforts to describe the basis and behavioural evidence of feedback are better than 'off the cuff' comments, impressions and evaluative judgements.

Conclusion: Attention and listening are interdependent human skills. Unlike technical skills, they rely on human consciousness, which enables humans to deploy the capability to think, feel and act. In other words, process skills are not one-dimensional but a complex set of abilities. Above all, they are the foundation of individual and collective learning and development.

In short, process skills focus on the 'how it is carried out' aspect of human behaviours. It balances the overemphasis of conventional communication on content and information rather than care, tact and concern for relatedness with others. Those interested in building and developing institutions will benefit if process skills are practised. There is ample opportunity to do so in daily life because they are life skills.

REFERENCES

1. Argyle, M. (1975) *Bodily Communication.* Methuen, London
2. Amman Luis A. (1991) *Self Liberation.* Bharatiya Vidya Bhavan, Bombay.
3. McGill, I. & Brockl, A. (2004) *Action Learning Handbook.* Routledge Falmer, London.
4. McCracken, G. (1989) *The Long Interview.* Sage Publications, Inc. London.
5. Rogers, C. (1979) *Personal Power.* Constable, London.
6. http://silo.net (2022)

B: Self-Driven Learning System for College and PG Students

Introduction

The old assumption that education is complete after passing out from college is no longer valid. There has been continuous advancement of knowledge on account of rapid changes in the economic-technological environment. New problems emerge, which demand new responses and new thinking. Education, thus, becomes a life-long process. A professional has to review and overhaul his knowledge base every five years. In a career span of 30 years, this process will have to be undertaken at least six times. A person who was competent at one stage may not remain so at the next stage if he/she has not seriously pursued the model of Lifelong Education. While at the institute, you thus need to acquire not only a knowledge base but also *an ability to learn on your own.* This ability will help you to update, review and overhaul your knowledge base once you start working. Notably, the ability to learn is also related to your ability to perform on the job and develop yourself.

Common Learning System

By the time you come to a post-graduate course, you have spent about 15 years in education. The system of school, teachers, examinations and parents made demands on you and you learnt to deal with them in some way. All this experience is now with you in the form of habits and behaviour patterns. Some new elements were added as you entered college and experienced some enlargement of choices. However, the basic pattern rarely changed. The most common pattern or learning system is to react to the demands of the system. The system decides what you will study, what will be taught, how it will be taught and how you will be tested. Your role was to do as demanded and to keep on the right side of your teachers and parents. In college, you faced some pressure to make choices, and so you may have found it easier to go along with seniors and peers. Perhaps the subject matter of learning did not seem connected with life around you and your own experience. Studies could be seen as a burden.

So, most students study just before the exams, take the help of classmates or seniors, and think their job is done by passing the exams. Learning may or may not take place, even with and in passing. The assumption is that learning would take place if one reproduced the answers in the books/guides at the time of the examination.

In short, the system sets the goals, plans, and methods for the inspection of performance. You are not concerned so much with the goals, the plans and the methods. You are only concerned with passing the inspection.

The New Situation

When you start working and face the need to update your knowledge, and if you are still locked in the common learning system, you postpone picking up the book as much as you can till the time comes to face your boss. Then, a mad search begins for shortcuts. Sometimes, you manage to pass muster and compliment yourself on scampering home. The habit now gets entrenched until the day of reckoning comes, when you are unable to answer simple questions from a knowledgeable audience. It could be a big occasion, and the loss could be significant, too. You decide to work and study and be up-to-date with your knowledge base and start wondering about your study habits.

Self-Driven Learning System (SDLS)

The time to develop the ability to learn is NOW. Basically, it means taking charge of your learning in your own hands by cultivating effective study habits. Learning means a relatively durable change in behaviour and mental maps. So, the SDLS has two main components: Management of the Learning Process and the Learning Process itself.

Let us look at the Management part. It involves setting goals for yourself, working out a plan of study, implementing the plan, and controlling the process. Fortunately, our curriculum documents clearly state the goals of the programme. They set the stage in which you can work out your personal goals. These can take the form of expressing the level of mastery you desire in different subjects: Tolerable, Competent, Proficient. The plan includes different activities, such as reading, visits, discussion, problem-solving and their schedule. It also takes into account the time required for each one. There is usually an element of search for sources. Fortunately, there are now many sources available in the form of people, print and non-print media. There are many places which can be visited for first-hand observation. Once you start implementing the plan, you encounter difficulties that you have to overcome in the present and prevent in the future. From time to time, you sit down and review your progress and modify the plan. *This is an important opportunity for you to develop basic managerial skills.*

Let us now turn to the Learning Process. Earlier, it was believed that the more you read, and the more times you read the same thing, the better you will learn it. Now, with insights from Cognitive Psychology, we know a little bit more about the process.

It seems to consist of four stages: procurement, processing, storage, and retrieval.

- In higher education, procurement consists of recording new data, which may be textual, numerical, and imaginal (audio, visual, kinesthetics). It could come from the class, the library and other sources.
- Processing has two stages: initial processing to identify, label and recognise phenomena and deeper processing to relate it to already held knowledge.
- Storage is both physical and mental. Physical storage consists of maintaining files of learning material, such as notes, handouts, etc. Mental storage is organised around key concepts, principles, procedures, and problems.
- Retrieval takes place when dealing with similar situations and information. It calls for *deliberate and unaided* rehearsals.

Learning Practices

If learning and learning to learn are important to you, then you must set aside time for the different activities required and carry out those activities within the time schedule. Then only you can change old habits and cultivate new ones. So, the **first** good practice is to stick to a timetable for different learning activities.

The **second** good practice is to make a list of all learning resources available to you. These include your faculty, classmates, and other students on the campus. The conventional resources of texts are no longer adequate. These are supplemented by journals, handbooks, encyclopaedia, project reports, reference books, and audio and video cassettes. There are magazines and newspapers, too. Review how you have utilised these resources until now.

The **third** good practice is to organise the procurement by *preparing* for it. You prepare by having an *overview* first and thinking about the various aspects of the subject matter before receiving it. You also prepare by familiarising yourself with the *things* to which the words or concepts are connected. You need to *hear and see things for yourself, especially if you do not possess experience in that field.* Please remember you already know something about or related to the context in which new knowledge is located. If you are attending a class, you go into it knowing well what is going to be discussed. If you are reading a book, you have already surveyed the whole book or the chapter and have formed the questions in your mind about the subject matter. You just don't attend a class or read a book mechanically. You are involved with it entirely.

The **fourth** good practice is to have your class notes and own notes filed topic-wise. Many students take class notes but never prepare their own notes when they read on their own. The reading may evaporate in a matter of hours or days. The notes condense what has been heard, discussed, or read. The notes can take a more sophisticated form when you prepare concept cards and structure diagrams.

The **fifth** good practice is to examine what you have learnt by asking questions of oneself, solving practice problems in the text, doing assignments, relating what you learn in one subject with other subjects, and discussing it with others. The first few contacts with the learning material are not as productive as subsequent ones. *It is always easier to understand things when you revisit them.* You need a lot of tenacity to do this.

The **sixth** good practice is to relate verbal and conceptual material with real-life phenomena, such as people, objects, events, and activities, with which you are familiar. Our memory not only stores words but also pictorial, sound, and kinesthetic images. Concepts embedded in images are stored much longer and retrieved faster. The closer the concepts to your living process, the better would be their assimilation.

The **seventh** good practice is to take stock of how well you are studying and make changes in the pattern according to your own needs and those of the situation. There are two internal registers (your own feelings at the end of an experience) that are most reliable in determining how well you are studying. The first is the feeling that *I am enjoying what I am doing,* and the second is that *I don't feel satisfied with what I have learned. I am still hungry or thirsty for learning.*

These good practices help you in your work life as well, and it is a mistake to think that good study habits make you into a bookworm or a scholar who has minimal touch with practical reality. It is worthwhile to remember what *Ronnie Lessem* says in his essay, *Management Thinking*:

> *"The underlying structures of successful achievement, of learning and of intelligent counselling and of what we call scientific method are logically identical."*

REFERENCES

1. Learning Library: Study skills, *World Book*
2. Learning Library: Memory skills, reading skills etc, *World Book*
3. Independent Study Techniques: *PD Kulkarni*
4. Developing Attitude towards Learning: *Mager, Robert*

(This note is prepared for students by Dr A.P. Bhupatkar, former Director of IMDR, Pune).

C: Art of Coaching and Mentoring in Institutions of Higher Education

Context: The dependence on individual talent may not be a sufficient factor to reach organisational excellence because collectivity is more than the sum of talented individuals. Organisational capability exists as a potential to be realised, and there are many possibilities at individual and collective levels to identify, nurture and sustain talent. Realising and developing human potential depends on devices or tools used by human resource and people management function. The important thing to remember is that developing employees at the workplace or students in schools and colleges cannot be outsourced to machines or technology because it is connected with relationships between managers, administrators, faculty, teachers, consultants and employees, students and the staff. Coaching and mentoring are processes that facilitate the maximisation of human talent for collective good.

The development of individual talent and capability building is possible when organisational learning takes place at interpersonal, departmental and inter-departmental levels. Hence, a systematic plan of coaching and mentoring of talent is needed to increase organisational learning of the collectivity. This kind of approach focuses on integrating individual talent with the organisation to contribute to productivity, creativity and quality. It also emphasizes on the improvement of organisational processes in communication, decision making and the well-being of individuals.

Mentoring and coaching

Mentoring is a value-driven relationship between two persons, and it is based on mutual understanding, acceptance and confidentiality. When young people join organisations, they need guidance and support from experienced people whom they admire, who they can confide in and receive advice from. The emotional support and guidance given by a senior and experienced person to a younger and less experienced person is called a protégé. Her guide is called a mentor, who may or may not be his/ her immediate superior, boss, faculty, or teacher. In the context of research and teaching, mentoring and coaching processes resemble the traditional *guru-shishya (master-disciple)* relationship.

Coaching distinguishes itself from mentoring as a process because it does not lead to dependency as it happens in the case of a mentee on the mentor. Coaching nurtures a trusting and supportive relationship between the employee, faculty, staff, student and the internal or external coach, who shares expert knowledge and gives guidance. Together, they set challenging work goals and provide support in case of difficulties by analysing barriers to achieving better performance. More importantly, they act as a team to plan personal and work-related goals for the future. This kind of helping relationship of coaching promotes autonomy and self-reliance in the person who is coached. In other words, the coach helps the (staff) employees, faculty, or students in such a way that they are able to help themselves. This is the principle that guides all successful developmental role relationships because, in the ultimate analysis, development or *vikaas* is about the development of the people by empowering them to be self-reliant rather than making them dependent on those in power positions.

Unlike training or teaching, coaching is a distinct skill because the primary motive of most teachers and trainers happens to be 'personal power' and control over others. This observation is based on research on the motivation of those in the teaching/training profession. The trainer's ego is satisfied when he/she gets applause, positive feedback or admiration from the trainees. In contrast, coaching requires different kinds of temperament, attitude and abilities. *Rahul Dravid* is an example of these qualities in sports, with an emphasis on self-control and perfection rather than on self-promotion and control over others.

Ideally, coaching provides a non-threatening climate wherein employees and students can freely express their tensions, conflicts, concerns, and problems to their coaches, who may be their superiors or seniors, faculty or professional coaches. This process helps employees understand their strengths and weaknesses. At the same time, it helps them understand the issues and challenges in their careers and how they would engage with the realities in an organisation or institution. In this way, the coaching process creates an awareness of the processes within and outside the individual at the workplace. In order to achieve this goal, the coaches usually decide to engage in the following developmental activities and processes for employees, faculty, and students.

1. Conducting workshops on interpersonal and behavioural competence in order to develop openness, risk-taking, communication and problem-solving.

2. Review discussions with employees, students, and faculty on progress in areas of work projects, self-study, assignments and so on.
3. Assisting employees and students in identifying problems, creating alternatives and developing an action plan for resolving the problem identified.
4. Encouraging employees and students for continuous improvement and lifelong learning.
5. Giving feedback about day-to-day behaviour followed by analysis of observed behaviours

Mentoring, however, is a somewhat different process. A mentor is an insider who knows the organisational dynamics and its work culture due to her long association. She knows what is the priority of management and what kind of behaviour leads to performance and success in the field she operates. Hence, a mentor's guidance is critical for the career success of the mentee. Moreover, it is a non-formal relationship based on mutual trust and respect. However, mentors are also human, not always idealised *Gurus* and may hold negative qualities, like jealousy, anger, and pettiness, which may harm mentees' prospects.

In this context, it would be relevant to describe at length an interesting experience of being mentored in the context of higher education institution. Prof *Rajen Harshe* (as a researcher) had described his relationship as a student with his PhD guide at *Jawaharlal Nehru University*, Delhi. Academic research at university is a long-duration project of three to six years. As mentioned earlier, the research guide in India is considered a *Guru,* which implies an unequal relation since he is bestowed with more authority and power over the student. Mentoring in academic research is a demanding process for both sides as it impacts in many ways the development of intellectual competencies, commitment to research goals.

It requires tenacity to remain with the project despite failures and delays in completion, and a desire for perfection and thoroughness. The researcher's account, (*Harshe R*, 2023) of this relationship with his guide/ mentor provides insights into the risks in this unique process. For example, in this case, the guide read the first chapter of the thesis carefully but did not approve it. He mentioned in the review that it was less organised, with many untested controversial statements. He commented on inadequate reading and the fact that there were many research gaps. The researcher, as a young student, was depressed when he read it only to find relief in the last sentence of the report! 'Don't feel discouraged by these remarks; take it as if I am sitting next to you and guiding you so that you shall not feel bad'. This was an eye-opener to the student, and subsequently, he revised the draft of the chapter several times without being dejected and took it as a challenge. Later, both of them decided to read the whole thesis together. In the process, he was learning the rigour of writing a research thesis in terms of constructing simple sentences with the right choice of words and connecting each sentence and paragraph with subsequent sentences and paragraphs without diluting the complexity of thought behind it. In short, he learned how to think and write in such a way that all chapters were well-connected and also learned the importance of brevity for impact on readers. It was an experience that the researcher remembers as the most memorable and productive in his academic career of four decades. At the end, some of the weaknesses of the guide as a mentor are mentioned in the researcher's account. He was jealous when a student attained success in his career and never trusted his junior colleagues in the department. In short, coaches, guides, and mentors are also human and not perfect, though they are depicted as depicted as Gurus, who are highly respected in the Indian tradition.

To sum up, coaching and mentoring are highly personalised and intense processes that help employees, faculty, and students achieve their potential without making them feel dependent or controlled. The purpose of coaching and mentoring is to help adults learn and develop necessary skills, attitudes, and abilities so that they can help themselves in future. If properly conducted, it can be a truly liberating and developmental process for employees and students, as well as for the coach, mentor, and faculty.

It is essential to recognise that both coaching and mentoring will not be effective if it is done mechanically, without involvement, lacking the right mind set and values, or taken as a routine part of administrative procedure. Also, it is not a set of techniques but an art based on wisdom, judgement, discerning sensitivity, care, and concern of the person, couched or mentored and shared values of the institution.

REFERENCES

1. Harshe, R. (2023). *Pakshi Unhacha: Inside seven university campuses.* Sadhana Prakashan. Pune
2. Pareek, U. (2011). *Person-focused OD interventions.* Sage.
3. Ramnarayan, S. & Rao, T. V. (2011). *Organisation development.* Sage.

D: Role and Competencies of Faculty, Head of the Department and Vice Chancellor in Universities

Abstract: Educational institutions in contemporary times face complex challenges due to rapid changes in socio-economic and technological conditions. Students, faculty, and top leaders like HOD and VC require special abilities and competencies to engage with and manage themselves in roles in order to face these challenges. The note gives examples of the process of 'role-taking' by HOD and Vice-chancellor of central and state universities. It describes the problems they encounter and how they are managed by taking and making roles needed for task performance. A framework of Thinking, Self-managing and Influencing competencies, along with specific behavioral indicators, is provided to highlight the importance of roles and competencies to effectively manage the challenges of building HEIs in the Indian context.

Definition of Role: Role is the pattern of behaviour expected by others from a person occupying a certain position in an organisation's hierarchy. (*Buchanan D. A, 1985*) Work organisations generally provide 'job description' to the role holder which explains tasks she is expected to perform. However, 'Role' is a more complex and dynamic concept since it is based on expectations of other related task holders in specific context. It is not formally described or told to the employee but she is expected to sense and learn about her role from on-the job experiences. At higher levels of hierarchy of authority, learning about role expectations is influenced by how the role holder understands the primary purpose and mission of the insitituion and its specific context. Hence she has to learn '*role making*' because, '*role taking*', based on job description, would not lead to superior performance. The former requires development of *thinking, self-managing,* and *influencing* competencies which are described below.

Purpose of HE institution : In India, families or parents of students often consider getting good grades as a kind of passport to get jobs that shall ensure survival for their wards in today's competitive climate. Then, the goal of an educational institution becomes like a production center where people, faculty and students are engaged with a huge amount of information. The role of the students ceases to be one of the partners in knowledge creation, instead faculty converts them into receivers of information as if they are empty heads to be filled in with loads of information. Here, teachers' role is to make efficient use of time and resources to give as much information as possible. In the way, institutions of higher learning become production centers for well-informed young people rather than a centers for the development of knowledge and wisdom. (*Chattopadhyay G.P.,* 2004) These two versions of the purpose and roles mentioned above, are: (a) knowledge creation, and (b) producing information centers, that in turn, determine the direction and strategy of higher education. When the purpose of higher education is knowledge creation, '*role-making*' is essential which implies that a conscious use of personal 'authority' by the facutly and students to engage with primary task of creating knowledge and wisdom rather than a focus on the secondary tasks like grades and career prospects. On the other hand, *role taking*, is oriented towards passive acceptance of the authority of the faculty and student's role to collect information and use it for examinations. The focus has to shift from *role-taking* to *role-making* where thinking, analyzing, self-managing, and influencing competencies are deployed by the role incumbent for better performance at work place.

Definitions of Competency

An observable skill or ability to complete a task successfully. (*Jacob.*)

An underlying characteristic of an individual that is causally related to superior performance. (*Evarts*)

A motive, trait, skill, aspect of one's self-image, social role or body of knowledge. (*Boyatzis*)

Two types of competencies: (a) Threshold, and (b) Superior performance. For instance, 'decision-making' is a generic or threshold competency, which is necessary for a normal performance. However, decision-making with sensitivity to people issues is not generic but related to superior performance in the context of service organisations, like airlines, hospitals, and education. In this note, the focus is mainly on competencies leading to superior performance in the context of educational institutions.

Competency is reflected in demonstrated behaviors while performing a task. Therefore, it is always located in the work context. For example, a faculty, assistant, and associate professor in a university is expected to have 'Thinking' competencies such as conceptual, analytical, and critical information seeking. They also require '*self–management*' competencies like *self-control, tenacity, self-development orientation*, and *efficiency*. At higher levels of positions in university, for *HOD* and *VC*, another set of competencies like '*Influencing*' competencies such as *rational persuasion, strategic influencing, concern for impact, consensus building* and *ability to learn* are needed.

Before we look into the specific behaviors in each of the competencies mentioned above, let us look 'behavioural' examples of what faculty, HOD and Vice-Chancellor (*VC*) of state and central universities in India actually do. Given below are some of the real-life experiences of *Prof Rajén Harshe,* as a faculty and later as the HOD at *Hyderabad University*. He is referred to as the professor below.

Context: **1.** University is an institution located in a specific geographical, social, political and cultural context. The incident below occurred at *Hyderabad University* in 1981. A lady student submitted a complaint alleging sexual harassment by a faculty member in one of the university departments. It later turned into a riot-like situation on the campus, and the university was closed for a month. The faculty behavior was investigated by a fact-finding committee. The professor, in this case, resigned from his post as General Secretary of the teachers' union along with other Union members from the faculty group on ethical grounds that they failed to protect the male faculty colleague whose services were suspended without due procedure of natural justice (*Concern with Impact*). Faculty who belonged to other states, outside AP, faced discrimination in the backdrop of regional identity politics on the campus of Hyderabad University. The professor mentioned above was 31 years old, as a new faculty, he was unaware of the complexity of gender-based, man-woman relations mixed with regional identity politics on campus. In retrospect, the professor thinks that he was unable to resolve this delicate issue adequately. (*Interpersonal Awareness*) It had a serious impact on the life of the accused faculty, who was acquitted in court later but suffered severe damage to his personal and family life.

2. In another incident, a student from Orissa complained about the professor and his teaching on the grounds that some students did not understand the lectures, which was in the backdrop of the fact that the professor was articulate about the injustice done in the university at large. Local faculty from *Andhra* state behaved rudely, but the professor continued a regular dialogue with his counterparts and remained open with students from all sections of society. In response to the above complaint of the student, the professor changed his teaching method so that students from underdeveloped regions could understand what he taught (*Concern with*

Impact, Self development orientation). In the process, he lost his weight due to pressure to perform but persisted, and it was appreciated by all students. The professor could succeed in maintaining a congenial dialogue with the student community. (*Adaptability*) However, it was rather painful for him to accept that in a cosmopolitan space governed by the democratic ideals of the modern university, educated faculty members held values that were feudal and regressive. It shows that *role-taking* as faculty is a demanding process that needs maturity, skills, and positive attitude and other behavioral competencies.

Later, at the *Allahabad University* (*UoA*) campus, Prof. *Harshe*, as the first Vice-Chancellor of the newly formed central university, encountered many challenges in getting necessary support of *HRD* minister, Shri *Arjun Singh* and members of the executive council on important decisions. The pending promotion of 18 faculty members was to be finalised based on the rules of central universities rather than state universities, as it was followed earlier. It was a court ruling, but the vested interests of local political leaders brought pressure on the VC through the executive council to promote them. The VC maintained a constant dialogue with the HRD minister during this transition period at the university. (*Self-control)* When given an opportunity in a special joint meeting with the minister and executive council, the professor spoke with courage of conviction. "I have come to Allahabad to work honestly, but the members of the council are not allowing me to do any constructive work. These people do not have any respect for scholarship but respect bullies; I am ashamed of them," he said. (*Independence*) The minister supported VC and said, "After much effort, we have an excellent VC. Allow him to work. I shall give you three months to change your behaviors..." (*Strategic Influencing)*

The VC always thought about the future prospects of the faculty. Many of them had not received due promotions, which affected their intellectual performance. University administration worked on a plan to promote all those eligible candidates, which reduced their apathy and depression. Later, the VC worked with senior faculty to recruit the best talent from the national level as professors in *UoA* university. The admission process for students at Allahabad University was now conducted at six centers in different states so that more students from other states could join the campus community of learners. (*Innovativeness*) In retrospect, the professor believes that it was a collective effort of the faculty to establish an academic climate and intellectual culture on campus and together, they worked hard for change and transformation. The VC contributed a fortnightly column in the *Hindustan Times* (2008), called *Vice Chancellor's Diary*, which was responded to by scholars and citizens from the city. (*Positive Self Image, Teancity*)

The work of institution building is thus linked with contributions from external stakeholders like intellectuals, scholars, government officers, and above all, media support. It requires '*role-making*', which goes beyond '*role-taking*' for the office of VC. Also, it demands specific competencies to give superior performance. Some of the relevant competencies are mentioned below.

Roles and Competencies

A theoretical framework for identifying competencies is available (*Boyatzis,* 2006) for those interested in its application in the process of selection and development of personnel in all kinds of work organisations. It is helpful as it describes specifically demonstrated behaviors or indicators of such behaviors, which enables a role-holder to achieve superior performance in organisations. Thus, with the help of the Behavioral Event Interview (*BEI*) technique, human resource *(HR)* experts can identify and recruit the right persons for specific jobs and institutions.

Thinking Competencies

Analytical Thinking

Essence statement of Analytical Thinking: *"Logically breaking down problems into their essential elements, carrying out diagnosis and developing solutions."*

1. Behavioural Indicators

1. Develops and uses clear criteria of guiding decisions (e.g. Resources, constraints, organisational values)
2. Identifies cause and effect relationship,
3. Identifies root causes
4. Thinking through priorities
5. Makes sense of information by organising it

2. Conceptual Thinking

Essence statement: *"Identifying Key issues, seeking relationships and drawing elements together into a broad, coherent framework."*

3. Behavioural Indicators

1. Makes connections between facts and events that are not readily obvious
2. Develops models and sees the 'big picture.
3. Identifies key factors in a complex problem
4. Forms a general impression about a group or organisation from the way people behave within that group or organisation.

Self-managing Competencies

1. Self-Development Orientation

Essence statement: "*Taking continuous action to improve personal capability*".

2. Behavioural Indicators

1. Explores personal strengths and weaknesses with a view to improving
2. Critiques own performance as a means of self-improvement, seeks opportunities to build knowledge in work-related matters
3. Actively seeks feedback as a significant source of learning and improvement
4. Learns from mistakes, Seeks developmental projects and tasks

3. Self-Control

Essence statement: "*Continuing to perform effectively in stressful and difficult circumstances*".

4. Behavioural Indicators

1. Remains calm when personally attacked. Keeps things in perspective despite fatigue and frustration,
2. Maintains effectiveness and commitment in the face of disappointment.
3. Works effectively under a tight schedule.
4. Maintains objectivity when interpreting information and defining problems

Influencing Competencies

1. Concern with Impact

Essence statement: "*Actively anticipating and responding to the feelings, needs and concerns of others.*"

2. Behavioral Indicators

1. Takes action to have an intended or desired effect on others.
2. Effectively communicates in order to influence.
3. Considers in advance the impact of actions on others and adjusts actions in order to influence others
4. Acts to ensure others will understand complex information.
5. Shows concern for and responds to the feelings and needs of the subordinates, peers, superiors and other stakeholders.

3. Strategic Influencing

Essence statement: "*Being aware of different forms and sources of influencing in choosing between different influencing strategies.*"

4. Behavioural Indicators

1. Identifies different needs of key people and adjusts strategies to influence them.
2. Considers the merits of different influencing strategies and acts on the best-perceived approach.
3. Is guided by a range of considerations in deciding the best course of action in influencing people. (e.g., political, cultural, and personal relationships, personal impact, hierarchical positions)
4. Works with 'informal' as well as formal systems to influence situations.

Summary: It is important to recognise that roles in work organisations are defined by the expectations of the stakeholders, like students, parents, industry employers, as well as role-holders like faculty, staff, HoD, VC. Role-*taking* and role-*making* are two processes that define the behaviour of the role-holders. *Role-taking* is uncritical conformity to the expectations of other role-holders. *Role-making* suggests negotiating role expectations for their relevance to the primary task or purpose of the organisation and is based on competencies of the role incumbent. For example, the primary task of an educational institution of higher learning can be described as 'engaging with activities that will create new knowledge, which in turn can be transformed into wisdom by those involved in the task of application of learning.' Thus, acquiring wisdom through the application of knowledge that one can utilise in all kinds of situations in one's work life is considered as primary task of higher education. Specific competencies are needed to accomplish this task by the role holders at the work place.

REFERENCES

1. Boyatzis R.E. (2006) *Leadership Competencies*, Routledge
2. Buchanan, D.A. (1985) *Organisation Behaviour*, Prentice Hall International, London.
3. Chattopadhyay, G.P. (2004) *IMDR Convocation Address*, Pune.
4. Harshe, R. (2023) *Pakshi Unhacha; Inside Seven University Campuses*, Sadhana Prakashan, Pune.

Epilogue: A Way Forward

Charting a way forward on institutional building *(IB)* for higher education in India would be an appropriate concluding note for the book. The epilogue first presents a brief review of prevalent perspectives in practice on higher educational institutions *(HEIs)* in India and how they tend to determine institutional designs and stakeholders' behaviours. It is relevant to revisit the 2by2 model of institutional processes, depicted as four quadrants mentioned in Essay One they are *Rational, Emotional, Instrumental, and Expressive.* The four dimensions are complementary processes and not mutually exclusive orientations of behaviours in institutions. The key premise of the book is that the effectiveness of institutional building for higher education would depend on how these four quadrants of 1) *Work, 2) Professionalism, 3) Identity, and 4) Articulation* are balanced in an appropriate way in specific contexts of each institution and how they are deployed for enhancing institutional performance. Moreover, the vision, competence and quality of top leadership are of paramount importance because higher education institutions have to play a unique role in sustaining and strengthening academic and societal purposes and, at the same time, fulfilling the aspirations of many generations of youth in India.

To recap the first quadrant of the '*rational-instrumental*' dimension, the model presupposes 'institution as a collectivity or community' with a purpose rather than merely a legal or economic entity. Therefore, the basic question addressed in institutions is, '*What*' is our work?' and thus emphasises those work-related tasks performed by the collectivity. Like other work organisations, it uses the logic of technical rationality (*TR*) and structures of bureaucracy. The authority is impersonal and uses procedures and rules to guide behaviours. The engagement of the staff and faculty with students is mainly transactional or task-related. The meaning of work for faculty and staff is limited to the number of hours put into teaching and administrative tasks. Needless to say, work is broadly considered as a 'load' or necessary evil and a means of survival. If institutional behaviours remain in this quadrant, there is less chance for the institutional building process to take root because survival rather than purposeful achievement is the institutional goal. It is feared that most of the state-run universities and affiliated colleges in India show a tendency to remain complacent in this mode, as mentioned in Essay Five on *Understanding Behavioural Processes of HEIs.* In order to improve the performance of quality and service of these institutions, which are trapped in the first quadrant of the institutional model, substantial investment in organisation development and interventions for change are critical; the tools and methods are explained in Essay Six on *OD* and *ID*. These interventions for *IB* would require initial handholding and the help of consultants or experts in the field of management and education. Promoters and leaders of public and private universities, affiliated colleges, and policymakers of the education ministry of the State *(MoE)* are expected to take appropriate interventions in this direction.

It is seen that privately owned and managed institutions of higher education in India tend to be 'person-centred', wherein decisions are centralised. Sometimes, there is a mismatch between the competence and role expectations of persons appointed to top positions and actual behaviours. The purpose and mission of such institutions remain on paper, and institutions are used for career growth and for the benefit of a few individuals. Such institutions also show stunted growth and negatively impact the attitudes of faculty and students. They are governed by feudal values that breed a tendency to build empires rather than institutions.

The second quadrant combines *Emotional and Instrumental* processes of collectivity. It addresses the question of '*How* the collectivity engages with its work'. It is concerned about efficiency at the workplace and the quality of outcomes. In an educational context, institutions in the second quadrant focus on professionalism and care about student learning, governance, student counselling, and attention to faculty and staff behaviours. The professional commitment of internal stakeholders, that is, of faculty members, staff, and management, to work is much evident as institutional efforts are taken to design robust systems like *PMS* and planning systems to improve institutional performance. Elite institutions from public and private sectors, like IITs, IIMs TISS, and some top universities/institutes in India, belong to this second quadrant. They emphasise professional values and good governance practices to deliver better quality of education

However, these institutions do not show similar excellence in the dimension of the '*Expressive - Emotional*' aspect of the third quadrant that focuses on the identity of the institution or addresses '***Who*** we are?' as a collective. For example, promoters of an elite and professionally managed private institution like *Ashoka* University in *Haryana* failed to protect one of its reputed faculty, who had written a series of critical articles for the *Indian Express.* Freedom of expression and a reasoned articulation of truth is a risky step in educational campuses in the present socio-political context. This kind of intellectual courage needs the support of shared values and commitment from the promoters, to begin with, and it is seriously lacking in the climate or culture of many universities and colleges in India. This is evident increasingly in many *HEI* campuses on unilateral interventions by authorities to suppress independent views that are critical of the State. Indeed, it is not a conducive climate for building innovative and liberal institutions and for the growth of democracy in general. The issue is also debated and discussed in Essay Four on the topic of *Corporatisation of HEIs.*

The impact of the third quadrant involving *Emotional-Expressive* processes of identity is evident, and is described in the illustrative case study on the *JNU Story - Rise and Decline of an Academic Institution. JNU* has a rich institutional legacy that promotes free expression and supports and aggressively celebrates its unique institutional identity. It has a tradition of demonstrating distinct creative energy of the collectivity of students and faculty via a democratic process of holding students' union elections consistently and having open spaces for debates and discussions. The academic excellence of *JNU* faculty and students has helped enhance its international reputation or 'brand value', as is the case of some elite private universities in India. However, *JNU's* identity is rooted in the aspirations of young men and women at the pan-India level, and it is committed to reaching all sections of society without gender, caste, class, or community discrimination. It represents India's inclusive, egalitarian ethos. No wonder the critical voices and dissenting opinions that belong to the *emotional-expressive* dimension of the third quadrant in *JNU* had led to its suppression through campus violence with the tacit support of the State. Hence, it justifies an urgent need for the institutional processes of the fourth quadrant, that is, articulation of the *Expressive and Rational* dimension focusing on conscious articulation of the vision and mission and the 'purpose' through behaviours on educational campuses. This would require convictions and courage to articulate them consistently and through democratic means. It is hard to find examples of such *HEIs* where faculty and students' thinking, feelings, and actions are coherent and expressed with integrity as a collectivity. This is a serious deficiency in the intellectual climate, not only in *HEIs* but in several social and cultural institutions in India in contemporary times. It is worthwhile to repeat Professor *Pankaj Chandra's* observation (Essay Ten) on the role of faculty in quality improving of higher education in India. *Dr Chandra* laments that university faculty, who are expected to be 'thought leaders' have given up their commitment to values of autonomy and freedom in terms of a) deciding what constitutes learning, b) how it is to be delivered, c) how engagement with and between students is organised, d) how rules of assessment are defined, and e) how learning would take place on and outside campuses.

In other words, building and developing *HEIs* need a deeper commitment to learning, which is distinct from managing institutions well. *IB* needs conscious nurturing of individual and collective 'being' or the value-based identity of the institution. It requires visionary leadership to build and transform institutions to this level where they are respected as 'seekers and promoters of truth', with an ability to articulate 'what is right and what is wrong, and what is important' to society at large. However, *HEIs* with good governance (*emotional-instrumental* processes) of the second quadrant and *emotional-expressive* processes of the third quadrant are equally required in India to provide education with access, equity and quality.

With a recap of the four-dimensional model, it would now be helpful to evaluate the performance of Institution Building *(IB)* around four dimensions and initiate interventions to strengthen institutions for a positive role in implementing the *National Education Policy, 2020 (NEP 2020).* This would impact the nation-building of a democratic country like India. With holistic development of higher education institutions a country can balance the complementary forces of emotionality, rationality, articulation, purposiveness, innovation and continuity so that the values and ideals embedded in the vision and mission of the institution and also of the Constitution of India are realised in practice.

Proposals for Solutions

Based on the experiential and qualitative data covered in the eleven essays and nine case studies of this book, along with conceptual discussions of the themes, it is appropriate to make specific proposals or suggestions on *IB for HEIs* in India in order to chart a way forward:

1. The first proposal is to initiate a macro or umbrella institution, which would be a federation of colleges, universities, and institutes to coordinate and share resources, represent and perform functions on behalf of its members, such as a) building an information base and its exchange with its members, b) optimisation of gains, c) resolving conflicts, d) strategic visioning and planning e) advocacy and lobbying, f) developing norms and accreditation, g) providing services with shared resources and costs. This kind of macro institution(s) would overcome and reduce the gap between elite *HEIs* and the hundreds of state universities and colleges in India by sharing resources, collaborating and building synergy among public universities and affiliated colleges.

2. The second proposal is to strengthen the established institutions that survive and operate as a weak link in the higher education system, as in the case of resource-starved affiliated colleges of the state universities embedded in specific geographical locations with distinct missions and identities. The main aim would be to safeguard the interests of faculty, students and local communities of these colleges with a strategic focus on the resolution of critical issues like (a) academia-society-industry connections, (b) designing inter-disciplinary courses, (c) financial funding, (d) provision for filling the backlog of recruitment and fair remuneration and terms of employment of faculty, (e) upgradation of quality of teaching-learning processes and (f) representation of students on governing councils. Against the backdrop of the apathy of the State and *MoE* in financing, it may use radial structural interventions like *Cluster University*, with a small residential college campus, a semi-autonomous division of the university, specialising in one branch of knowledge as suitable for specific colleges. It can be an initiative to create new universities by a) upgrading existing colleges and b) converting colleges into clusters (*RUSA*). In western Maharashtra, reputed private colleges have been given a semi-autonomous status as universities by *UGC* in recent years *(2020-21).* However, few state universities and affiliated colleges have opted for cluster design till date. The latter would require a commonality of purpose and collaborative values for building such institutions. It is still not clear which stakeholders would benefit from cluster universities; students, promoters, the State, and society at large. The design and application of this proposal are at an early stage and somewhat elusive. Structural changes would require strategic considerations based on the location and purpose of the institution; there is no best model for all.
3. The third equally important proposal is to develop a vibrant intellectual climate and academic culture on *HEI* campuses, which is very critical for preserving and promoting academic autonomy and intellectual freedom of institutional builders, faculty and students of *HEIs* in India. In the contemporary context, this could be achieved by questioning and loosening the prevalent practice of total control of regulators in academic and policy matters. It would involve resisting the covert and overt attempt of the *MoE* and its regulators to corporatise *HEIs* in the name of global competition and competitiveness. So-called 'autonomy' bestowed on affiliated colleges in recent years (2022-23) would benefit the promoters of these institutions rather than their faculty and students, as is evident in autonomous private universities. A collective and amalgamative representation of *HEIs* through a 'macro umbrella institution', mentioned

in the first proposal, is essential to protect the core values of autonomy in higher education to maintain cognitive processes like critical thinking, inquiry, promoting and sustaining liberal-democratic values such as independent thinking, diversity, equality and solidarity. It is rare to find university teachers' unions raise academic issues of students' learning, assessment, faculty research.

The main predicament of the higher education system in India emerges from its failure to balance continuity and innovation. Positive aspects of the traditional university system and initiating reforms to face new challenges are both necessary. As mentioned earlier, the weakest link in the higher education system is affiliated colleges of the Indian universities, which offer outdated courses and remain resource-starved. Bestowing autonomy to selected colleges without preparation for building academic culture with faculty committed to knowledge creation, lifelong learning, and related norms appropriate for self-regulation and autonomy results in giving more power to promoters or management rather than to the faculty, staff and students. What is missing in granting autonomy to institutions is the promotion of inter-organisational collaboration to strengthen institutions so that limited resources are utilised effectively. The core idea behind the theory of institution building (*IB)* is to strengthen its inherent, permeable structures to empower learning communities in order to help create spaces for democratic values of freedom and equality so that it can achieve epistemological goals of knowledge generation and innovative ideas.

Structures, processes and values should be synergetic rather than contradictory. The institutional performance of *HEIs* primarily depends on the core values and concepts that sustain them. Openness to other institutions and adapting to the changes in the environment, commitment to learning and development, the welfare of students, and mutual respect and trust between faculty and students are some of the values that nourish educational institutions. The recent trend in higher education seems to promote individual excellence and privatisation of institutions that consider higher education as a part of private goods. Though elite institutions like IIMs and IITs are funded by public exchequer, the benefit goes mainly to the individual student rather than to the institution and society at large, and many of them leave the country for better prospects. Moreover, non-elite institutions that serve the needs of the masses compromise on the quality of education due to neglect, lack of resources and policy bias of the State. This requires serious attention from the policymakers and can be resolved only by an equitable distribution of recourses to all *HEIs* and a review of the prevalent ideas of academic merit.

4. Macro institutions of higher education can use their resources to push for these reforms. The theory and practice of macro institution building, for example, in the form of cluster university, though in a nascent and idea stage, may provide a direction in future to improve *HEIs* in the following ways as mentioned below.

   In the pandemic period 2020-21, institutions of university and affiliated colleges struggled with many problems. One was about helping students prepare for classroom teaching, learning and conducting examinations. Promoters and management of colleges were unprepared for the tasks of online education on such a scale. In the city of Nasik in western Maharashtra, affiliated undergraduate colleges shared resources and distinct competency and strengths of colleges and other autonomous institutes in areas of curriculum design, delivery of online lectures, IT infrastructure, learning resources and faculty in order to mobilise and share information and resources to serve the needs of the students and colleges. It was an exercise in building a temporary macro institution to collaborate on specific tasks and functions, and it was done voluntarily. Such experiments deserve to be documented as case studies and action learning projects so that local innovations and experiences on institution building can be conceptualised for developing the theory and methodology of *IB* for higher education institutions. Informal, partnership-based para universities of this kind have not been adequately experimented in India.

5. The fifth proposal is to positively encourage and deploy the research methodology of Action Research *(AR)* with a focus on institutions, Phenomenological research *(PR)* on community of students-faculty relatedness and Reflective Practice *(RP)* for professional development of faculty and administrators to sustain intellectually vibrant process-driven institutions. It would bring action orientation to applied research and promote egalitarian and inclusive values conducive to the professional, cognitive and emotive development of faculty and staff of *HEIs*. The perspective of Phenomenology with a focus on individual-level experiential learning and reflective documentation is essential for effective and imaginative pedagogy in higher-order teaching–learning–researching. They can be used to develop a deeper understanding of human experiences so that students' engagement with their everyday situations can be more thoughtful and sensitive. These humanistic values would act as a foundation of *HEIs*, which are essential to protect the democratic processes for nation-building.

6. Also, there is an urgent need to work on new institutional designs and solutions at national and local levels so that clusters and network partnership models can be developed as an answer to the unresolved problems of industry-academia collaborations, applied inter-disciplinary research, teaching and consultancy. These issues emerge from the overdependence of *HEIs* on state bureaucracy to solve higher education problems that do not have expertise in the field. Strengthening the self-confidence, dignity and identity of academicians and researchers is critical at this juncture. Available experiments in innovative designs of *IB* (*refer to three cases in Section Two*) need to be formalised and supported by the state on the basis of their performance on the criteria of institution building, such as service to students, innovations in institutional designs and curriculum, and faculty development. Balancing conformity and innovation in *HEIs* is a way forward.

The above example shows how the prevalent competitive mode of affiliated colleges and their operations can become collaborative, which creates synergic processes to utilise the available resources more effectively. It is a learning lesson for universities and colleges to recognise that higher education is a community resource and social capital rather than a private good and ownership when the involvement of the larger community in higher education is ensured. The collaboration based on the community model can be expanded further in areas of inter-disciplinary research in natural and social sciences, as well as in humanities, sciences and languages.

The root cause of problems in building robust *HEIs* in India lies in the fact that they operate within the education policy of the State that covertly encourages private universities and corporate norms and values. It is claimed that it would lead to competitiveness and quality improvement. The neoliberal economic policy expects them to consider students as customers and faculty as service providers and treat higher education as a part of private and individual goods rather than part of public goods. Courses in *STEM,* that is, science, technology, engineering and medicine, are preferred over courses in languages, humanities and social sciences. The state policy is to withdraw funding and instead expects *HEIs* and the students, which practically means parents, to bear all costs of higher education. Higher fees have made higher education exclusive, and reputation is equated with the promotion of institutional brand images.

It is unlikely that such global forces of neoliberal ideology would change in the immediate future. In this scenario, the only hope lies in the response and initiatives of conscientious, competent faculty, socially responsible and deserving student communities and unions within *HEIs* in India. Institutions which engage in sound processes of reflective learning, stand a good chance to evolving rational strategies of addressing challenges of increasing number of aspirants to higher education and explosion of knowledge in the last century. Institutions' main resource lies in the wisdom of key stakeholders led by faculty, along with leaders from other fields like industry, commerce, media etc. Similarly, Reflective Learning, Collegiate Decision making would HEIs evolve strategic directions and initiatives in times of transition and change. It needs to be recognized that 800 years old Oxford and Cambridge have become robust institutions based on their research excellence, collegiate system and strong alumni network. HEIs in India can plan strategically on the basis of their unique strengths and opportunities to build robust institutions. (Essay Eight on Institutional Purpose and Strategic Planning)

Promoters of private universities and educators should consider new designs to build a para-institution, a kind of parallel and emerging structure and academic sub-culture that exists as an imaginary or phantom institution within the existing institution, dedicated to nurturing an intellectual culture of thought, collegiality in order to subvert dominant market-oriented objectives and curriculum by the state policy. This kind of parallel-university, consisting of an informal network of talented faculty, students, alumni and associations, would be an emerging, semi-autonomous sub-culture to uphold those values of higher education that promotes the excitement of inquiry, the collective effort of cooperation, constructive criticism, mutual encouragement and self-criticism. In this way, the four quadrants of *IB* mentioned earlier can be balanced in spite of the constraints imposed by the macro higher education system. Such parallel universities within universities would be sustainable to the extent they can resist the pressure of the State to conform and standardise.

In the final analysis, the democratisation of knowledge and opportunity for higher education is both a political and epistemic or knowledge-generating process, which would sustain *HEIs* in India. However, the real threat to state-funded universities and institutions of professional courses, is an overemphasis on market orientation reflected in the craze for tutorial colleges and institutes at Kota and Delhi which provides coaching for students aspiring for admission to elite *HEIs* in India. Similarly, a challenge for the academic faculty of undergraduate colleges is the temptation to earn additional money from working for coaching classes and private tuitions. They make faculty and students prefer teaching content that is digestible, simple and utilitarian so that it is without dissent, doubts, curiosity, inquiry and scientific temper. This is a climate that discourages faculty and students from struggling for academic excellence, competence building, dignity, and freedom of individuals and to sustain robust institutions wherein their collective intellectual energies are preserved, spread and shared. The outcomes of *IB* in higher education have long-term consequences and impact on future generations in India. It is not just a platitude to say that institution building for higher education is equivalent to nation-building.

In the contemporary context of India, it is necessary to remind ourselves that important institutions such as the judiciary, armed forces, police, and universities, act as a buffer or safety net between the state power and society at large. Also, they protect individual freedom and dignity from regressive social, political and cultural forces. Moreover, due to the systematic weakening of higher education and other social institutions, it is the community of students and their parents/families who suffer the most. In fact, they desperately need quality education and an egalitarian culture on campuses. Building, strengthening and sustaining autonomy and high quality institutions of higher education, deserve to be a top priority on the agenda of 21st century India. Robust Institution Building for higher education deserves to be a nationwide movement.

REFERENCES

1. Orsini, F. (2018). *Academic Unfreedoms. The Idea of a University*. Context.
2. Padaki, V., & Vaz, M. (2003). *Institutional Development in Social Interventions: Towards Inter-organisational Effectiveness*. Sage.
3. Thompson, Q. (2018). *International Reflections on University Autonomy and Freedoms. The Idea of a University*. Context.
4. Vishvanathan, S. (2018). *Logic of Academic Freedom. The Idea of a University*. Context.

Index

D

E

F

G

H

I